Math and Nonfiction

Grades 3–5

Math and Nonfiction

Grades 3–5

Stephanie Sheffield

Kathleen Gallagher

Introduction by

Marilyn Burns

Math Solutions

Sausalito, California, USA

Math Solutions
150 Gate 5 Road
Sausalito, CA 94965
www.mathsolutions.com

Library of Congress Cataloging-in-Publication Data

Sheffield, Stephanie.
　Math and nonfiction. Grades 3–5 / Stephanie Sheffield, Kathleen Gallagher.
　　p. cm.
　Includes bibliographical references and index.
　 ISBN 0-941355-62-4　(alk. paper)
1.　Mathematics—Study and teaching (Elementary) 2.　Children's literature in mathematics education. I.　Gallagher, Kathleen, 1963– ill. II.　Title.
　QA135.6.S482 2004
　372.7—dc22

2004018524

ISBN-13: 978-0-941355-62-9

Editor: Toby Gordon
Production: Melissa L. Inglis
Cover and interior design: Catherine Hawkes/Cat and Mouse
Composition: Interactive Composition Corporation

Printed in the United States of America on acid-free paper
13　12　11　10　09　　ML　　　　　　　4　5

A Message from Math Solutions

We at Math Solutions believe that teaching math well calls for increasing our understanding of the math we teach, seeking deeper insights into how children learn mathematics, and refining our lessons to best promote students' learning.

Math Solutions shares classroom-tested lessons and teaching expertise from our faculty of professional development instructors as well as from other respected math educators. Our publications are part of the nationwide effort we've made since 1984 that now includes

- more than five hundred face-to-face professional development programs each year for teachers and administrators in districts across the country;
- annually publishing professional development books, now totaling more than seventy titles and spanning the teaching of all math topics in kindergarten through grade 8;
- four series of videos for teachers, plus a video for parents, that show math lessons taught in actual classrooms;
- on-site visits to schools to help refine teaching strategies and assess student learning; and
- free online support, including grade-level lessons, book reviews, inservice information, and district feedback, all in our *Math Solutions Online Newsletter*.

For information about all of the products and services we have available, please visit our website at *www.mathsolutions.com*. You can also contact us to discuss math professional development needs by calling (800) 868-9092 or by sending an email to *info@mathsolutions.com*.

We're always eager for your feedback and interested in learning about your particular needs. We look forward to hearing from you.

*To Sondra, who talked me into this,
and to Megan, who made it possible, my love and thanks. —S. S.*

*To my colleagues, who shared their wonderful students and classrooms,
to my family, who allowed me to write about it,
and to my writing group, who provided
thoughtful and constructive criticism, thank you. —K. G.*

Contents

Acknowledgments   *ix*
Introduction by Marilyn Burns   *xi*

Bananas   1
Berries, Nuts, and Seeds   10
Biggest, Strongest, Fastest   19
Chimp Math   29
Dealing with Addition   39
Ed Emberley's Picture Pie   47
From Seashells to Smart Cards   58
G Is for Googol   66
Hottest, Coldest, Highest, Deepest   78
How Much, How Many, How Far, How Heavy, How Long,
  How Tall Is 1000?   88
Icebergs and Glaciers   100
If the World Were a Village   107
If You Hopped Like a Frog   118
In the Next Three Seconds . . . Predictions for the Millennium   132
A More Perfect Union   138
One Tiny Turtle   148
Roman Numerals I to MM   160
Ten Times Better   169
Tiger Math   181
Wilma Unlimited   192

Blackline Masters   203
  One-Inch Grid Paper   205
  My Baby Milestones   206
  Hottest, Coldest, Highest, Deepest *Worksheet*   207

Grid and Circle Worksheet   208
Half-Inch Grid Paper   209
1–100 Chart   210
Birth Weight Record Sheet   211

References   213
Index   215

Acknowledgments

Thanks to those teachers who allowed our lessons to be taught in their classrooms—at Dingeman Elementary School, San Diego, California: Charlene Barad, Wendy Karch, and Kris Lee; at Beneke Elementary School, Houston, Texas: Tamara Barr, Gloria Cantu, Emily Diaz, Mary Karnick, Trang LeQuang, Linda McClosky, Maralyn Reid, Cynthia Tapscott, and Heather Watt; at Kennedy Elementary School, San Diego: Gloria Moses; and at Washington Elementary School, San Diego: Ruth Reyes.

Introduction

For months before publishing this resource of classroom-tested lessons, I was surrounded by children's books. They were stacked practically up to my ears on my desk and additional piles were all around on the floor. It took some fancy shuffling at times to make space for other things that needed my attention. But I never complained. I love children's books and it was pure pleasure to be immersed in reading them and then teaching, writing, revising, and editing lessons that use them as springboards for teaching children mathematics.

This book is one in our new Math Solutions Publications series for teaching mathematics using children's literature, and I'm pleased to present the complete series:

Math and Literature, Grades K–1
Math and Literature, Grades 2–3
Math and Literature, Grades 4–6, Second Edition
Math and Literature, Grades 6–8
Math and Nonfiction, Grades K–2
Math and Nonfiction, Grades 3–5

More than ten years ago we published my book *Math and Literature (K–3)*. My premise for that book was that children's books can be effective vehicles for motivating children to think and reason mathematically. I searched for books that I knew would stimulate children's imaginations and that also could be used to teach important math concepts and skills.

After that first book's publication, my colleague Stephanie Sheffield began sending me the titles of children's books she had discovered and descriptions of the lessons she had taught based on them. Three years after publishing my book, we published Stephanie's *Math and Literature (K–3), Book Two*. And the following year we published Rusty Bresser's *Math and Literature (Grades 4–6)*, a companion to the existing books.

Over the years, some of the children's books we initially included in our resources have, sadly, gone out of print. However, other wonderful titles have emerged. For this new series, we did a thorough review of our three original resources. Stephanie and I collaborated on substantially revising our two K–3 books and reorganizing them into two different books, one for grades K–1 and the other for grades 2–3. Rusty produced a second edition of his book for grades 4–6.

In response to the feedback we received from teachers, we became interested in creating a book that would offer lessons based on children's books for middle school students, and we were fortunate enough to find two wonderful teachers, Jennifer M. Bay-Williams and Sherri L. Martinie, to collaborate on this project. I'm pleased to present their book, *Math and Literature, Grades 6–8*.

The two books that round out our series use children's nonfiction as springboards for lessons. Jamee Petersen created *Math and Nonfiction, Grades K–2*, and Stephanie Sheffield built on her experience with the Math and Literature books to team with her colleague Kathleen Gallagher to write *Math and Nonfiction, Grades 3–5*. Hearing nonfiction books read aloud to them requires children to listen in a different way than usual. With nonfiction, students listen to the facts presented and assimilate that information into what they already know about that particular subject. And rather than reading from cover to cover as with fiction, it sometimes makes more sense to read only a small portion of a nonfiction book and investigate the subject matter presented in that portion. The authors of these Math and Nonfiction books are sensitive to the demands of nonfiction and how to present new information in order to make it accessible to children.

We're still fond of the lessons that were based on children's books that are now out of print, and we know that through libraries, the Internet, and used bookstores, teachers have access to some of those books. Therefore, we've made all of the older lessons that are not included in the new series of books available online at *www.mathsolutions.com*. Please visit our Web site for those lessons and for additional support for teaching math.

I'm pleased and proud to present these new books. It was a joy to work on them, and I'm convinced that you and your students will benefit from the lessons we offer.

MARILYN BURNS
2004

Bananas

Taught by Stephanie Sheffield

Jacqueline Farmer's *Bananas* (1999) is packed with information, recipes, jokes, and interesting facts about—you guessed it—bananas! A fun read-aloud, it is full of mathematical facts about bananas that can be used to integrate mathematics into an everyday context. In this lesson taught in a fourth-grade class, children use multiplication to find the number of bananas produced by a single plant, compute the differences between various nutritional values of bananas and apples, and think about percents to figure the amount of vitamin B_6 they should have each day.

MATERIALS

I asked the fourth-grade students to look at the cover of *Bananas* and think about what genre the book might be.

Tristan called out without raising his hand: "A fairy tale, or a story."

Roland raised his hand after thinking for a moment. "A book about bananas?" The rest of the class chuckled, then settled down.

I called on Thomas next. "It looks like a real book about bananas, like nonfiction," he said.

"You're right," I told him. "Although the cartoon-like pictures may lead you to believe that this is a fictional story, it is really a non-fiction book."

After this spirited beginning, the class settled down to listen to the book. I showed them the title page and told them about how I had met the author at a math conference and had her autograph the book. The children were excited about having this connection with the author, which added to their interest in listening to the book.

The very first paragraph gave us something mathematical to talk about: "It's the most popular fruit in America, where each person eats an average of twenty-eight pounds of bananas annually. Now that's a bunch of bananas!" I paused, and the class began commenting in a lively manner.

"I hate bananas!" Tristan announced. "I don't eat twenty-eight pounds of them!"

Brianna countered, "I love them! I eat one every day."

A loud and heated conversation about the merits of bananas ensued. After about a minute, I interrupted with a question: "What does it mean when they say that Americans eat an average of twenty-eight pounds of bananas annually?"

Marra answered, "Well, I think annually means every year."

"That's right, Marra," I said. "Does anyone know what *average* means?" Only three children raised their hands. I called on Jordan.

"Typical?" he asked. At first I didn't understand his answer because I was expecting an explanation of mathematical average. I asked him to repeat himself, and then I realized what he was thinking.

"Do you mean typical like, the average fourth grader is nine years old?" I asked. Jordan nodded.

"So you could say, the average fourth grader is nine years old," I said. Again he nodded.

"So in this context we would say that the typical American eats twenty-eight pounds of bananas a year," I explained. "Does that mean that *every* American eats twenty-eight pounds of bananas?" The class answered together: "No."

I went on. "Some people in America probably eat more bananas than that in a year, and some eat fewer than that. But it sounds as if Americans eat a lot of bananas every year."

This short conversation made me realize that this class needed additional experience with the concept of *average,* and I made a note to myself to explore that idea with them at a later date.

I read page two, which states that a banana plant can grow up to thirty feet tall in one year. I initiated another mathematical discussion by asking, "How tall is that?"

When no one responded right away, I stood up and said, "I'm five feet tall. How many people my height would have to stand on each other's shoulders to reach the top of the banana plant?"

Immediately Mohammed called out, "Twenty!"

I responded, "I think that twenty people my height would be one hundred feet tall if they stood on each other's shoulders. Think about my height—five feet—and the height of a banana plant—thirty feet."

Katrina raised her hand. "Six," she said.

"How did you figure that out Katrina?" I asked.

"Because you're five feet tall, and six times five is thirty," she said.

I continued reading. The students were interested to learn that bananas grow not on trees, but on really tall plants, and they were surprised that the plants grow from rhizomes and have "eyes" like potatoes. The following page gave us our next mathematical challenge. I read that very small new bananas look like, and in fact are called, fingers. They grow in groups of ten to twenty, and each group is called a hand. One banana plant can produce up to fifteen hands. (**Note:** This page states that fifteen hands form a "bunch . . . that can weigh more than one hundred pounds!" We generally think of a bunch as a cluster of six or so bananas, like the ones we find at the store. To prevent confusion about the meaning of *bunch,* especially for limited English speakers, I didn't read that part of the text.)

On the board I wrote:

10 to 20 fingers in a hand

15 hands on a plant

"That sounds like a lot of bananas," I said. "Do you think we could figure out how many bananas might be on one plant?" The class nodded eagerly, but no one spoke up to get things started.

"What will we have to do to figure this out?" I asked.

Brianna said, "You have to multiply ten times fifteen." I saw Milo begin to count on his fingers, but Sergio looked lost, as did a few others.

I drew a rough sketch of a plant with a few elongated circles hanging off it. "Let's suppose each of these is a hand of bananas," I said, pointing to the elongated circles. "How many of these should I draw on the plant?"

"Fifteen," Austin said, "'cause there are fifteen hands on a plant."

I added elongated circles until there were fifteen. "What else does the picture need?" I asked.

Milo jumped up and took the marker from me. He wrote *ten* in each circle on the banana plant. "The book said there were ten to twenty little bananas in each hand," he said.

"Fingers," Andre corrected him.

"OK, fingers," Milo said. "So they each have at least ten."

"So you have to count by tens," Tristan advised, and other students nodded. Tristan and some others didn't immediately see this as a multiplication problem, the way Brianna had, but I decided to let them solve it in a way that made sense to them, then try to make the connection to multiplication.

Tristan began counting by tens, pointing to the elongated circles I had drawn on the plant. The class counted with him, continuing until they reached 150.

"What does the number one hundred fifty tell us?" I asked.

Marra said, "It means how many baby bananas are on the tree. I mean *plant*."

"So are there always one hundred fifty banana fingers on a plant?" I asked.

Mohammed answered, "That's only if there are ten banana fingers in each hand."

"What other numbers could represent how many banana fingers could be in one hand?" I asked.

Thomas said, "It said ten to twenty in each hand."

"Yes, they're saying that there is a *range* of bananas in a hand. Some may have only ten, and some could have as many as twenty. So we need to find the range of bananas that could be on a plant. We found the number at the low end of that range, one hundred fifty. What would the high end of the range be?" I asked.

Several students raised their hands. I called on Sergio. "Two times fifteen is thirty, and just add a zero. You get three hundred," he said.

"Does anybody have a different way to think about it?" I asked.

"I do," Roland offered. "Ten each is one hundred fifty, so twenty each would be the same amount again. Like, fifteen and fifteen is thirty, so one hundred fifty and one hundred fifty is three hundred."

I continued reading *Bananas*. We learned how bananas are grown and shipped to market, about their history, which animals like to eat bananas, and the nutritional benefits of bananas. The last section of the book has banana riddles and easy-to-make banana recipes.

After I finished reading, I returned to the page that compares the nutritional components of apples and bananas. On an overhead transparency, I made a chart with three columns and labeled them *Apple*, *Difference*, and *Banana*.

I said, "Let's compare the two kinds of fruit and see if we can tell how much better for you a banana is than an apple. We'll look at each nutritional component and find the difference between the values given for the apple and the banana." On the chart, I wrote the calorie counts the book gives for an apple and a banana.

	Apple	Difference	Banana
Calories	100		128

"What's the difference between these two numbers?" I asked.

"That's easy!" Katrina said. "Twenty-eight. One hundred twenty-eight minus one hundred is twenty-eight." I recorded the difference in the middle column of the chart. The next set of data was for iron content: an apple has 0.3 mg and a banana has 1.1 mg. I recorded the two numbers on the chart and asked the class to compare them.

	Apple	Difference	Banana
Calories	100	28	128
Iron	0.3		1.1

Milo had this idea: "Eleven minus three is eight, and you just put the dot back in. I mean the decimal point." I invited him up to the overhead to record his thinking and fill in the *Difference* column on the chart. He wrote:

$$\begin{array}{r} 1.1 \\ -.3 \\ \hline .8 \end{array}$$

The next nutritional numbers were for phosphorus: an apple has 12 mg and a banana has 39 mg. I called on Brianna, who came to the overhead and figured the difference using the standard vertical algorithm. There was no regrouping needed, so this problem was easy for Brianna.

	Apple	Difference	Banana
Calories	100	28	128
Iron	0.3 mg	0.8 mg	1.1 mg
Phosphorus	12 mg	27 mg	39 mg
Potassium	196		555

The comparison for potassium involved bigger numbers: 196 mg and 555 mg. When I asked the students to compare the two numbers, Mohammed explained how he figured the difference between them. I recorded his thinking on the board as he spoke. "One hundred ninety-six and four more makes two hundred. Then three hundred more is five hundred and fifty-five more is five hundred fifty-five." He paused here and seemed to be counting something up on his fingers.

"Can you tell us what are you doing in your head?" I prompted.

"First I added four, then three hundred more, so that's three hundred four, then fifty-five more, so that's three hundred fifty-nine in all."

I wanted to help make Mohammed's reasoning clear to the rest of the class, so I concluded, "Mohammed added up from one hundred ninety-six to find the difference between one hundred ninety-six and five hundred fifty-five, which is three hundred fifty-nine."

$$196 + \boxed{} = 555$$
$$196 + 4 = 200$$
$$200 + 300 = 500$$
$$500 + 55 = 555$$
$$4 + 300 + 55 = 359$$

We continued in the same way with the rest of the information about nutritional values. Each set of numbers gave us another chance to compare either whole numbers or decimals. For each set, I asked the students to choose the strategy for comparing that best fit the numbers. For instance, when comparing 196 to 555, it makes sense to *add up*, since 196 is so close to 200. Marra used the same adding-up strategy to compare 90 and 285.

	Apples	Difference	Bananas
Calories	100	28	128
Iron	0.3 mg	0.8 mg	1.1 mg
Phosphorus	12 mg	27 mg	39 mg
Potassium	196 mg	359 mg	555 mg
Vitamin A	90 IU	195	285 IU
Vitamin B$_6$	0.08 mg	0.69 mg	0.77 mg
Vitamin C	10 mg	5 mg	15 mg
Magnesium	8.5 mg	41.0 mg	49.5 mg
Niacin	1.1 mg	0.1 mg	1.0 mg

After we finished the chart, we had one more mathematical discussion. Returning to the book, I read that a single banana contains 25 percent of the U.S. Recommended Daily Allowance of vitamin B$_6$. I pointed to our chart, which said that a banana has 0.77 mg of vitamin B$_6$. I asked, "Can you use that information to figure out how much vitamin B$_6$ you should have in a day? Talk to the person next to you and see if you can come up with an answer and a way to explain to the class how you figured it out."

When I called the students back together, several of them were eager to share their ideas, while others seemed to be not quite sure. I called on Thomas and Andre. Andre began, "We knew that twenty-five percent is like a quarter, because there are four twenty-fives in one hundred." He drew a circle on the board and divided it into four parts, then wrote 0.77 mg in one part. Then he wrote 0.77 in each of the other three parts of the circle.

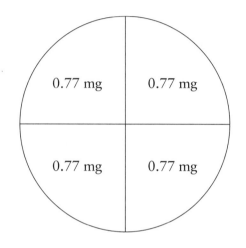

"Now I have to add all these point seventy-sevens up," Andre said.

"Show us how you do that," I suggested.

He responded, "Two sevens is fourteen, and fourteen and fourteen is twenty-eight. Since there's four sevens in the tens place, that's twenty-eight tens, or two hundred eighty, and then twenty-eight in the ones place. That makes two hundred, and another hundred from the twenty and eighty, so three hundred and eight. Then I go back and put in the decimal point, so the answer is three point zero eight."

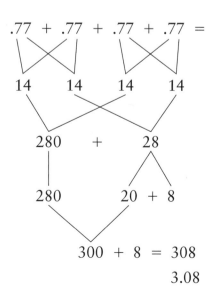

"And that's how much vitamin B_6 the government says we should have each day," I said.

"We'd better start eating bananas," Milo quipped.

To end the lesson, I added a question to the information on the board:

> *10 to 20 fingers in a hand*
> *15 hands on a plant*
> *How many bananas can there be on one plant?*

I asked the students to individually record their solutions to the problem. I was interested to know, after the discussion we had earlier, how each would make sense of the problem. Figures 1–1, 1–2, and 1–3 show some of their solutions.

Figure 1–1: Sergio drew a model of two banana plants, showing the hands. He labeled the hands to be sure he had fifteen of them. He counted by tens and then twenties to find the totals, but he wrote all fifteen as addition problems.

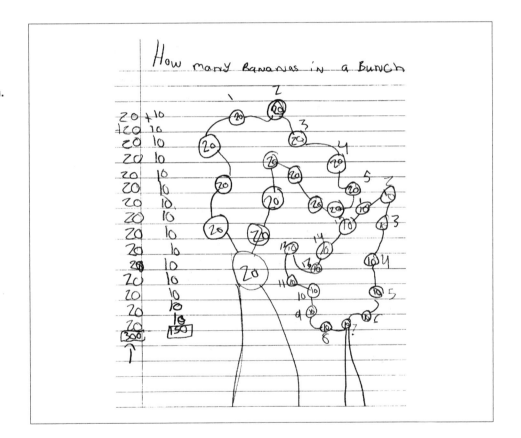

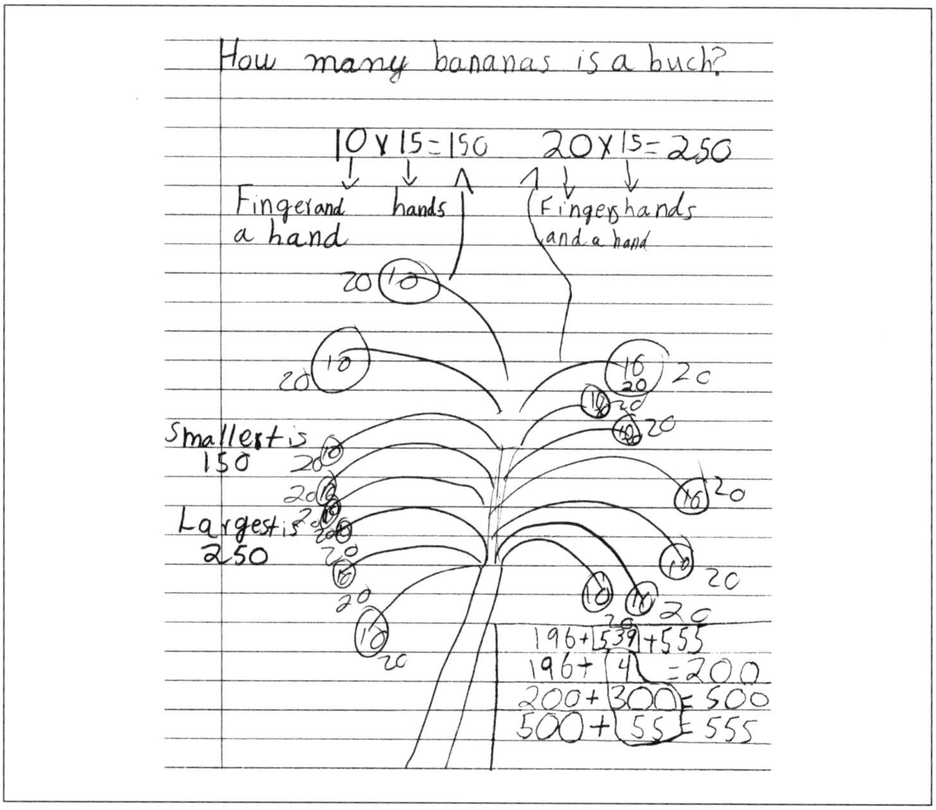

Figure 1–2: Roland also drew a sketch of the plant. He used words to label the numbers in his number sentences to make them clear.

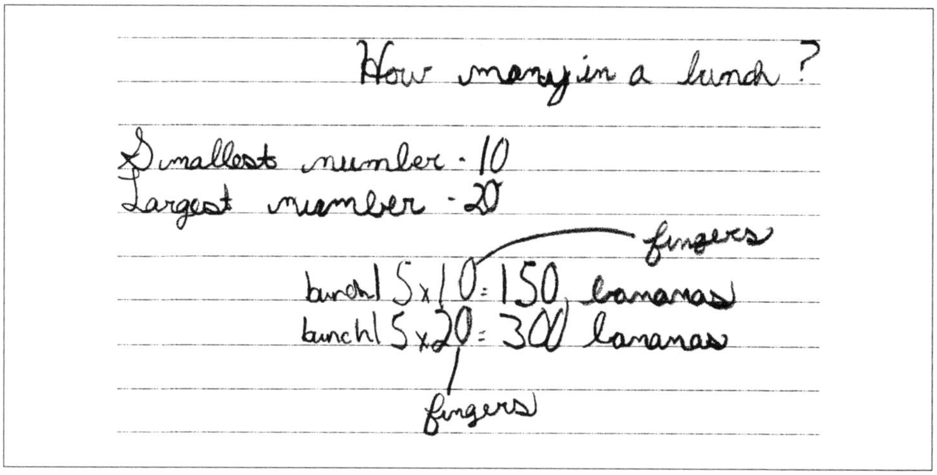

How many bananas is a buch?

10 X 15 = 150   20 X 15 = 250

Finger and   hands   (Fingers hands
a hand   and a hand)

Smallest is
150

Largest is
250

196 + 539 + 555
196 + 4 = 200
200 + 300 = 500
500 + 55 = 555

Figure 1–3: Katrina showed that she clearly understood why she multiplied the numbers and what the answers meant.

How many in a bunch?

Smallest number - 10
Largest number - 20

                                fingers
bunch1 5 x 10 = 150 bananas
bunch1 5 x 20 = 300 bananas
                    fingers

Berries, Nuts, and Seeds

Taught by Stephanie Sheffield

Diane L. Burns's *Berries, Nuts, and Seeds* (1996) is part of a series of books for young explorers. This field guide is designed to help children identify thirty common berries, nuts, and seeds. It describes each and tells where to find it, which type of wildlife eat it, and other interesting facts. In this graphing lesson for third graders, students sort, classify, and graph common nuts, berries, and seeds. The lesson gives them hands-on experience with picture graphs where a single symbol represents more than one item.

MATERIALS

mixed nuts and seeds from grocery store

other nuts or seeds to add to mix—acorns, sunflower seeds, pumpkin seeds, sycamore, or other nuts that are native to the area or easily obtained

plastic bowl or container, 1 per 2 pairs of students

12-by-18 inch drawing paper, 1 sheet per 2 pairs of students

one-inch grid paper, 1 sheet per student (see Blackline Masters)

tablespoons or small scoops, 1 per 2 pairs of students

To prepare for this lesson for third graders, I filled a large bowl with mixed nuts, sunflower seeds, and acorns, then divided the mixture into individual bowls, with about a cup and a half in each. I prepared one bowl for every 4 children in the class.

As I held up *Berries, Nuts, and Seeds*, the class seemed interested in the appealing cover. "Hey look! Strawberries!" Sailor exclaimed.

"And acorns," Kaleb added.

"I see that floaty thing that you wish on," Carlos said.

"That's a dandelion," I explained, "and it's one of the things we'll read about in this book."

I didn't intend to read the entire book to the class, because I knew it would be too much for one sitting. I wanted to read about plants that were familiar to these third graders and to give them basic background about nuts, berries, and seeds. "This book is intended to be used as a guide if you're out walking and want to identify some of the berries and nuts you see. I'll read you a few pages, then I have an activity for you to do using the nuts I've brought to class," I explained.

I read the introduction, then moved on to the page about cranberries. The class was interested to learn that cranberries grow on a vine that creeps along the ground. I skipped to the section about nuts and read about the sycamore. "I've seen those!" Colleen called out. "They're real spiky." I read about the pecan next, because it is native to our part of the country. Most of the children had eaten a pecan at some point, and they thought it was interesting that full-grown pecan trees produce about one hundred pounds of nuts each year. "The squirrels eat all the pecans that fall out of our tree," Braden commented. "My mom says we're lucky if we get a bowl full." We read about hickory nuts, milkweed, and dandelion, as well as wild rose and cattail. "You might be interested in reading about other plants in this book, so when I leave I'll put it on your teacher's desk, and you can look at it when you have more time. Right now I'd like to begin our lesson."

I gave the students a short break to stretch and go back to their desks before beginning the next part of the lesson. "Today we're going to be learning something new about graphing, and we're going to use nuts and seeds to do it. You're going to create a graph with the nut mixture I brought. Let's look at what's in the bowls." I held up a walnut, a pecan, an acorn, an almond, and a sunflower seed, and the class identified them correctly. Mary, the classroom teacher, and I had to name the Brazil nut and filbert for them.

Then I said, "We are going to demonstrate what to do with the nuts, then you'll go back to your seats and sort and classify your own collection."

Mary picked up a tablespoon and scooped a bunch of nuts and seeds from a bowl. She poured the mixture onto the table, scooped up another tablespoon, and asked, "Did you notice how I made sure the spoon went to the bottom of the bowl? That's because I want to be sure to get some of the small things in the bowl as well as the larger nuts. I want a variety of sizes in my scoop to make my graph interesting. How do you think I should sort them?"

"Put all the things that are alike together," Peyton suggested.

"Does anyone have another idea?" Mary asked.

"By size," Brooke suggested. "All the big ones together and all the little ones."

Alicia suggested, "You could put the nuts together, and the seeds together."

"Those are all good ideas, but I think I'll sort them as Peyton suggested." Mary made small piles, separating the mixture according to type. "OK, now I'm going to show how many I have of each kind. Let's start with the walnuts. I have two of them," she said, placing them on a piece of paper marked off into seventy squares. "I can't leave these walnuts on the paper, so I'll sketch the shape of a walnut for each one," she said.

Mary counted out the sunflower seeds and announced that she had eighteen.

"Wait!" Kaleb called out. "They're not going to fit!"

"What do you think we should do?" I asked.

"We could put some of them back in the bowl," Katrina suggested.

"I want to think of a way to represent all the seeds and nuts we actually scooped on the graph," Mary replied.

"I know," Sailor said, "we could tape another piece of paper to the one you've got."

"Good suggestion, Sailor, but I want you to think of a way to represent the data on one graph," Mary said. "I have an idea. If I draw symbols on the graph, I can decide what each one stands for. Often one symbol stands for one item, like the two little pictures I drew for the two walnuts. But I could change that and have one symbol stand for two nuts." Mary drew one small sunflower shape and said, "That will stand for two of the sunflower seeds." She moved two of the seeds on the desk in front of her apart from the others. "How many little sunflower seed shapes do I need to draw on the graph?"

Allison raised her hand. "I think nine," she said.

"What makes you think that?" Mary asked.

"Because," Allison said, counting on her fingers, "two, four, six, eight, ten, twelve, fourteen, sixteen, eighteen."

Mary drew nine small symbols on the graph, then directed the class's attention to the top row.

"We might have a little problem now," she said. "In one of our rows the symbols mean one nut each, and in the other row they mean two nuts each. That might be confusing to someone looking at the graph. Remember that the point of a graph is to visually show data in a way that helps the viewer gather information quickly. Who has an idea about how we could avoid confusion?"

Several children raised their hands. Mary called on Delphina.

"You can't change the sunflower seeds, because we know it won't fit, so you have to do the same as we did with them to the walnuts. Count them by twos, too," Delphina suggested.

"If we make one symbol for every two walnuts, how many will we need?" Mary asked.

"Just one," Peyton said. "Every picture means two nuts, so just one." Mary erased one of the walnut symbols.

"But I have a question," Peyton continued. "What if someone else doesn't know what those things are you drew? Shouldn't the graph say what kind of nut it is?"

"That's a good observation, Peyton," Mary said. "You're right in saying that every graph needs to have labels. Since my graph paper is one big grid, there's no place to write. So I'm going to glue it to a piece of drawing paper."

Mary attached the graph to a 12-by-18-inch sheet of drawing paper, taped the whole thing to the board, then continued: "Now I have lots of room to write. You'll want to be sure to label each row to tell what kind of seed or nut you are representing. What else does every graph need?"

"I know," Medani said. "Your name."

"Right. And what else?"

Booker said, "A title."

Braden waved his hand in the air excitedly, asking to be called on. "A key!" he exclaimed proudly. "You've got to draw a little picture in a box and tell what it stand for. Like your little pictures on the graph mean two nuts or two seeds."

"Will you come to the board and demonstrate what you mean?" Mary asked. Braden came up and wrote at the bottom of the drawing paper:

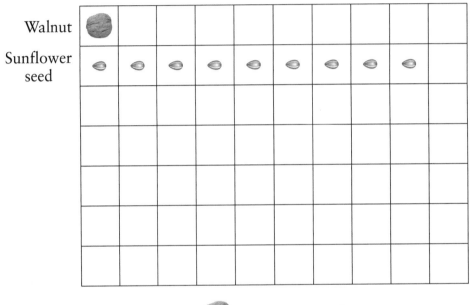

= 2 nuts or seeds

"I have one more question for you to think about before you begin working," Mary said. "What if I had scooped a whole bunch of sunflower seeds, even more than I did scoop? Could I have the little picture symbols represent something else, or do they always have to represent two?"

Mary waited while the class thought about this for a few seconds. Then she called on Peyton, who said, "If you had a really lot of them, you could make the picture represent ten at a time, or three or four or five. It can be anything."

"But you have to have a key so you'll know how many there really are," Sailor added.

I stepped back to the front of the room to give some last-minute directions. "You may work with a partner, or by yourself. Each group will need one piece of drawing paper and one piece of graph paper. The paper is on the reading table. When you and your partner are ready for it, please help yourselves."

I turned to the board and wrote:

1. *your names*

2. *a title*

3. *labels for the nuts and seeds*

4. *a key*

"These are the things that must be on your paper," I said. "Now it's time for you to do your own graphs. Mrs. Karnick and I will bring a bowl of nuts and seeds to each group, along with a spoon. Take turns at your table and scoop twice. Remember to scoop all the way to the bottom so you'll have some of each kind of nut and seed."

The students got right to work, scooping nuts and seeds and gluing their pieces of graph paper to drawing paper. Mary and I walked around and checked with each pair of children.

Booker and Alicia called me over with a question. "We have five Brazil nuts," Booker explained. "But every picture means two nuts, and five is an odd number. What should we do?"

"Do either of you have an idea?" I asked.

"Well, maybe we could just draw half a nut," Alicia suggested.

"I think that will work," I said. Figure 2–1 shows Booker and Alicia's finished graph.

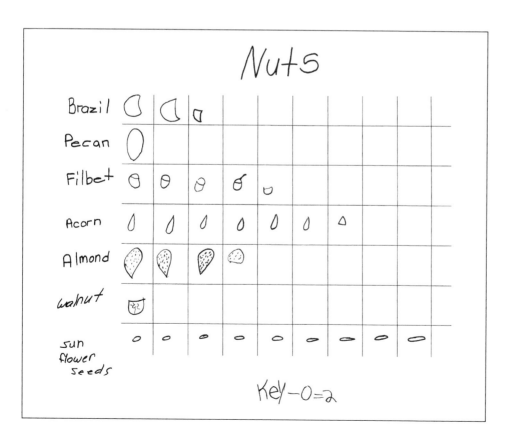

Figure 2–1: Booker and Alicia solved the problem of having an odd number of nuts by drawing half a symbol to represent just one nut.

There were very few questions from the children as they sorted their nuts and seeds and counted them carefully. Because the students were using spoons of the same size, the number of nuts and seeds they got in each scoop was roughly the same from group to group. The distribution was different, though, and that made every graph different.

As students raised their hands to say they were finished, Mary directed them to look at the front board. "Check to be sure your paper is complete," she told them.

After several groups had finished, Mary called for the class's attention. "When you finish your graph, you and your partner should look at it carefully and write sentences about what you notice."

Kaleb and Colleen were really struggling with their graph. I asked them if they needed help. "We have so many sunflower seeds!" Kaleb wailed. "We don't know how to put them on our graph."

"How many do you have?" I asked.

"Thirty-two!" Colleen said dramatically. "We thought we could count by fives, but we only have two walnuts. How can we make a picture of that?"

It seemed clear to me that Colleen and Kaleb were not going to be able to work this out on their own, and I didn't want them to get bogged down. Removing some of the seeds seemed the simplest way to address the problem, so I reached down and took away several of their sunflower seeds. "There," I said. "Try again."

Mary noticed that Katrina and Analeigh had a long list of statements on their paper. (See Figure 2–2.) She stopped to read the first one: "A brazil nut is a long brown nut that is bumpy." We had in mind that the students would write about the mathematical things they noticed, but Katrina and Analeigh had described the nuts and seeds themselves.

After getting the class's attention, Mary made an announcement. "Be sure that your sentences are mathematical statements about the graph, rather than statements about the nuts and seeds." Peyton and Braden looked at each other with a "Whoops!" kind of look, and started writing again. (See Figure 2–3.)

To bring the lesson to a close, rather than having all the students share in whole group, Mary had each pair of partners share their graph and sentences with another pair. She sometime uses this alternate method of sharing, which allows for more children to interact, and less time for them to wait to share their work.

Figure 2–4 is Colleen and Kaleb's picture graph, while Figure 2–5 shows Booker and Alicia's sentences.

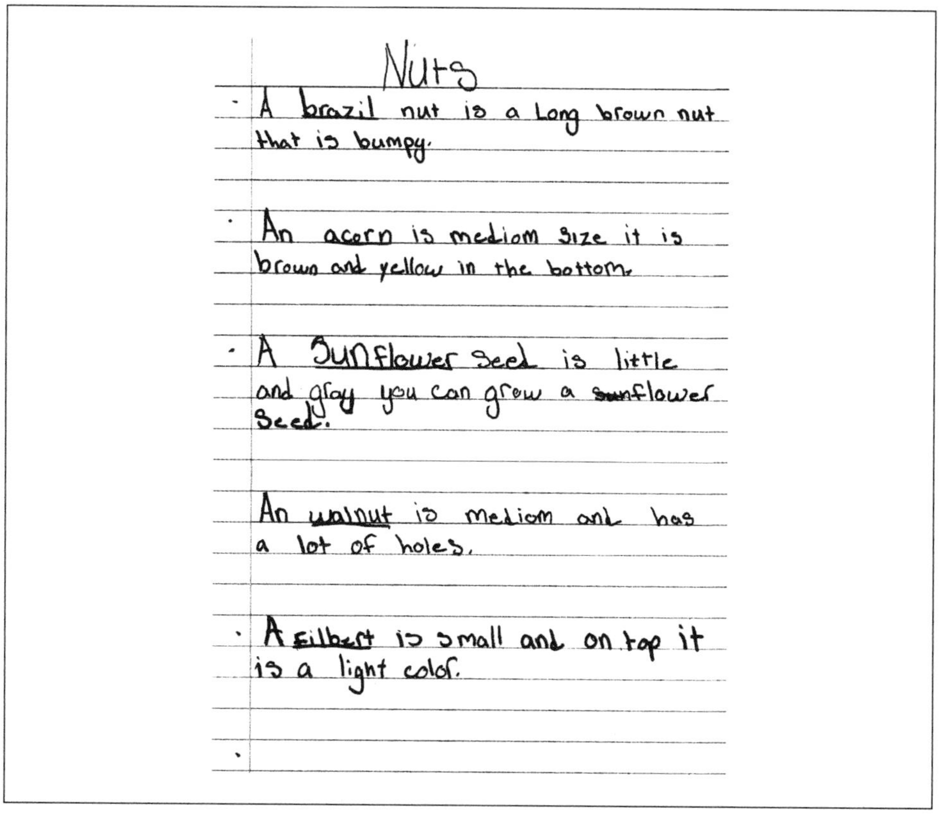

Nuts

- A brazil nut is a long brown nut that is bumpy.

- An acorn is mediom size it is brown and yellow in the bottom.

- A Sunflower seed is little and gray you can grow a sunflower Seed.

An walnut is mediom and has a lot of holes.

- A Filbert is small and on top it is a light color.

Figure 2–2: Katrina and Analeigh wrote sentences describing the nuts and seeds.

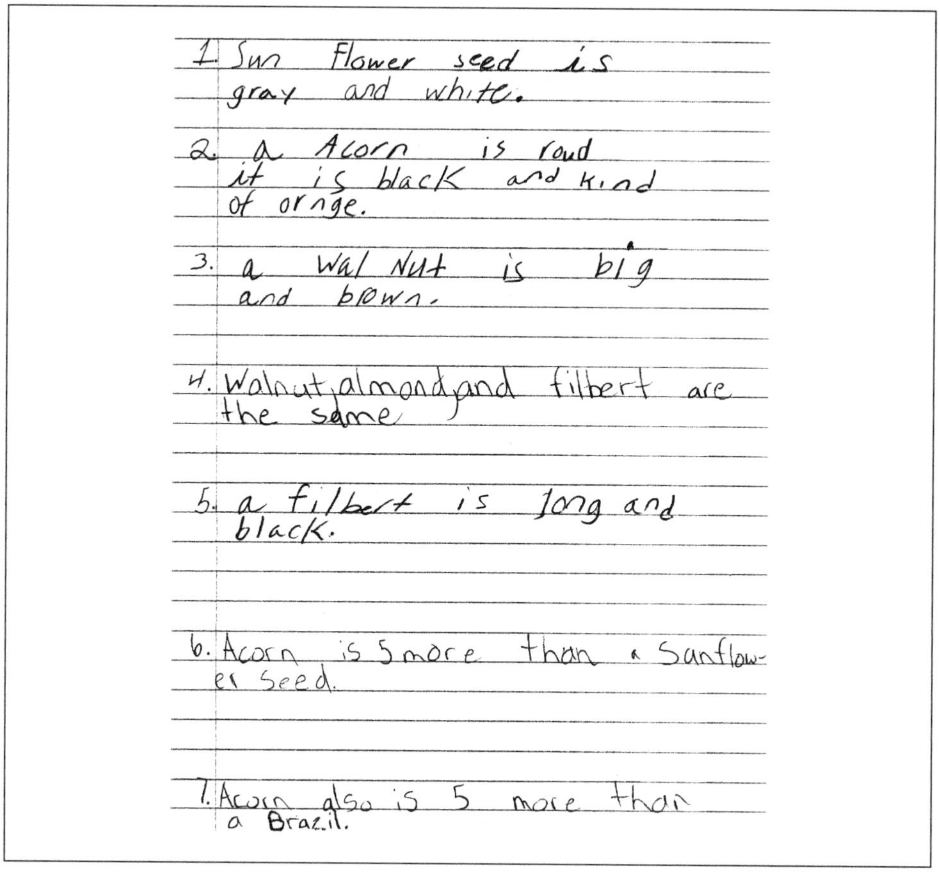

1. Sun Flower seed is gray and white.

2. A Acorn is roud it is black and kind of ornge.

3. a Wal Nut is big and brown.

4. Walnut, almond, and filbert are the same.

5. a filbert is long and black.

6. Acorn is 5 more than a Sunflower seed.

7. Acorn also is 5 more than a Brazil.

Figure 2–3: Braden and Peyton wrote both descriptive sentences about the nuts and mathematical statements.

Figure 2–4: Colleen and Kaleb spent a lot of time on their graph and were proud of their results.

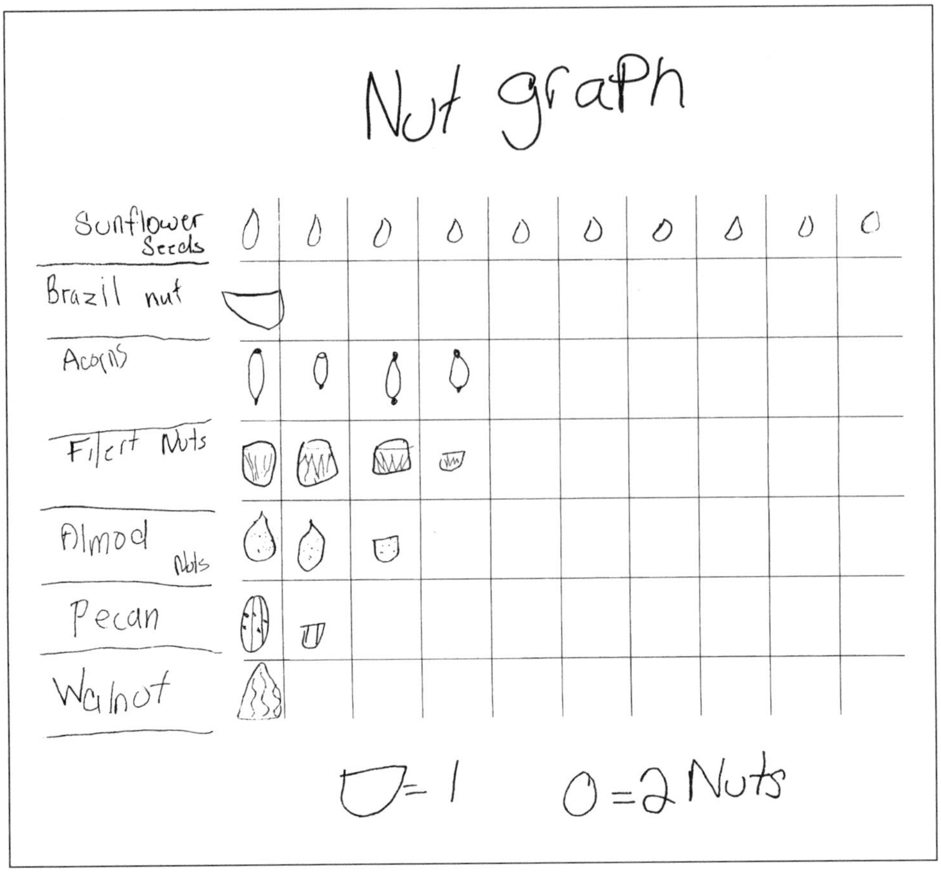

Figure 2–5: Alicia and Booker took turns writing statements about their graph. They counted each row, then compared rows.

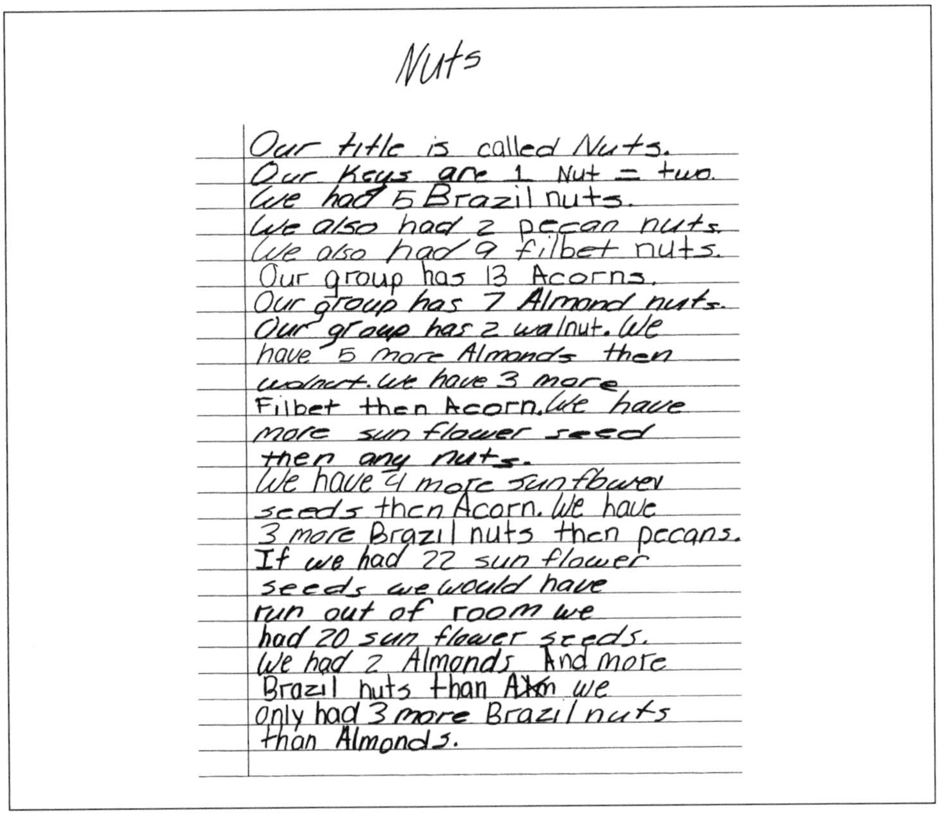

Math and Nonfiction, Grades 3–5

Biggest, Strongest, Fastest

Taught by Kathleen Gallagher

Steve Jenkins's *Biggest, Strongest, Fastest* (1995) is a joy to read with children. Jenkins has collected facts about the height, weight, speed, and strength of a variety of creatures and has included a human reference for each so children can make better sense of the particular animal's specialty. In this lesson, fourth graders prove that the author's comparisons are true and convince others that their own computational methods for verifying the comparisons are sound.

MATERIALS

I gathered the fourth-grade children on the rug to listen to *Biggest, Strongest, Fastest*. As I read the first page, I stopped and asked the children to predict which animals were "too small to see without a microscope."

"I bet it's like some kind of bacteria or something," predicted Samson.

"Maybe it's plankton," said Rocio.

"I think there's lots of things crawling around that we can't see," said Diego boldly. "Like I heard little bugs you can't even see live in your mattresses and pillows and stuff."

"What about lice? That's a really small animal," said Vivian.

"Eww, gross," replied Duane.

As I continued reading, I had the children predict which animals would match the text's superlatives of *biggest, fastest*, etc. When

I turned to the page about elephants, I read, "The African elephant is the biggest land animal."

"How does the author know this?" I asked the children.

"He probably measured it," said Angel.

"How?" I asked.

"Maybe they have a way to lift it up to see how much it weighs," suggested Antonette.

"Yeah, like they put a strap under its belly and lift it in the air and there's one of those scales like with the needle thing that moves to show the weight," said Angel.

"Wow, that must be a pretty strong scale," I said.

"Yeah, but they weigh cars and planes and stuff like that," said Samson.

I continued reading. "'The largest elephant ever measured was more than 13 feet tall and weighed 22,000 pounds. An African elephant eats over 300 pounds of grass or leaves every day.' Could we actually prove that?" I asked.

"It would be kind of hard to weigh the food after it was already eaten," Alex contemplated.

"How could they know that?" asked Rocio.

"Maybe they keep track of the food they feed the elephants in the zoo," Samson speculated.

"It would be kind of hard to keep track of leaves and grass," countered Diego.

"So, again, what is the biggest land animal?" I asked as I showed them the picture.

"The African elephant," they answered.

I turned the page and read about the animal that is strongest for its size, the ant. As I continued to read, I asked more questions to help the students realize that asking how people know things is a smart thing to do. I asked questions like:

How does the author know that?
How could that be tested?
Could that really be true?

When we got to the page about the blue whale, I read, "'A blue whale can grow to be 110 feet long and weigh over 168 tons—as much as 20 elephants.' Could that really be true?" I asked. "Do twenty elephants really weigh 168 tons? What do you think?"

"I think it's probably true, because a blue whale is the biggest thing," said Diego.

"But how could we find out if it's really true?" I asked.

"We could test it out," said Carmen.

"How?" I asked.

"Look on the page about the elephants," suggested Rocio. "Didn't he say how much an elephant weighs?"

I turned back to the page about the African elephant. On the board I wrote:

The largest elephant ever measured weighed 22,000 pounds.

"What else do we need to know to test whether a blue whale weighs as much as twenty elephants?" I asked.

"How much does the blue whale weigh?" asked Diego.

I returned to the blue whale page and wrote:

A blue whale weighs 168 tons.

"Now what?" I asked.

"It seems like the elephant weighs more, 'cause it weighs twenty-two thousand and that's more than one hundred sixty-eight," said Alex.

"Yeah, but the whale is one hundred sixty-eight *tons,* not *pounds!*" countered Kenny.

"How much is a ton?" asked Rocio.

I could have just told them, but I wanted to model the use of reference materials. I grabbed one of the children's math books and read the definition of *ton:* "A customary unit for measuring weight. One ton (T) = 2000 pounds." I wrote it on the board under the other facts.

Is it true that a blue whale weighs the same as 20 elephants?

The largest elephant ever measured weighed 22,000 pounds.
A blue whale weighs 168 tons.
One ton (T) = 2000 pounds.

"Do you have enough information to figure out if it's true that a blue whale weighs the same as twenty elephants?" I asked.

"We have to figure out how many tons an elephant is," said Samson.

"That's one way to get started," I said. "How would you do that?"

"I think if there's two thousand pounds in one ton, then two, four, six, eight, ten, twelve, fourteen, sixteen, eighteen, twenty, twenty-two—an elephant would weigh eleven tons," he reasoned, using his fingers to keep track as he counted.

"It sounds like you have a good plan for figuring it out. Grab a piece of paper and write that down. Then think what you will do next." Samson went to his seat and started working. I asked the class, "What are the rest of you thinking?"

"Since a ton is two thousand pounds, I think we could figure out how many pounds the blue whale weighs," said Carmen. "Wouldn't it be like two thousand times one hundred sixty-eight?"

"That's also a good way to start," I said. "Go ahead and take a piece of paper, and write your idea down, Carmen."

I wanted to make sure all of the children had a plan before I excused them to their seats. "Who has an idea about how to get started?" I asked.

About half the students raised their hands and I told them to get started. "What questions do you have?" I asked the remaining children.

"What are we trying to find out again?" asked Eduardo.

"Look at the question I wrote on the board, Eduardo: 'Is it true that a blue whale weighs the same as 20 elephants?' Can you figure out if that's true? The author gave us this information," I said, pointing to the statements I had written beneath the question.

We read the words out loud as a group. Eduardo said, "I think I can figure it out."

"Me, too," said a few more students as they got up to get paper.

I told the rest of the children to go get paper and a hard surface to write on and we could work on the problem together. When they returned to the rug with their materials, I said, "As soon as you think you can finish it on your own, go to your seat and continue working."

"OK," they agreed.

"What are we trying to figure out?" I asked.

"If a blue whale and an elephant weigh the same amount," replied Jasmine.

"Not one elephant, twenty elephants," Catherine corrected.

"So how much do twenty elephants weigh?" I asked.

"We don't know. We only know one elephant," answered Jasmine.

"But if we know one elephant, can we figure out twenty elephants?" On the board, I circled the weight of the biggest elephant ever measured. "If this is the weight of one elephant, how much would twenty of them weigh? Try to figure it out on your piece of paper."

All of the children wrote *22,000*. Alex diligently began making a neat column, writing *22,000* repeatedly. Before long, Vivian said, "I know what it is. It's four, four, zero, zero, zero."

I wrote *44,000* on the board. "Let's see what other people get. Vivian, you think about what the next step might be."

Alex was still making his list when I leaned in and whispered, "Alex, would it make sense to see how much ten of that number equals and then double it?" I asked.

Paul said, "It's four hundred and eighteen thousand." He held up his paper to show how he had added up the numbers.

$$
\begin{array}{r}
3 \\
22000 \\
22000 \\
22000 \\
22 \\
22 \\
22 \\
22 \\
22 \\
22 \\
22 \\
22 \\
22 \\
22 \\
22 \\
22 \\
22 \\
22 \\
22 \\
\hline
1 \\
418{,}000 \\
22000 \\
\hline
440{,}000
\end{array}
$$

I wrote *418,000* on the board and said, "You think about the next step, too, while other people finish."

"I think it's four hundred and forty thousand," said Duane. "I did it two times and got the same answer."

"Now we have three different answers," I said. "Let's let the others finish and see if we can get a consensus. Alex added up ten of his twenty-two thousands and got two hundred twenty thousand. What does that number tell you?"

"How much ten elephants weigh," Alex said.

"Can you use the number two hundred twenty thousand to figure out how much *twenty* elephants weigh?" I asked.

Alex wrote *220,000* on his paper a second time, then added it to his previous total. "Forty-four thousand!" he called out.

$$
\begin{array}{r}
2\\
22{,}000\\
22{,}000\\
22{,}000\\
22{,}000\\
22{,}000\\
22{,}000\\
22{,}000\\
22{,}000\\
22{,}000\\
22{,}000\\
\hline
220{,}000\\
220{,}000\\
\hline
440{,}000
\end{array}
$$

"Read the numerals in your answer," I instructed.

As Alex read, I wrote *440,000* on the board. "What is this number, boys and girls?" I asked.

"Four hundred and forty thousand," they said.

"I got that too," said Jasmine.

"Can you explain what you did, Alex?" I asked.

"I added up ten twenty-two thousands and got two hundred twenty thousand. Then I added another one of those and I got four hundred forty thousand."

"I did the same, but I added twenty, twenty thousands. But I got four hundred and eighteen thousand," said Paul.

"That's 'four hundred eighteen thousand,'" I corrected. "You don't say the word *and* in a number unless there's a decimal point. Are you sure you wrote down twenty numbers?"

Paul counted the numbers on his paper and said, "Oh no, there's only nineteen."

He started to erase his answer to make room for another 22,000 but I said, "Can you add one more 22,000 to your total?"

Paul wrote *22,000* under the *418,000*.

"We think we know what to do next," said Jasmine and Vivian.

"Do you both agree on the answer?" I asked.

"Yeah, it's four hundred forty thousand. I messed up when I timesed it 'cause I forgot to put the zero," Jasmine admitted.

$$
\begin{array}{r}
22000\\
\times\ 20\\
\hline
00000\\
44000\\
\hline
44{,}000
\end{array}
$$

"But now I know what to do."

"OK, go ahead and go."

Carmen began to walk over to me. I wanted a little more time with the group on the rug, so I said, "Will all of you who are working on your own do me a favor? I really want to understand how you figured this out, so will you please write down in words what you did so I can understand your thinking?"

Carmen sat back down and began writing.

Angel said, "I got the answer with multiplication."

"How did you do it, Angel?" I asked. "Everybody lean over and look at Angel's paper."

"I know if you're multiplying by a number with a zero, you can just put a zero and multiply the next number," he explained. "So I put a zero and then did two times zero is zero, then two more zeros, then two times two is four and another two times two is four."

$$
\begin{array}{r}
22000 \\
\times\ 20 \\
\hline
440{,}000
\end{array}
\qquad
\begin{array}{r}
22000 \\
\times\ 20 \\
\hline
00000 \\
440000 \\
\hline
440{,}000
\end{array}
$$

"OK, so what does this number tell us?" I asked.

"How much twenty elephants weigh," answered Alex and Duane.

"And what are we trying to find out?" I asked.

"If twenty elephants weigh the same as a blue whale," said Angel.

"Let's see what the rest of the class has done. I want you to listen to what they say, and ask them questions if you don't understand something," I said.

I asked for the class's attention and said, "Is anybody ready to share what they learned?"

"It's not true! They don't weigh the same!" exclaimed Donald.

"Who agrees with Donald?" I asked.

Most of the children raised their hands. A few were still working. "Who will share how they did it?" I asked.

Several children raised their hands and I called on Diego. I asked the children to bring their papers to the meeting area, so it would be easier for them to see each other's work.

Diego said, "First I saw how much four elephants weigh, and I found out it was eighty-eight thousand. Then I said, 'How many tons is that?' So I divided two thousand into eighty-eight thousand and got forty-four. Then I did eighty-eight plus eighty-eight plus forty-four equals two hundred twenty tons. That's how much the twenty elephants weigh. So if a blue whale equals one hundred sixty-eight tons, then they're not the same."

"Did you add up all the twenty-two thousands?" asked Paul.

"No. I found out that four equaled eighty-eight thousand pounds. Then I figured out that eighty-eight thousand pounds equaled forty-four tons. So I added forty-four tons five times."

"Why five times?" I asked. "Show us on your paper."

"Because they go with these five eighty-eights," he said, pointing to the five eighty-eight thousands that represented five groups of four twenty-two thousands. (See Figure 3–1.)

"Do you understand, Paul? That was a great question. He converted the weight of the elephants to tons before he added them up."

"Oh," said Paul, not quite sure what to say next.

"Let's listen to someone else's solution," I suggested. I taped Diego's paper to the board. "Who else would like to share?"

"I would," offered Rocio. She read from her paper (see Figure 3–2):

I think it's not true because I found out one elephant weighs eleven tons and eleven times twenty is two hundred twenty tons for twenty elephants, and a blue whale only weighs one hundred sixty-eight tons. That's what I think. I think the author was wrong or maybe gave the wrong weights in his book.

"Rocio, you got the same numbers as Diego, but you did it very differently," I said. "Will you explain what your picture means?"

Rocio said, "I knew the elephant was twenty-two thousand pounds, so I said, 'How many tons is that?' So I kept drawing a ton

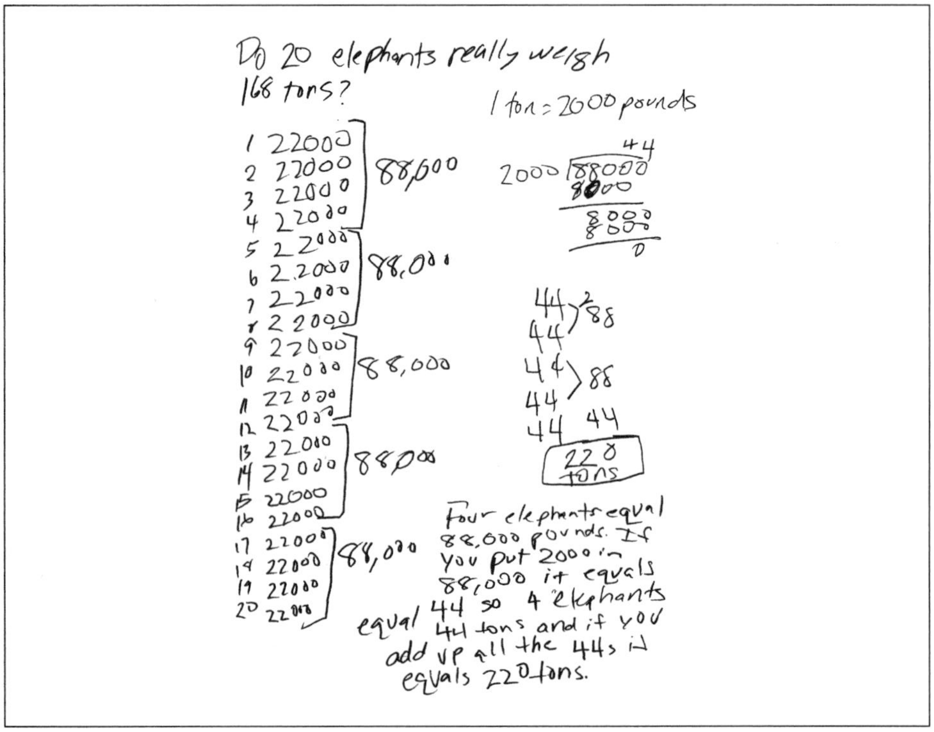

Figure 3–1: Paul changed the elephants' weight to tons, then added.

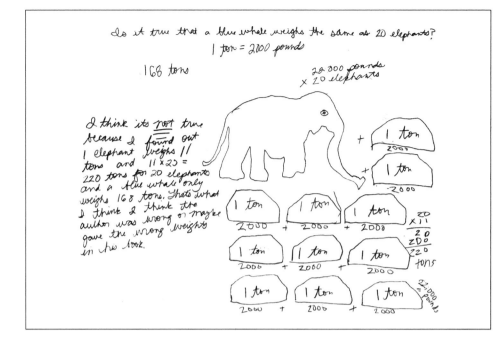

Figure 3–2: Rocio provided a convincing argument about why a blue whale does not weigh the same as twenty elephants.

until it added up to twenty-two thousand, and that's how I knew it was eleven. Then I multiplied that by twenty and got two hundred twenty tons like Diego, so I knew it was more than the whale."

"How come you figured out the tons first?" asked Donald.

"I don't know. That's just what I thought to do," answered Rocio.

"Thanks Rocio. I think we have time to hear from one more person," I said.

"Can I share mine?" Donald asked.

"Sure, Donald," I said as I taped up Rocio's paper.

"I first multiplied one hundred sixty-eight times two thousand to see if I could figure out how many pounds the blue whale weighed. I think it weighs three hundred thirty-six thousand pounds. But when I figured out how many pounds twenty elephants weighed it was four hundred forty thousand, so I knew it was more than the blue whale." (See Figure 3–3.)

"We got four hundred forty thousand for the twenty elephants, too," said Jasmine.

"That's interesting that you converted the whale's weight to pounds," I said. "Can you explain how you did that?"

"Since a ton is two thousand pounds, I multiplied two thousand times one hundred sixty-eight since the whale weighs one hundred sixty-eight tons."

"So it seems like everyone agrees that twenty elephants are heavier than the blue whale. Is that true?" I asked.

Even though not all the students had finished, they were all convinced that the weight of twenty elephants wasn't equal to the weight of one blue whale. "What do you think happened?" I asked. "Steve

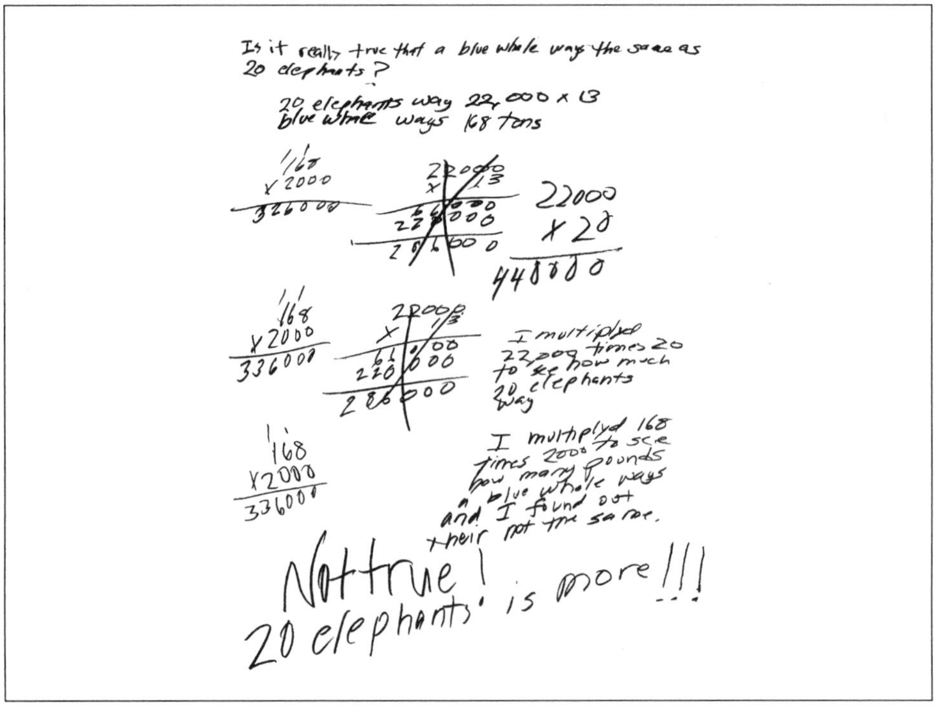

Figure 3–3: Donald found
the weight of twenty
elephants and one blue
whale in pounds and
determined they were not
the same.

Jenkins's books are usually pretty accurate. It surprises me that there would be that much of a discrepancy."

The children didn't have any ideas about what might have happened. I thought the discrepancy might be because we had used the weight of the heaviest elephant ever measured, not the average weight of an elephant. Before I excused the students for lunch, I gave them a homework assignment: "I want everyone to try to find out what a typical elephant weighs. You can go to the library, or search on the Internet, or look in an encyclopedia. Let's see if using the weight of a more typical elephant instead of the heaviest of all time makes a difference."

I collected the children's papers as the children walked out to lunch. I was pleased with their thinking during the lesson and looked forward to reading them the rest of the book.

Additional Ideas

- Use the page about the land snail to have the children explore the statement that if a snail moves 8 inches in a minute it would need $5\frac{1}{2}$ days to travel a mile. Ask them, "Is this true? Can you prove it?"

- Using the page about the flea, ask the students, "If a flea is only $\frac{1}{16}$ of an inch tall and can jump 8 inches into the air, is it really true that it jumps 130 times its own height? How do you know?"

Chimp Math

Taught by Stephanie Sheffield

Ann Whitehead Nagda and Cindy Bickel's *Chimp Math: Learning About Time from a Baby Chimpanzee* (2002) documents the early life of a chimpanzee born in a zoo in Kansas. The chimp's mother was not able to care for it, so zookeepers took over the job. On each of the book's two-page spreads, the right page tells the chimp's story in narrative form, while the left page uses graphs, time lines, charts, and tables to give information about the chimp. In this lesson, third graders are presented with numerical problems to solve mentally and gain experience with graphing data.

MATERIALS

My Baby Milestones chart, 1 per student
(see Blackline Masters)

12-by-18-inch white construction paper,
2 sheets per student

Day 1

I gathered the third graders on the rug to read them *Chimp Math: Learning About Time from a Baby Chimpanzee*. They were interested as soon as they saw the back of the book, which is covered with images of bananas and has the photo of a tiny baby chimp in the center.

"Oh, what a cute monkey," Arabella exclaimed.

"Not a monkey," Jesus corrected, "a chimpanzee."

"OK, a chimpanzee," Arabella allowed.

The book's end papers give a glimpse of its content: We see Jiggs the chimpanzee swinging from a branch, sitting in a car seat, and pulling the ear of a deer. The students were immediately drawn to the little chimp and were excited about hearing the story. I began by reading the introduction, which explains how the book uses time lines, charts, graphs, and other visuals to help tell the story of Jiggs. I told the class that we would be reading the story and examining some of the visuals.

One of the first pages tells about how Jiggs was so small when he went to live in the zoo nursery that he had to be fed two ounces of milk from a bottle every two hours.

"How many feedings did Jiggs have in a day?" I asked. I waited before calling on anyone. I wanted all the students to have a chance to figure out the answer.

"That's easy," Ophelia said when I called on her. "They fed him twelve times."

"That's what I was going to say!" Cedric exclaimed.

"Cedric, can you explain why Jiggs was fed twelve times?" I asked.

"Sure. Twelve plus twelve is twenty-four, so there are two twelves in twenty-four. That means he had twelve feedings."

"Huh? I don't get that," Kayla said.

"How did you get the answer twelve, Ophelia?" I questioned.

"I did it a different way. I used my fingers." Ophelia counted by twos to twenty-four, using her fingers. After reaching twenty, with ten fingers showing, she started over on her fingers to count the last two groups of two. "See, that's twelve twos. That means in twenty-four hours, they fed Jiggs twelve times. But some of that was in the middle of the night." The others seemed to agree, so I went on with the reading.

A graph on page twelve shows Jiggs's weight from birth to seventeen weeks. I read that, although most chimps weigh around four pounds at birth, Jiggs weighed only two pounds, twelve ounces. I asked, "What is the difference between Jiggs's weight and the weight of an average newborn chimp?"

"I think we have to subtract to find out," Jasmine commented.

"What should we subtract?" I asked.

Jasmine thought for a few seconds. While she was thinking, I wrote on the board:

Jiggs's weight: 2 pounds, 12 ounces
Average chimp weight: 4 pounds

I thought about setting up the problem for subtraction, as Jasmine had suggested, by writing the larger weight on top, but, I decided to give the students the opportunity to think about the numbers and solve the problem in their own ways.

Several children raised their hands. I called on Jesus, who said, "Well, Jiggs weighs less, so we have to subtract what he weighs from the bigger number."

Rex said, "Yeah, it should be four pounds take away two pounds, twelve ounces."

"Hmm," I said, "how are we going to do that?"

"Well, four take away two is two," Jasmine said, "Then we have to take twelve ounces away from that."

"Any idea how we might do that?" I asked.

Rex knew there were sixteen ounces in a pound: "I think it would be sixteen ounces minus twelve ounces, so four ounces left. So the answer is one pound, four ounces."

I continued going through the book, stopping every few pages for the students to look at the time lines, graphs, calendars, and charts. Rather than read the text on each page, I showed the graphics to the class and discussed them. The students were delighted with the story of Jiggs, especially because it is illustrated with photographs, and they were interested in the charts and time lines.

Introducing the Investigation

After reading the whole book, I turned back to the chart that compares when a wild chimp and Jiggs learned to walk, suck their thumbs, eat solid food, and attempt other typical childhood events. "Who knows what a milestone is?" I asked. The class was quiet, and I saw a few students shrugging their shoulders.

"Think about the word for a minute, then tell me what comes to mind." After a few moments I called on Jasmine.

"Is it like a stone that marks a mile on a road?" she asked.

"That's one meaning, Jasmine," I replied, "but we also think of a milestone as a different kind of marker. A milestone is an important event that we use to mark a particular stage in a person's life. Most parents keep up with the milestones in a child's life, because they show how the child is growing up. The events listed here on the chart are milestones in Jiggs's life. Why do you think the zookeepers recorded these events?"

Jesus said, "Maybe they wanted to see if Jiggs did things like a wild chimp did."

"Yeah," Carlos added, "Jiggs was too small when he was born, so they had to see if he grew up like the wild chimp. That's why they're both on the chart."

"My baby sister just started to walk, and she's almost one year old," Natalie commented. "Jiggs was only five months old when he took his first step."

"But he was nine months old when he walked alone," Tahlia said. "I think I was eight months old when I walked alone."

"No way!" exclaimed Jesus. "Babies can't walk when they're eight months old!"

I decided to step into this disagreement. "Human babies don't all start walking at the same time, just like Jiggs didn't walk at the same time as most wild chimps. There's a lot of variety in the times when children reach different milestones. That's why I thought you'd be interested in finding out about your own milestones. I've written a letter to your parents for you to take home. The letter explains a bit about the book we read and asks your parents to think about the important milestones in your early life." I held up the letter.

My Baby Milestones

Dear Parents,

Today we read a book which used information about a baby chimp to help us learn math. We are going to gather information about our childhoods to compare them to Jiggs the Chimp. Please help your child fill in his or her ages for each of the milestones below. If you can't remember exact ages, please give us your best guess. We will use this information for a graphing activity.

Thank you.

1. How old was I when I first sucked my thumb or pacifier? _____

2. How old was I when I got my first tooth? _____

3. How old was I when I ate solid food for the first time? _____

4. How old was I when I could sit up by myself? _____

5. How old was I when I began crawling? _____

6. How old was I when I took my first steps? _____

7. How old was I when I could walk alone? _____

"At the bottom of the page are some questions that I want you to ask your parents about your own baby milestones. You can record their answers on these lines." I had chosen milestones that were included in the book about Jiggs so that students could compare their growth with the baby chimp's. The children were excited about this activity, and chatted about it as they put the papers in their homework folders.

Day 2

The next day, the students were eager to share their information. I gave them a few minutes to talk about their milestones with each other before I started the lesson. (See Figures 4–1 and 4–2.)

"Today you're going to compare your milestones with Jiggs's milestones and choose how you want to present the comparison to others. Yesterday we looked at several different ways to represent data related to events and time. What were some of the graphic devices we saw

Figure 4–1: Arabella added
information about her birth
weight to her milestones.

My Baby Milestones

1. How old was I when I first sucked my thumb or a pacifier?
   October 25, 1993 right after I was born

2. How old was I when I got my first tooth? 9 months

3. How old was I when I ate solid food for the first time? 10 months

4. How old was I when I could sit up by myself? 8 months

5. How old was I when I began crawling? 8 months

6. How old was I when I took my first steps? 12 months

7. How old was I when I could walk alone? 14 months

8. How many lbs and oz did you weight 6 lbs & 9 oz

Figure 4–1: Arabella added
information about her birth
weight to her milestones.

Figure 4–2: Tisha's mother
added information about
Tisha and her twin brother.

My Baby Milestones

1. How old was I when I first sucked my thumb or a pacifier?
   4 mos.

2. How old was I when I got my first tooth? 3 months

3. How old was I when I ate solid food for the first time? 8 mos.

4. How old was I when I could sit up by myself? 8 mos.

5. How old was I when I began crawling? 10 mos.

6. How old was I when I took my first steps? 15 mos.

7. How old was I when I could walk alone? 15 mos.

Tisha came quietly into the world at 12:06 PM on January 21, 1994. She weighed only 4 pounds, 5 ounces, but she was a very long 21 inches, and it didn't take her very long to catch up with her twin brother in every way. They cut their first teeth within days of each other, and they began walking on the same day.

used in the book we read?" I listed the graphics on the board as the students called them out.

time lines
bar graphs
charts
calendars

"Today you'll choose one of these to represent your data and Jiggs's data, so that someone looking at your paper could easily see how your milestones compare. Your first step will be to sketch out a rough draft of whatever you choose to do, whether it's a chart, a graph, a time line, or a calendar. I want you to think about which of these will most clearly present the information you have. On the board, I've written the ages at which Jiggs reached the same milestones you asked your parents about. Think about what you need to have on your graph. Who can name one thing your graph will need?" I waited a bit until there were several hands in the air, then I called on Giovanni.

"You have to have a title," he said, "but what should the title be?"

"Each one of you will have to decide on a title for your graph or time line," I replied.

Ophelia said, "You need numbers to tell how many months, like how many months I was when I sucked my thumb and how many months Jiggs was."

"Yes," I said, "you'll need to think about how many months you need to represent on your graph, and what kind of interval you'll need to get all those months to fit on your paper."

The students went back to their desks in high spirits. I passed out plain white paper for their rough drafts, and they got started immediately. Most of the children talked about making bar graphs or time lines. They worked on their rough drafts until it was time for science. (See Figures 4–3 and 4–4.) I asked them to finish their rough drafts for homework.

Day 3

The next day the students were eager to get started again. I distributed sheets of 12-by-18-inch white construction paper, and I circulated as they began their final graphs. The two children who had originally chosen to create time lines had changed their minds, and all the students were now making either bar graphs or some form of chart. Some used rulers to draw straight lines and make the intervals on the sides of their graphs equal. Others weren't as interested in being precise. (See Figures 4–5 and 4–6.)

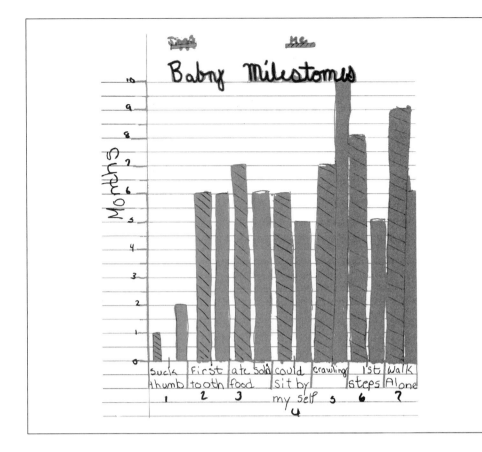

Figure 4-3: On Sylvia's rough draft, the bars representing her milestones have diagonal lines while Jiggs's bars are solid.

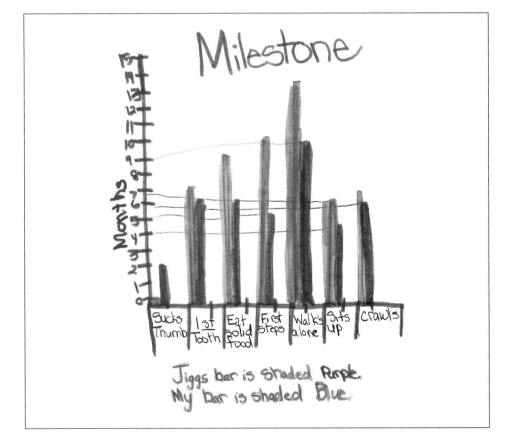

Figure 4-4: Jessie used horizontal pencil marks to connect the tops of her milestone bars with the "Months" numbers on the side.

Figure 4–5: Tisha used tally marks to represent her age at each milestone, but she forgot to include a key to explain how much time each tally represented.

Figure 4–6: Chelsie's bar graph was clear and easy to read.

Math and Nonfiction, Grades 3–5

About fifteen minutes before the end of class, I called the students to the floor at the front of the room and invited Arabella to come up to share her graph. She had drawn side-by-side bars to represent herself and Jiggs. Before I asked for the other children's comments, I explained the purpose of this part of the activity:

"Arabella's graph is really looking good so far, as many of yours are. But sometimes it's a good idea to get feedback along the way when we are trying to represent information. Sometimes someone else can look at our work and easily see something we could do to improve it, when we didn't notice that same thing. This helps us revise our work and make it the best it can be. Try to remember, when you offer a suggestion, that everyone has worked hard on their graphs so far, so keep your suggestions kind and positive. Is there anything Arabella could do to make her graph better?" Several children had ideas to share. I called on Courtney first.

"She could color in the bars, one color for Jiggs and a different color for herself," Courtney suggested.

Sylvia said, "I think she should write her words bigger at the bottom so they are easier to read."

Ophelia commented, "Her title needs to be at the top."

I asked Cedric to bring up his graph for the others to see. I began by asking him a question: "Before we listen to others' opinions, is there anything you would like to change?" I wanted to know if Cedric could see his work in a new light after hearing the suggestions about Arabella's work.

"Yes," he answered. "I need to write *months* on the side. And I need a key so it shows which bars are me and which are Jiggs."

After one more student shared with the class, I sent the children back to their desks to finish their graphs. Many of them used the suggestions from the class discussion to improve their work, making it clearer to read or easier to understand. In math, when we ask students to answer questions, we typically check the answers and give the students a grade. We seldom allow students to revise their mathematical work after getting feedback, as we would in a composition class. I want students to develop the habit of examining their mathematical work and thinking about how to make it more complete. As Figure 4–7 shows, a student can revise a rough draft and create a neat, easy-to-read graph.

As the students finished their graphs, I suggested that they write questions that could be answered by looking at their graphs. (See Figure 4–8.) After the graphs were posted on the wall, the children could read and try to answer each other's questions.

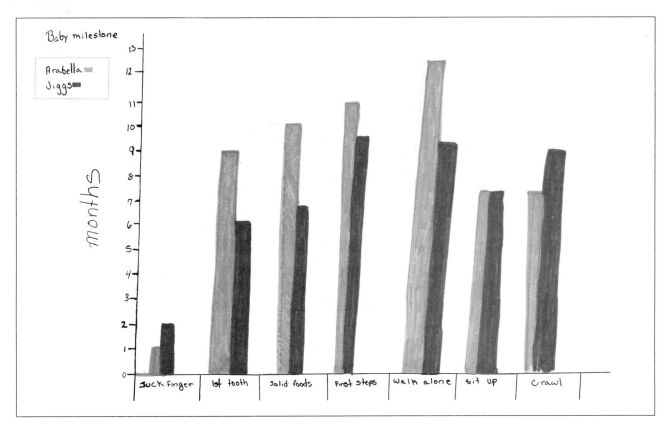

Figure 4–7: Arabella took many of the suggestions given to her and created a neat, easy-to-read graph.

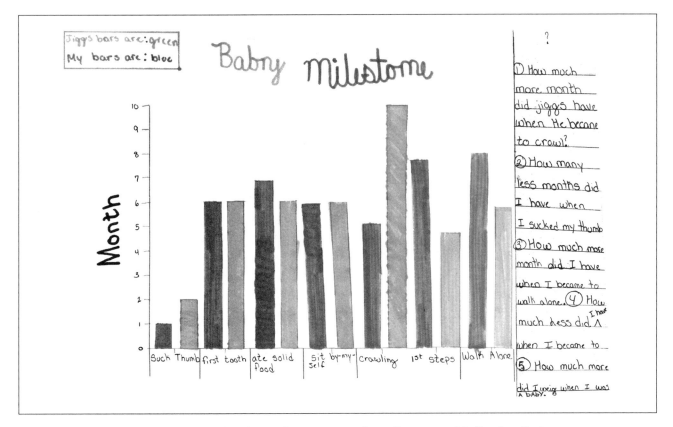

Figure 4–8: Sylvia wrote questions asking the reader to compare her milestones with Jiggs's milestones.

Dealing with Addition

Taught by Stephanie Sheffield

Lynette Long's *Dealing with Addition* (1998) introduces opportunities for children to explore a deck of playing cards by asking them to find different combinations of cards that add up to the numbers from one to ten. In this lesson in a third-grade classroom, students use cards to find number combinations for various sums.

MATERIALS

standard playing cards, 1 deck per student

optional: overhead playing cards or large playing cards for demonstration

The third graders were waiting for me on the rug when I arrived. They knew I was coming to read a book to them, and they were anxious to find out what it was. I held up *Dealing with Addition.*

"Look! It's cards!" Terrance exclaimed.

"I'll bet you can tell what this book will be about, can't you?" I asked.

"Sure," Samud said. "It's about adding with cards."

"And what does *dealing* mean?" I asked.

Keith responded, "It's the way you pass out the cards. Like one by one. But you can't look at them and pick the ones you want. My mom taught me how to deal cards, and I can shuffle, too." Keith was excited to be able to contribute his knowledge to our conversation.

"Why do we shuffle cards?" I asked.

Theo, Trevor, and Terracita raised their hands. I called on Terracita, who said, "You have to mix them up, so you don't know who is getting which cards. That's fair."

I took one deck out of its box and fanned out the cards in one hand. Walking around the group on the floor, I showed them to the students and asked, "What do you notice about these cards?"

"There's a pattern," Tracy observed. "Red, black, red, black."

"Anything else?" I asked.

"They're all in order," Aaron said. "I think that's why you have to shuffle them."

I began to read the book out loud. The first few pages introduce the four suits of cards and explain what pairs and face cards are. The book then introduces the idea of making number combinations by adding the numbers on cards. We went through the page that asks readers to find two different ways to make the number two by combining the cards pictured: the ace of diamonds, ace of clubs, ace of hearts, and 2 of clubs.

Theo suggested, "Add the ace of diamonds and the ace of clubs." I recorded $1 + 1 = 2$ on the board using 1s to represent the aces. (The books explain that there aren't any cards with the number one, but only cards with an A, which stands for *ace*.)

"What about the two by itself?" Samud asked.

"What number sentence could we use to represent that?" I asked.

I wrote Samud's answer on the board: $2 + 0 = 2$.

"Are there any other cards that could be combined to make a sum of two?" I asked.

Trevor responded, "I think that's all, unless the different aces count different."

"No, we'll count them as the same because they'll give the same math sentence," I replied. I turned the page and we saw that the author shows two ways to make the number two. The book doesn't show the sentence $2 + 0 = 2$, but just a 2. The children agreed that our number sentence meant the same thing. I think it's valuable to incorporate zero into math discussions wherever possible.

I explained again, "For this activity we'll use each number only once. For example, an ace of clubs plus an ace of hearts is the same as an ace of diamonds plus an ace of hearts. Does everybody understand what I mean?" Although all the students nodded, I expected to have to go over that rule again when the combinations became more complicated.

I read the challenge on the next page, which asks how many ways the reader can make the sum of three using combinations of the following cards: 3 of diamonds, ace of hearts, ace of clubs, ace of spades, and 2 of hearts. As students suggested combinations, I recorded them on the board: $2 + 1 = 3$, $3 + 0 = 3$, and $1 + 1 + 1 = 3$. Then I turned the page and we checked our results, again agreeing that our $3 + 0 = 3$ meant the same as the 3 shown on the page. We repeated the activity for the number four, as suggested on the next page, finding the combinations and recording them.

I then said, "Before I show you the page for five, I'd like you all to go back to your seats. I've put notebook paper on your desks, and you're going to find the combinations that make five on your own. On your way to your desk, please pick up a deck of cards from the table." I went to the overhead projector and laid out the seven cards shown in the book on the five page: ace of diamonds, 5 of hearts, ace of spades, 3 of clubs, 2 of spades, ace of clubs, and 4 of diamonds. If I didn't have overhead or large-size playing cards to demonstrate, I would list the cards on the board using symbols for the suits.

"You'll need to find these cards in your deck and take them out," I directed. The students didn't have much trouble finding the cards because I had given them new decks to use, and they were still in order. If we were using decks that weren't in order, I might have the students put them in order, or I might discuss the fact that the suit of each card doesn't matter in this problem. As long as students have enough cards depicting the particular numbers they need, their combinations will be correct.

"Using these cards, make combinations that equal five, the same way we did for the smaller numbers," I directed. "Write a number sentence for each way you find. In a few minutes we'll share your solutions." The room became quiet as the children moved the cards around on their desks and recorded or sketched the combinations. I walked around the room observing and offering help when needed.

After a few minutes, Theo announced, "I'm done. I've got five." Samud and Thomas both agreed. Not everyone had found all five combinations possible with the cards given, but I wanted to move on to a more challenging problem and deal with an issue I knew was going to come up.

As Samud, Sarah, and Aaron reported their solutions in turn, I wrote them on the board:

$$1 + 1 + 1 + 2 = 5$$

$$3 + 1 + 1 = 5$$

$$2 + 2 + 1 = 5$$

Samud, Thomas, and Terrance objected to Aaron's combination: "That's not right, there aren't two 2s!" After briefly reminding the class that mistakes are opportunities for learning and that we were all there to help each other learn, I asked Terrance to explain.

"You can only use the cards on the overhead. He used two 2s, but there's only one on the overhead," he said.

"That's right," I confirmed. "The problem I gave you was to use this set of cards to make the sum of five, so this last combination won't work. Do you have another combination you'd like to share, Aaron?"

I could see Aaron erasing the combination he had just given, but he stopped and looked at his paper. (See Figure 5–1.) "How about three plus two equals five?" he asked. I looked around the room for confirming nods and added it to the list on the board: *3 + 2 = 5*. Two other students contributed *4 + 1 = 5* and *5 + 0 = 5*.

Lupe raised her hand tentatively. "I know another one, but I don't think it's right. Is it different if you say 'two plus three equals five'?"

"That's a good question, Lupe," I replied. "Of course the sum stays the same when you change the order of the numbers, and in some games or problems each number sentence would count separately, but not for this activity. Once you've used a set of addends, you can't use them again in a different order. Does that make sense to everyone?"

La'vonda asked, "What's an *addend*?" I looked around the room and called on Huong, whose hand was up.

"It means a number you add together to get a sum," she said.

"That's right, Huong. Now, are you all ready for a bigger challenge?" I asked. I saw smiles and nods of assent.

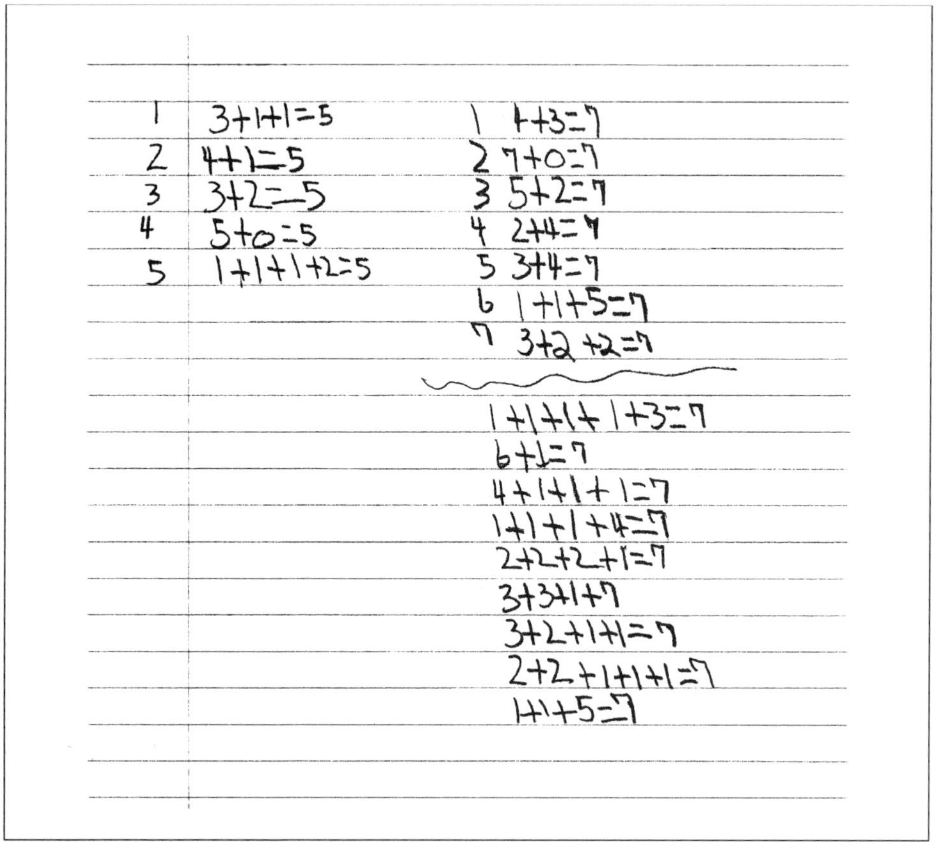

Figure 5–1: Aaron erased the combination he had written with two twos. He also found all the combinations possible with the given cards.

Math and Nonfiction, Grades 3–5

"We're going to skip the page on six, and go straight to seven. Here are the cards you'll need to use," I said, putting the eight cards shown in the book on the overhead: 3 of clubs, 7 of hearts, ace of diamonds, 5 of spades, 4 of hearts, 2 of diamonds, ace of clubs, 2 of spades.

"Before you begin, think about this," I said. "How many combinations of seven do you think there will be using these cards?"

The students yelled out together, "Seven!"

Valentina added, "It's seven for seven. There were five ways to make five, so there will be seven ways to make seven." The children were correct. The cards were purposely chosen so that there were seven combinations for seven, just as there had been five combinations for five. With other cards, another three for example, there would be more ways to make seven.

"Let's see if you're right," I said. "You can get to work now finding these cards and then using them to make combinations of seven."

The students went through their decks of cards looking for the ones on the overhead. Lupe looked frustrated and asked, "Do they have to match exactly?"

"What do you mean?" I asked.

"Well, I found a 2, but it isn't diamonds. Can I use any 2?"

"For this problem, Lupe, yes, you can use cards of any suit, as long as you have the same numbers on your cards as are on the ones I put up." She looked relieved and continued to go through her deck. This question came up once or twice more, and I answered the same way each time.

As I walked around I noticed that Samud seemed to be wrestling with a question. "Can we use two 2s?" he asked.

I asked another question in reply: "Do we have two 2s in your set to start with?"

"Yes," he replied. "Oh, it's OK then," he said and went on working.

Keith said to Samud, "I got seven combinations."

Tracy said, "I got six combinations."

"I got nine," Nakita said.

Keith looked at the girls. "It's always going to be the same number as the number of combinations."

"What do you mean?" Nakita asked.

"Since the number we're trying to get is seven, there should be seven ways to get it," he explained. "It's a pattern." Nakita searched her paper and found two duplicate combinations.

As some students decided that they were finished with finding combinations of seven, I presented an extension to the problem. "I want you to think about this problem in an expanded way. What if you could use all the numbered cards in the deck? How many new combinations could you find using all the cards?" (At the back of the book, the author lists all the possible combinations for the numbers from one to ten using all the cards from aces through 10s. There are thirteen combinations for seven.)

The students who had found the basic seven combinations got to work on the extension. When I was sure that all of the students had completed the initial problem, I asked the children to return to the meeting place on the rug.

"Let's look at the combinations you found for the first part of the problem," I said. As the students reported their seven combinations, I recorded them on the board:

$$7 + 0 = 7$$
$$3 + 4 = 7$$
$$5 + 2 = 7$$
$$3 + 2 + 2 = 7$$
$$3 + 2 + 1 + 1 = 7$$
$$5 + 1 + 1 = 7$$
$$4 + 2 + 1 = 7$$

"What are some other ways you made seven?" I asked.

At Santos's suggestion, I recorded $3 + 3 + 1 = 7$.

As Lupe spoke, I wrote $2 + 2 + 1 + 1 + 1 = 7$.

"I have a different one," Mitchell said, and I recorded $2 + 4 + 1 = 7$.

When I wrote Tracy's suggestion, $1 + 1 + 2 + 2 + 1 = 7$, Sarah raised her hand right away. "I think that's the same as Lupe's," she said. "They both have two 2s and three 1s." Others agreed, as did Tracy, so I erased her suggestion.

We continued in this way, recording additional combinations of seven. As more and more combinations got repeated, I decided to end the lesson because we were spending more time looking for repetition than was valuable for the experience. The class time was just about over, and I was interested to hear the students' reactions to the lesson.

"Who can tell me something you learned today, or something you found interesting about the activity?" I asked.

Valentina raised her hand. "I learned that if you have the same numbers, it doesn't matter which one comes first or second or third, the answer is the same."

"I learned that there are four suits of cards," Thomas contributed.

Lupe added, "Yeah, spades, clubs, hearts, and diamonds. Two red and two black."

I called on Trevor. "I found out there are four of every card in the box. Like four 5s, four 6s, four kings. Like that."

"I learned that there are lots of ways of making seven," Aaron said.

Terrance said, "There's always a plus zero, and there's always a plus one."

"I found that out too," Valentina agreed. "If you want to be sure you get them all, you can do the one pluses, then add two, like that."

When there were no more hands raised, I said, "Before class ends, I want to go back to the book for a minute." I showed the class the page with the combinations of seven. "You were right, there are seven combinations of seven using the cards on the previous page." Indicating the facing page, I said, "There are other sets of cards here for eight, then nine, then ten. I'll leave the book here for you to explore these other number combinations if you're interested. There's also a game on the last page that you may be interested in playing."

This activity was just right for this class of third graders. Because the addition was easy enough for them to do, they were able to focus on the problem-solving aspect of finding all the possible combinations. They worked hard and steadily, sharing the solutions and strategies depicted in Figures 5–2, 5–3, and 5–4.

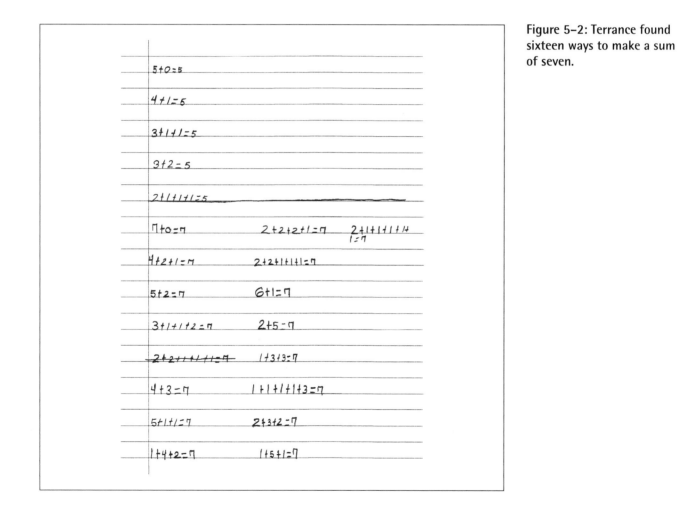

Figure 5–2: Terrance found sixteen ways to make a sum of seven.

Figure 5–3: When Kerry began the extension he used all four aces first, then moved on to other combinations with fewer aces.

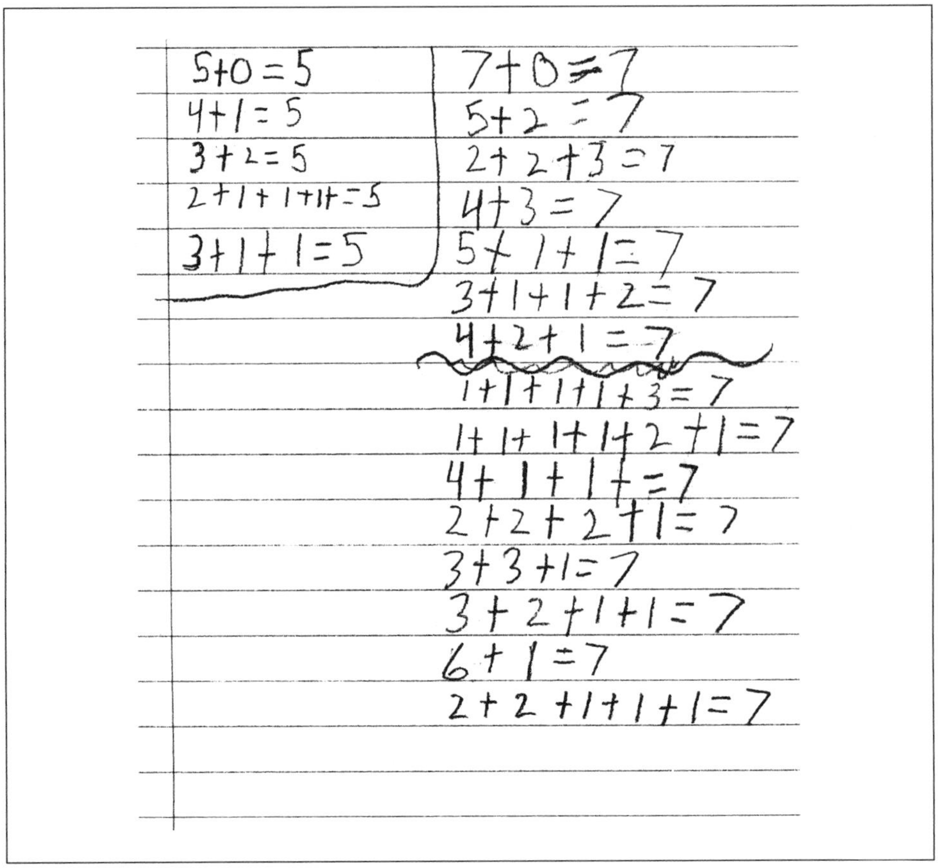

$5 + 0 = 5$ $7 + 0 = 7$
$4 + 1 = 5$ $5 + 2 = 7$
$3 + 2 = 5$ $2 + 2 + 3 = 7$
$2 + 1 + 1 + 1 = 5$ $4 + 3 = 7$
$3 + 1 + 1 = 5$ $5 + 1 + 1 = 7$
                     $3 + 1 + 1 + 2 = 7$
                     $4 + 2 + 1 = 7$
                     $1 + 1 + 1 + 1 + 3 = 7$
                     $1 + 1 + 1 + 1 + 2 + 1 = 7$
                     $4 + 1 + 1 = 7$
                     $2 + 2 + 2 + 1 = 7$
                     $3 + 3 + 1 = 7$
                     $3 + 2 + 1 + 1 = 7$
                     $6 + 1 = 7$
                     $2 + 2 + 1 + 1 + 1 = 7$

Figure 5–4: Mitchell struggled to find combinations of seven and erased them as he found duplicates.

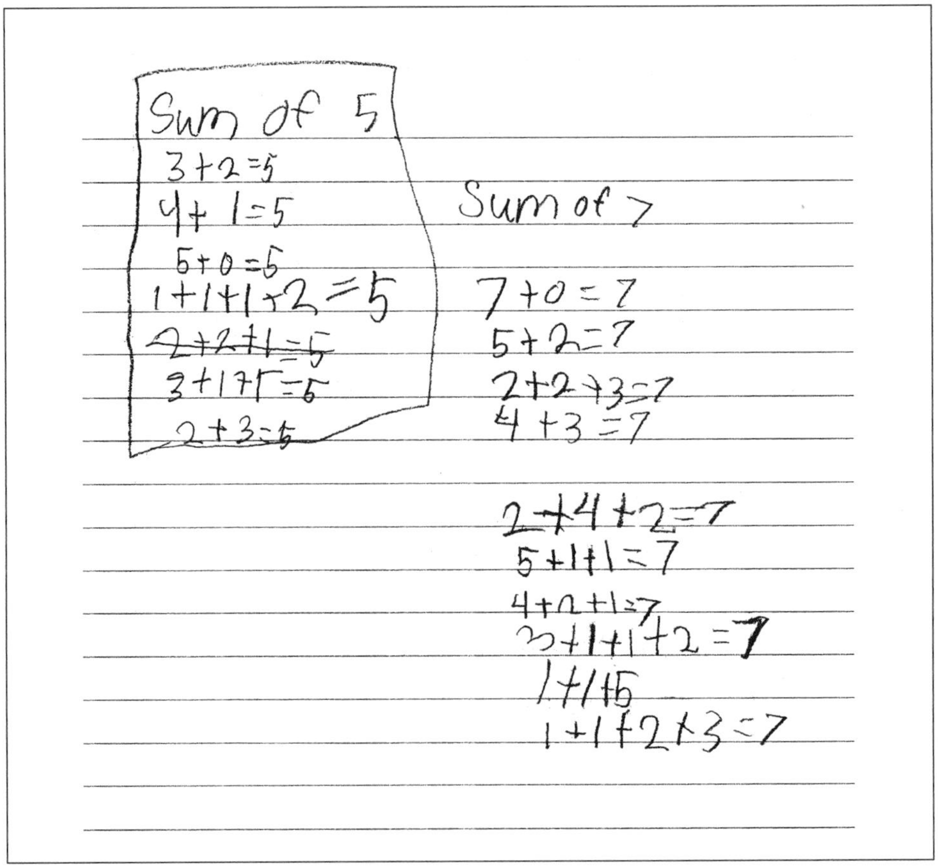

Sum of 5
$3 + 2 = 5$
$4 + 1 = 5$
$5 + 0 = 5$
$1 + 1 + 1 + 2 = 5$
$2 + 2 + 1 = 5$
$3 + 1 + 1 = 5$
$2 + 3 = 5$

Sum of 7
$7 + 0 = 7$
$5 + 2 = 7$
$2 + 2 + 3 = 7$
$4 + 3 = 7$

$2 + 4 + 2 = 7$
$5 + 1 + 1 = 7$
$4 + 2 + 1 = 7$
$3 + 1 + 1 + 2 = 7$
$1 + 1 + 5$
$1 + 1 + 2 + 3 = 7$

Ed Emberley's Picture Pie
Taught by Stephanie Sheffield

In *Ed Emberley's Picture Pie: A Circle Drawing Book* (1984), the author shows readers how to use simple shapes—whole circles and circles in halves, fourths, and eighths—to create beautiful pictures. The pieces used are all cut from the same size circle, which makes the book work well as an introduction to fractions. In the first lesson described here, third graders explore fractions as parts of a whole, using circle pieces to create symmetrical pictures and identifying the fractional part of the original circle each piece represents. In the second lesson, taught in a fifth-grade class, students create pictures with different-colored halves, fourths, and eighths of circles, then figure out the total fractional value of each color in their pictures.

MATERIALS

circles, 3- or 4-inch in diameter, cut out of different colors of construction paper, 6–10 per student

12-by-18-inch black construction paper, 1 sheet per student

Third-Grade Lesson

I began the lesson by sharing *Ed Emberley's Picture Pie* with the class. The children delighted in his illustrious.

I then held up a construction paper circle, folded it in half, and asked, "If I fold this circle like this, how many parts will I have?"

The students responded confidently together, "Two."

Peyton added, "It's half."

"How do you know it's half?" I asked, as I wrote the word *Half* on the board.

"Because you're folding it in the middle," he answered.

I pressed down the fold to make a sharp crease, then opened the circle and cut it in half on the fold. I held up the two pieces and asked, "What can you tell me about these two pieces?"

"They're both halves," Gustavo said.

Lauren added, "They're the same size . . . exactly."

"OK," I said holding up half the circle, "what name would I use for this piece of the circle?"

"That's one-half," Thui said.

"How do I write that number?" I asked.

Jourdyn stood up and directed me: "You write a one, then a line under it, then a two."

I wrote $\frac{1}{2}$ as she spoke, then wrote it again with a slanted line: *1/2*.

"Some people write one-half with a horizontal line between the one and the two, and some people use a slanted line. Both ways are correct," I explained. I held up one of the halves and I said, "The two on the bottom means the whole circle was cut into two equal pieces. The one on top refers to the one piece I'm holding."

Next, I folded another circle, not in half but into one small section and one larger one. The students immediately began making disapproving sounds.

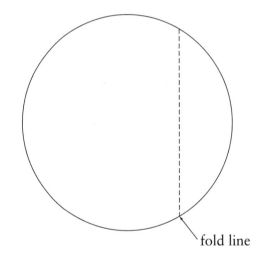

fold line

"That's not half!" Christina complained. "It's not fair."

"What do you mean by *fair*?" I asked.

"The pieces have to be the same to be fair," she replied.

"Can someone rephrase what Christina is telling us?" I asked.

"I can," Jenny said confidently. "One-half means you have one piece of something that is cut into two equal parts." On the board I wrote:

$$\frac{1}{2} \qquad \frac{one\ part}{two\ equal\ parts}$$

As I placed a stack of cut-out circles at each table, I directed the students to each take a paper circle, fold it in half, cut, and then label both halves. "As you write $\frac{1}{2}$ I want you to say quietly to yourself, 'one out of two equal parts.'" I walked around the room and watched the children cut and label their halves.

Next, I held up another uncut circle and asked for the class's attention again. This time I folded the circle in half and then in half again, to make fourths. Before I unfolded it I asked, "How many parts will the paper circle have when I unfold it now?"

Many children answered out loud: "Four."

I directed them to each take a circle, fold it in half and then in half again, and then unfold the circle and see how many parts it had. The children seemed pleased when they counted and found four parts, as they had expected.

"Before we cut this circle apart, let's label each section. What fraction can we use to name one part of the circle?" I asked.

I called on Braden after waiting to be sure most of the class had had time to think about it. "I think one-fourth," he said.

"Will you come to the board and write that number, please?" I asked Braden.

As other students began to label each of their four parts with $\frac{1}{4}$, I pointed to the fraction Braden wrote and asked, "Who can explain what this means?"

Booker answered, "Each little pizza piece is *one*, and there are four altogether, so one out of four. I think they look like pizza slices," he explained.

I directed the students to take another circle, fold it into fourths, then fold it in half one more time. "Now how many parts do you think you'll have when you unfold your circle?" I asked.

This time there was disagreement. Most of the class thought there would be six parts, but Booker, Sailor, and Peyton were convinced there would be eight. When they unfolded their circles and counted, I heard several surprised "Oh!"s.

Maria said, "I thought there would be six, but there are eight."

Colleen raised her hand and said, "I get it now. I thought it was like, two, four, six. But if you have four things, like the pizza, and you cut them in half, then each one has two pieces now, so it's two, four, eight."

I talked with the class about how to write the fraction $\frac{1}{8}$, then waited until all the students had finished labeling their eighths and cutting their circles. I asked for their attention again.

I explained, "You're going to use whole circles, halves, fourths, and eighths to make a design, and as you do it you'll be using two math concepts. One is the fractions we use to describe the pieces you've just cut, and the other is a concept we've talked about before—*symmetry*. Who remembers what *symmetry* means?" I gave the children several seconds to think and then called on Alicia.

"It's like a mirror. Both sides are the same," Alicia explained.

"That's right, Alicia," I confirmed. "If you fold a shape or a picture on a line of symmetry, the two sides will match up exactly. The design you will make today will be symmetrical. You will make your picture using the paper circles on your desks, cutting some of the circles into equal pieces. So there are two things you have to pay attention to as you make your design. Who can tell the class what those two things are?"

I called on Gustavo, who said, "It has to have symmetry."

"That's right," I replied. "If you use an eighth of a blue circle on one side, you have to use an eighth of a blue circle on the other side. What's the other thing to remember about the pictures?"

Several children raised their hands. "We're doing fractions, so you have to cut the circles into fractions," Kaleb said.

"Yes, Kaleb. You can cut any one circle into halves, fourths, or eighths, but the parts you cut it into must always be equal. You may use one whole circle in your picture, but only one."

I walked around passing out black construction paper that would be the background for the pictures, and the children quickly became engrossed in folding, cutting, and placing colored sections of circles. I watched to see how they were creating their symmetrical pictures, encouraging them to think about where they wanted to place their circles and circle parts, and to move the pieces around until they were sure they were ready to glue them down. As the students finished their pictures, they wrote their names on the back with white chalk and left them on their desks to dry. Each child chose a book to read until everyone had finished.

When the last student had completed his work, I called the class back to the meeting place and asked them to bring their pictures. "What mathematical ideas did you explore as you made your pictures?" I asked.

"We had to use symmetry," Delfina commented.

"How did you go about making your picture symmetrical?" I probed.

"I just made sure that whatever I put on one side I put the same thing on the other side," Delfina said.

I put the pictures on the walls so that all the students could appreciate them and discuss their symmetry over the next several days.

Fifth-Grade Lesson

When I showed the fifth graders *Ed Emberley's Picture Pie*, I focused their attention on geometry in art. "What kinds of geometric figures do you see in artwork?" I asked.

"Shapes," Miranda replied. "Like triangles, rectangles, squares, and stuff."

"What else?" I asked.

"Angles?" Tiffany said hesitantly.

"What kind of angles might you see?" I continued.

Noah said, "Right angles."

Chelsea followed immediately: "And obtuse angles, the big ones."

"How would you describe obtuse angles?" I asked.

Chelsea answered, "They're bigger than ninety degrees."

"And what if they are smaller than ninety degrees?"

"The little ones are *acute*," Lauren answered. "They're less than ninety degrees."

"Can you think of any other geometric figures or elements you might see in artwork?" I asked.

Lucas raised his hand. "I think symmetry."

"What do you mean by *symmetry*?"

"I think it means when both sides are exactly the same. Like if you have a red square on one side, there's a red square on the other side."

"You've thought of a lot of geometry words that name shapes and concepts that are used in artwork. In this book, the author, Ed Emberley, explores using another mathematical concept to create art." I held up the book. "He starts with many congruent circles and cuts them into pieces of equal size, then puts the pieces together to make pictures. Just to review, who can tell me what *congruent* means?" Several hands were raised and I called on Lauren.

"It means same shape and size," she explained.

As she answered I picked up a paper circle from my pile and folded it in half, then opened the circle and cut it in half on the fold. "What can you tell me about the value of one of these pieces?"

Miranda replied, "It's one out of two."

"One-half," Sherrod added. I asked Sherrod to write that fraction on the board. I picked up another circle and folded it in half and then in half again.

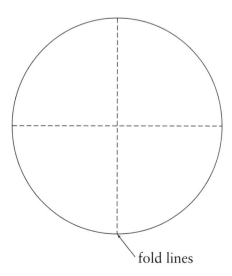

fold lines

"What am I doing now?" I asked.

"You're making it smaller," Sherrod said.

Miguel said, "You're making more."

I opened the circle and showed it to the students. I asked, cutting the circle into fourths, "How many congruent pieces are there?"

Lucas answered, "Four. The more you fold, the more pieces you get."

I held up one of the pieces and asked, "How much is this worth?"

Noah spoke up: "It was one whole, but you made it into four pieces. You're holding one of the pieces, so it's one-fourth."

Lucas came to the board and wrote $\frac{1}{4}$ to indicate the pieces I held up.

Next I cut a third circle into four uneven pieces. The class began to call out, "That's wrong," and "You can't do that!"

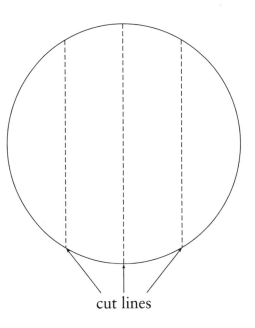

cut lines

Alex raised her hand and explained, "You can't do that. The pieces have to be equal."

"I agree," I said putting aside the oddly shaped pieces. "The four pieces must be equal in area to be fourths."

I picked up another circle and quickly folded it in half and then in half again. As the students watched, I folded it in half one more time. "What can you tell me about the parts you'll see when I open the circle?" I asked.

Several children in the class answered at once, "They're all congruent!"

I was surprised by their answer because I was expecting them to think about the number of parts. I asked, "How many parts will the circle have when I open it up?" About half the class answered, "Six" and the other half answered, "Eight." A loud argument ensued. I got the students' attention back. "Let's just find out," I said, and unfolded the circle. The class counted the parts together. When they discovered there were eight parts, there were a few "Told you so's" before I got their attention again.

"Rather than argue, who can tell me why someone might think there were going to be six parts?" I asked.

Sherrod answered, "Because it was two, then four, and then it would be six." I agreed with Sherrod that that pattern exists in many places, and recorded the pattern on the board:

2, 4, 6

Then I recorded this pattern:

2, 4, 8

"Who can explain what this pattern means in this context?" I asked.

Alyssa began, "The four pieces, if you cut them in half you get eight."

I took two of the one-fourth pieces and put a tiny bit of sticky tack on the back of each. I stuck them to the board like this:

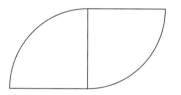

"If I put these two pieces together, how much do I have?"

Ethan called out, "Two-fourths." The rest of the class disagreed. They said, "One-half."

"You're both right," I said. "One-half and two-fourths are two names for the same amount." Then I picked up one of the fourths and turned it, creating the shape of half of the original circle.

Tiffany said, "You still have two-fourths. It doesn't matter how you put them."

"What if I put these together," I asked, holding up two one-fourth pieces and one one-eighth piece. "How much are these worth together?"

I waited for several children to raise their hands, then called on Ethan. He answered uncertainly, "One-third?"

"Hmm," I said. "There are three of these pieces. Can they be thirds?"

Miguel answered, "They aren't equal. They can't be thirds. Besides, that's almost the whole circle when you put it together."

"How does that help you think about the fractions, Miguel?"

He thought for a moment, then said, "Well, a third is smaller than a half, and when you hold those three pieces together, it's more than a half, so they can't be thirds."

Samantha said, "It's half of one piece and half of another."

"What if I want to name how much this is, using only one fraction?" I asked.

"Could we say *twelfths*?" Chelsea asked.

"How did you get twelfths, Chelsea?" Tiffany asked.

"I added eight and four, since one piece is a fourth and two pieces are eighths. But I don't think it's right."

To help her clarify her thinking I asked, "Are twelfths bigger or smaller than fourths?"

"Smaller," Chelsea answered.

Tiffany added, "When you cut them, the pieces get smaller."

"Let's think about the names we gave for these two pieces a few minutes ago," I encouraged.

"Well, it's two eighths because we cut the yellow circle into eight pieces, but two are the same size as the blue one-fourth," Chelsea explained.

"This is an important thing to know about fractions," I explained. "The same amount of the circle can be named using different fractions. This will be important to remember later in the activity."

I held up *Ed Emberley's Picture Pie* again and asked the students to notice that the pictures on the cover were made using pieces cut from circles, as we had just done. I gave them these directions: "You'll use circles and circle pieces to make pictures, too, and later you'll use fractions to describe your pictures. I've cut congruent circles from many colors of construction paper and you'll cut the circles into equal parts to use for your picture. You don't have to have a picture of an actual thing, like these pictures of birds Ed Emberley has done," I said, showing the pictures. "On some pages he just creates designs, but he always uses circles and parts of circles to create the design."

"How many circles can we use?" Lauren asked.

"I've cut lots, so you can use as many as you want. But you must cut them into equal parts so that you can describe each part using a fraction."

As the children walked back to their desks, I gave each a piece of black construction paper, then I put construction paper circles in various colors on their desks so that every student would have easy access to them. The students began cutting circles right away, and positioning the circle pieces on the black paper. I was amazed at how quiet the room became as the students carefully made their designs. The fifth graders were totally engrossin this project.

When most of the students had finished creating their pictures, I called the class back to the meeting area to give them the next directions. "Now that you have created your own works of art, I'd like you to go back and find out how much of each color you used in your design. Start by picking one color. Write a number sentence adding all the parts of that color and show how you combine all the fractions together. Then go on to another color. Do this for all the colors in your design."

"What if we used more than one whole circle of one color?" Tiffany asked.

"If you used enough parts to create a whole circle and then more, you'll be representing your number as a mixed number," I replied.

As the students worked on this new assignment, I walked around observing their work and helping when needed. Paige raised her hand for help. "I don't get what I'm supposed to do," she said.

"OK," I said, "what color would you like to start with?" Paige chose brown. "You need to start by writing a number sentence adding all the fractional parts of the circle that are brown," I explained. I pointed to one brown piece, which was one-eighth of a circle. "What fraction of a circle is this?" I asked.

"One eighth," Paige answered. She wrote: *Brown* $\frac{1}{8}$. Then she counted all her brown wedges. "There's seven of them. Do I just add them together?"

"Yes, just write a number sentence adding all the eighths," I said.

Paige moved on to her light-blue circle parts, and recorded her addition sentence with eighths and fourths. (See Figure 6–1 on page 56.)

Lucas used many different colors for his abstract design. He grouped the like fractions together to add, but didn't always rename them using the smallest denominator possible. (See Figure 6–2 on page 56.)

See Figures 6–3 and 6–4 on page 57 for other students' designs and addition sentences.

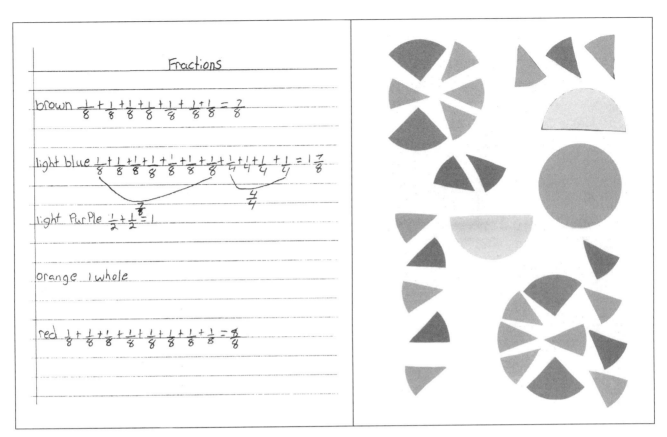

Figure 6–1: Paige had trouble getting started, but correctly wrote number sentences for all her colors.

Figure 6–2: Lucas used many colors and wrote addition sentences for them all.

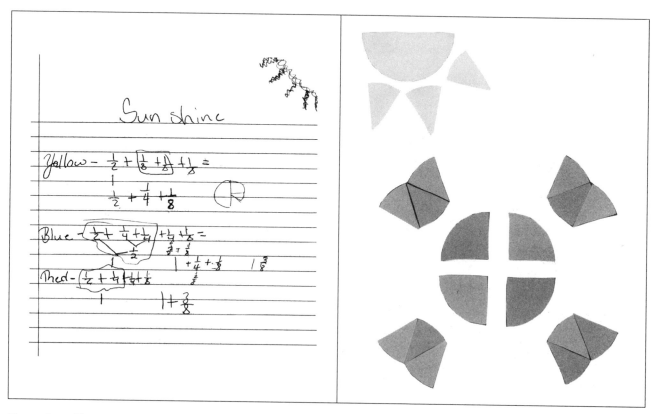

Figure 6–3: When Conchita added her blue eighths, she got $\frac{5}{4}$. She changed the improper fraction to a mixed number, then added it to two blue halves to get a sum of $2\frac{1}{4}$.

Figure 6–4: Alyssa drew a small circle to help her figure out that $\frac{1}{8}$ plus $\frac{1}{8}$ equals $\frac{1}{4}$.

Ed Emberley's Picture Pie

From Seashells to Smart Cards

Taught by Stephanie Sheffield

Ernestine Giesecke's *From Seashells to Smart Cards* (2003) gives an overview of an appealing topic—money—its history, how it's made, how it's protected, and the world of economics. The book's many interesting facts about money—and its photos, time lines, and diagrams present opportunities for mathematical explorations and investigations. This lesson, taught in a fifth-grade classroom, involves students in comparing a yearly salary to an hourly wage.

MATERIALS

When I brought *From Seashells to Smart Cards* into the fifth-grade class, we looked at the book's features before I began reading it. I showed the students the contents page first to help them get an overview of the information the book contains. The book is forty-eight pages long, and not suitable to read at one sitting. It addresses many different aspects of money and economics, and each section would benefit from a class discussion to make the ideas clear and to connect them to the students' own lives.

On this day, I read aloud only the two small sections that related to the lesson. I started with the first section, "What Is Money?" which explains that money is used by people in exchange for things they want and need. "We use money to purchase goods," I said. "Who knows what I mean by *goods*?"

"It means stuff," Ace said. "Like stuff you buy."

"Yeah," Roxanne added. "Stuff like clothes, food, video games."

"That's right. Goods are things that we want and need. But money is used to pay for another kind of thing, things we need that aren't actually things. Money is also used to pay for *services*." I read the first paragraph on page four and we discussed examples of services and service providers the students were familiar with, like doctors and dentists, trash collection, and lawn mowing.

"My parents own a restaurant," Ace said. "That's kind of like both goods and services together."

I read about how money is used to compare the value of things, and we talked about how money can be saved for future use.

Then I read the next section in the book, "Earning Money." This section describes wages and salary as different forms of income. I didn't stop to discuss these because I knew I'd be coming back to them later.

Before beginning the activity, I showed the class other illustrations in the book, skipping around, reading some of the captions and also reading a few pages the class was interested in. After giving the class a feel for the whole book, I went back to the section about earning money.

I read that a grocery store checker might earn $6.50 an hour, whereas a secretary might earn a salary of $25,000 a year. "Can you tell who actually earns more money in a year?" I asked.

"Well, probably the secretary," Cameron responded. "But I guess it depends on how many hours they both work."

"What do you mean?" I asked.

"Well, if the grocery checker doesn't work much, she wouldn't make much money, because she only gets paid for the hours she works," he reasoned. "But I don't know if she works the same as the secretary," he said.

"You've hit on an interesting aspect of this question," I said. "When I was in college I worked at McDonald's. I got paid an hourly wage. When I started I got minimum wage, then I got raises after I had been there and learned new things. That was a long time ago, so I didn't make what is now minimum wage, which is around $6.00."

"What do you mean by *minimum wage*?" Victoria asked.

"The government has set the least amount of money that employers must pay to hourly workers. That's the minimum wage. I'd have to do some research to find out what it is now. The government raises it from time to time to keep up with the economy, so it isn't the same as when I worked at McDonald's, but kids working at McDonald's now probably earn only the minimum wage. It's the amount that the government decides is fair to pay workers for an hour of work. Although it doesn't apply to all jobs and all employees, it does apply to many, so we can use it as a comparison here."

"So how much do you get paid an hour now?" Jose asked.

I laughed. "I might be afraid to find out, Jose. Teachers don't work for an hourly wage, we work for a salary. In a salaried job, you work until the work is finished, no matter how long it takes. At this school, teachers have to be here from 7:45 A.M. to 3:45 P.M. every day, but that doesn't mean our work stops at 3:45. We might have parent conferences, papers to grade, lesson plans to write, or materials to gather. After school we have to attend faculty meetings, workshops, and curriculum meetings with parents. When you're on a salary you're getting paid for doing the whole job, no matter how long it takes."

"So how do you know who makes more money, the grocery checker or the secretary?" Sepi asked.

"Twenty-five thousand dollars is a lot of money. That must be more!" Carissa exclaimed.

"That's actually what you are going to investigate today. We're going to assume that the grocery checker and the secretary both work forty-hour weeks, because that's a typical amount of work for a week," I said. "I want you to compare their earnings by finding out how much the secretary makes per month, per week, per day and, per hour. Who has an idea about how to get started?"

"I think we need to divide by twelve because there are twelve months in a year," Ranna said. Carissa nodded in agreement.

"Can we work with a partner?" Kyle asked.

"Sure," I said, "or you may work alone if you prefer."

The students spent a few minutes choosing partners. They were really curious to find out who made more money, and they got right to work.

After a few minutes Theresa and Victoria called me over for a question. "Some months have four weeks and some have five. Which one should we use?" Theresa asked.

"You'll need to decide that for yourselves," I said. "You might want to compare the results of figuring it out both ways."

Ace and Cameron had a harder time getting started. They argued over who was going to write and how to begin. I gave them a stern look and they settled down. They got past the first question fairly easily, deciding to divide 25,000 by 12 to find out how much money the secretary makes in a month. As Figure 7–1 shows, they correctly came up with $2083.33. But then they had trouble finding out the secretary's weekly earnings. They decided to divide 25,000 by 52, since there are 52 weeks in a year, but when Ace didn't put a decimal in the number 25,000, his answer didn't make sense. Cameron showed him his division problem, in which he remembered to place the decimal. He was in the process of deciding how to round the four numbers to the right of the decimal when Victoria looked over and said, "I divided by four for four weeks instead of by fifty-two, but I decided to round it after two decimal places because it was money." (See Figures 7–2, 7–3, and 7–4.)

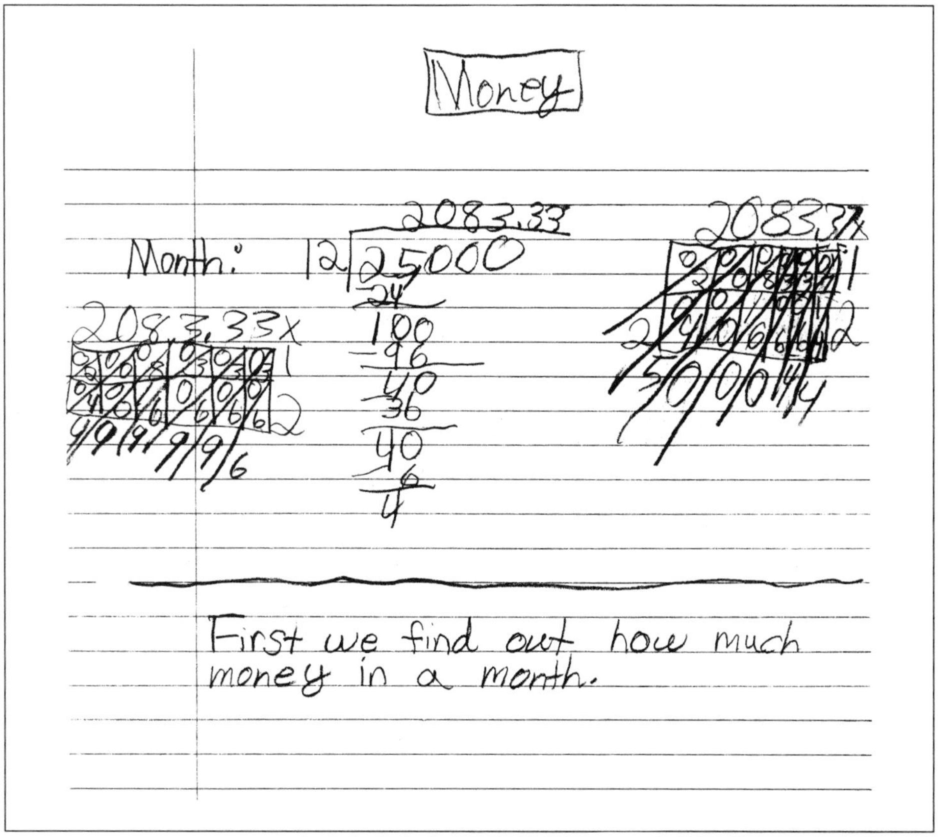

Figure 7–1: Ace and Cameron checked their division using lattice multiplication.

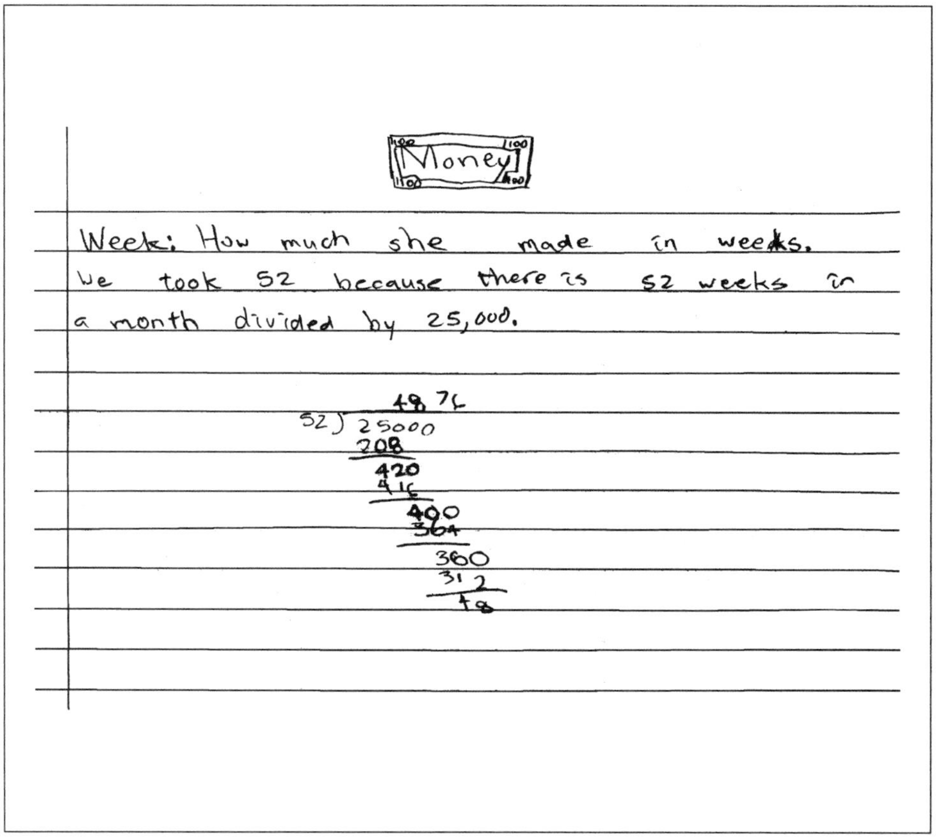

Money

Month: 12)25000 2083.33

2083.33x

First we find out how much money in a month.

Figure 7–2: Ace's problem with the decimal point meant that his answer didn't make sense.

Money

Week: How much she made in weeks. We took 52 because there is 52 weeks in a month divided by 25,000.

52)25000
   208
   420
   416
   400
   364
   360
   312
    48

Figure 7–3: Cameron wasn't sure how many places to leave at the right of the decimal.

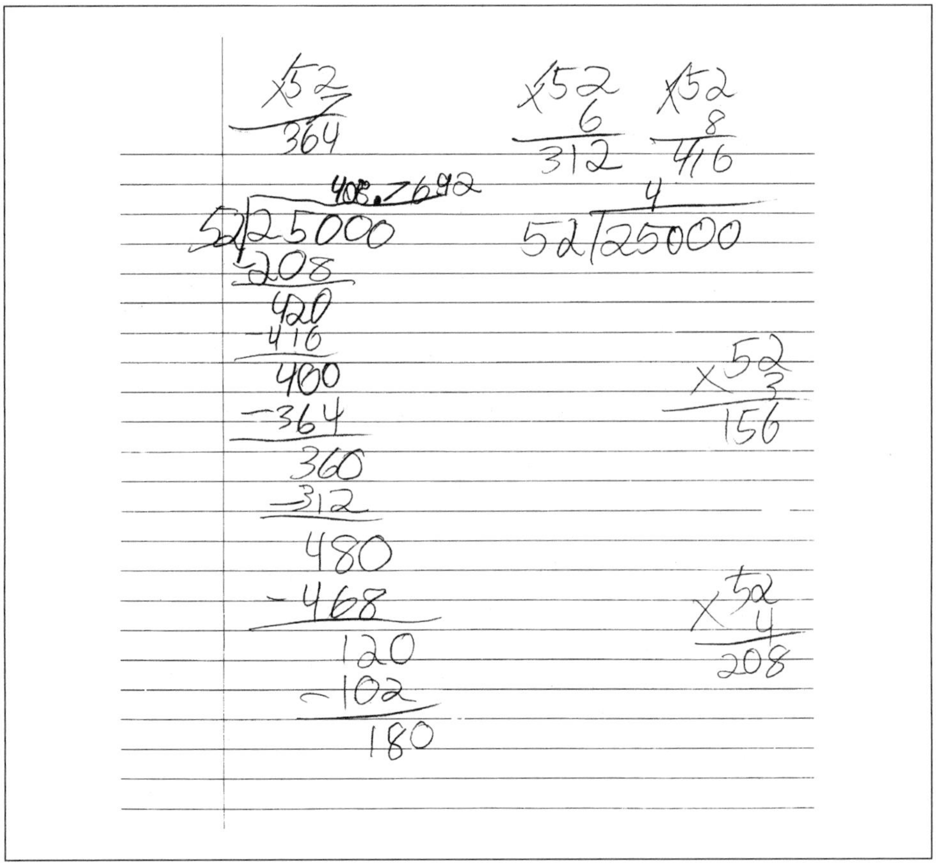

Figure 7–4: Victoria explained that she used two places after the decimal to represent cents.

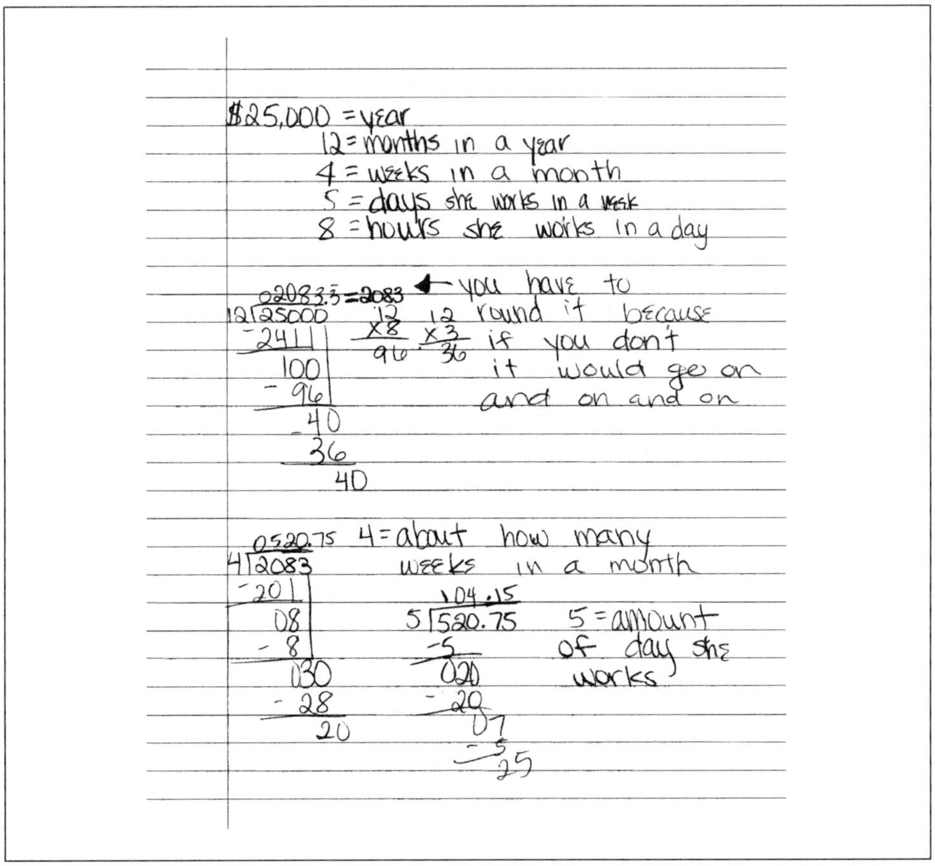

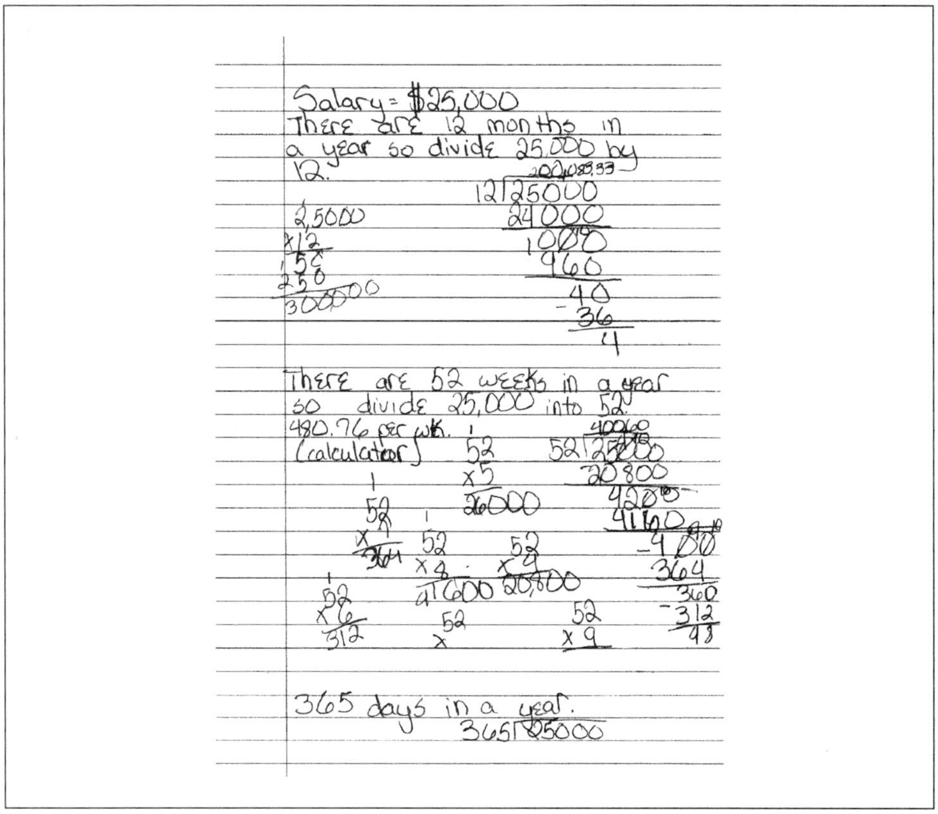

Figure 7–5: Roxanne used a calculator to check her answer.

Roxanne worked by herself. Although she knew what operations to perform, the calculations gave her trouble. She divided 25,000 by 12, but got mixed up with all the zeros. Her answer of $200,083.33 didn't make sense, but she left it and moved on to the next problem. (See Figure 7–5.) Once again she had difficulty with the traditional division algorithm, and finally approached me, exasperated.

"May I use a calculator?" she asked. "I don't think this is right."

"By all means," I said. "See if the calculator helps." I made a note to myself to give Roxanne help with doing the calculations by herself.

When everyone was close to being finished, I gave the class a five-minute warning: "Finish up what you're working on now, and let's meet back on the rug in five minutes to discuss your work so far."

The students brought their papers and settled onto the floor, talking and comparing their answers. "Who would like to share something about your work today?" I asked.

Rick, who is usually quiet, spoke up. "I think we made a big mistake," he said. "We got $52 an hour and that can't be right." He paused a few seconds. "I know what we did wrong. We started with $25,000 every time. Like we divided forty into $25,000 because she worked forty hours a week, but that's wrong." (See Figure 7–6.)

"Do you know what you should have done, Rick?" I asked.

"Hmm," he mused, then whispered something to Kyle. Kyle said, "I think we should have divided how much she made in a week by forty, since she worked forty hours a week. 'Cause all the money she made in a week has to be divided up by all the hours she worked."

"It sounds like you two have a bit more work to do," I commented. "Who else would like to share today?" I asked.

Jose reported next. "I divided 25,000 by 12 and got $2,083.33. That's how much the secretary makes in a month. Then I divided that by four because there are four weeks in a month and I got $520.83. But I did it the other way, too. I divided the yearly salary by fifty-two weeks in a year and got something different." (See Figure 7–7.)

"Which do you think is more accurate?" I asked, wondering if Jose would realize that each month doesn't have exactly four weeks.

"I don't know. I used the first one to do the money per day," he said.

"We used the same thing," Theresa reported. "We found out she made $104.15 a day. Then we divided that by eight, because she works eight hours a day. So we got that she makes $13.02 per hour, which is a lot more than a person makes at McDonald's. I think it's better to get a good job than to work for minimum wage," she concluded.

This was a fairly straightforward lesson that gave the class the chance to think about income in two forms and compare them. They used computation, rounding, and problem-solving skills to make the comparison. And even though students assured at different hourly wages for the secretary, depending how they figured, all calculations led to the same conclusion: that the secretary earned more than the store checker.

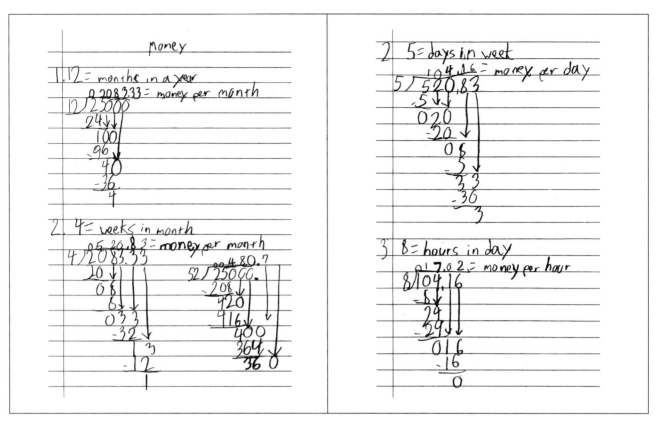

Figure 7–7: To get the secretary's weekly salary, Jose divided her yearly salary by fifty-two and her monthly salary by four. She wasn't sure which was more accurate.

G Is for Googol

Taught by Kathleen Gallagher

David Schwartz's *G Is for Googol* (1998) contains a wealth of interesting and engaging mathematical explanations. This lesson focuses on the page titled "O Is for Obtuse," because these fourth graders were just learning about the different classifications of angles. In this lesson, students connect their book knowledge to their real-world surroundings. They also learn to estimate angles using the benchmark measurements of 0 degrees, 90 degrees, and 180 degrees.

MATERIALS

$8\frac{1}{2}$-by-11-inch white copy paper cut lengthwise and then crosswise into fourths, 6 $4\frac{1}{4}$-by-$5\frac{1}{2}$-inch rectangles per student

chart paper, 2 sheets, one labeled *Three Kinds of Angles* and ruled into three columns

I began the lesson by showing the fourth graders the front of *G Is for Googol*. "Has anybody seen this book before?" I asked. Several students raised their hands, but most admitted that they had not read it. We first discussed the alphabetical organization of the book. Then I asked the children, "What do you think the author talks about on the A page?"

"Angles!" the students answered, since they were just studying about angles in a unit on geometry. When I showed them the A page, they were surprised to find out that the author was introducing the word *abacus*.

I skipped to the F page. I knew I wasn't going to read the whole book, and I wanted to get the class thinking about mathematical words for various letters of the alphabet. "What do you think the F page will be about?" I asked.

"Fractions," suggested Billy.

"I think the number five," said Antonette.

"Maybe it's fact family," Julia speculated.

"Or factor," added Marcus.

I showed them the page and read, "F is for Fibonacci." I told them, "Fibonacci was a famous mathematician from Italy who inspired the people of Europe to use Arabic numbers, like the ones we use, instead of roman numerals. He also discovered the Fibonacci sequence, which you can read about later if you'd like."

I closed the book and showed them the cover again. "What do you think the G page will be about?" I asked.

"Googol!" they answered.

"You're right!" I said. I told the class there was a lot to learn about mathematics in this book and there was no way we could read the whole book today. "Today we're going to focus on just one page, the one about O. "What do you think the author will introduce on the O page?"

"Octagon," predicted Billy.

"I think opposite," said Ashton.

"It could be the number one," added Antonette, who had predicted five when we were talking about the F page.

"Or maybe operation," suggested Javier, who had searched the room and found the word on a chart.

"All of those are good guesses," I said, "but this word has something to do with something you've been studying recently."

"Is it *odd*?" asked Kristin.

"No, but that is a good guess too. It has something to do with angles."

"Obtuse!" several students realized at once.

"Yes," I said. "Today we're going to learn more about obtuse angles, and other angles, too."

As I read the O page aloud, I had the children follow the author's directions, forming different sized angles with their hands. I listed the math words from the pages on chart paper and included a diagram to represent each. (See Figure 8–1.)

The children had a lot of fun with the author's suggestion that they shake out their hands and make hand shadows. When I said, "That's enough fooling around with shadows," and showed them that those are actually the author's words, they laughed and gave me their attention again.

When they had to try to make a 180 degree angle using two hands and keeping the bases of their palms together, many children claimed they could actually do it. It was Javier who pointed out, "Nobody really can, because look—if you put your hands flat on the floor, you really can't touch your palms together. It's more like your wrist."

When we finished reading, I explained the activity: "The book tells us what acute angles, right angles, and obtuse angles are. Let's see

Figure 8–1: A chart of math words and diagrams.

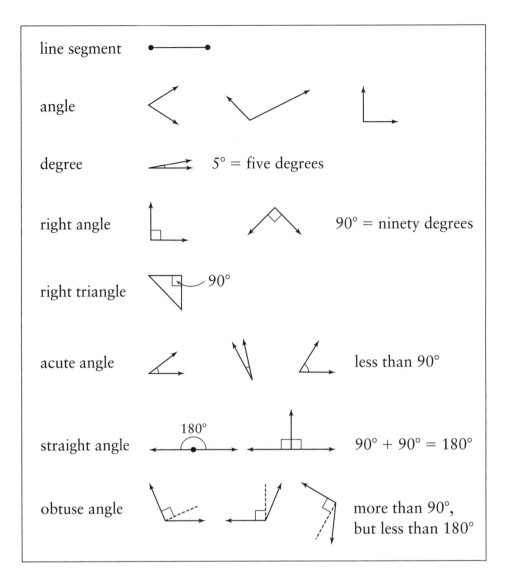

how many of these angles you can find if you take the time to really examine your surroundings. We're going to start off inside the classroom and then move outside. Your job is to try to find one of each type of angle in each place. Draw the object you've found, drawing the angle as precisely as possible, and label the object so we know what it is. Be sure to label the angle you are referring to as *acute, right,* or *obtuse.*" I pointed to these words on the chart paper. As an example, I sketched the state of California on the board and labeled the obtuse angle on the eastern border where California meets Nevada. (See Figure 8–2.)

Monitors passed out six small sheets of paper to each student and the children got right to work. I noticed that many students were drawn to the same objects: their desks, the window, a book, or a journal. "Try to look carefully for things other people might not notice," I encouraged. "Find at least three or four things before you decide on the one you will draw."

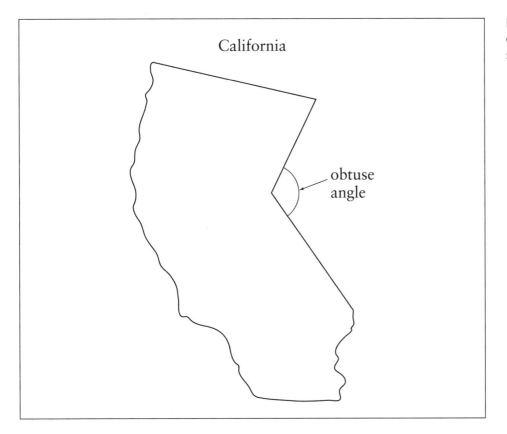

California

obtuse
angle

Figure 8–2: Using a sketch of the state of California to show an obtuse angle.

Ashton had already begun a careful drawing of the window. His drawing showed that it contained two right angles. I asked him to consider the angles created by the shutters and he counted thirteen. Then he said, "No, look! There's double, 'cause there's two angles for each shutter, plus it's double again because there's the same amount on the opposite side!" (See Figure 8–3.)

Julia drew a picture of the basket that held her independent reading books. When I asked her how she knew the angle drawn was obtuse, she said, "I drew an imaginary line, so I found out it's more than ninety."

"Will you show that in your drawing?" I requested, and Julia complied. (See Figure 8–4.)

I told the students that if they were finished, I'd like them to take a minute to think about how they knew what kind of angle they had drawn, then write what they were thinking. Moments when children reflect about their work can offer great opportunities for learning.

Daisy found a lot of angles in the word MAY. She explained on the back of her paper that obtuse angles would make a good chair and acute angles are shaped like an animal's mouth. I looked at the angle in the middle of the letter M and said, "Wow, that's a pretty straight chair. Are you sure it's obtuse?"

Daisy picked up another piece of paper and placed the corner carefully inside the angle of the M to test it. "Uh oh," she said. "That's

Figure 8–3: Ashton realized that the corner of each shutter slat created a right angle, for fifty-four right angles in all.

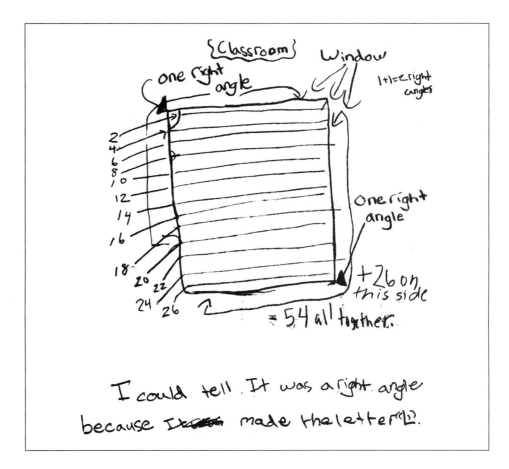

Figure 8–4: Julia used an imaginary line to create a right angle. This proved that the angle formed by the bottom of the basket she drew was obtuse.

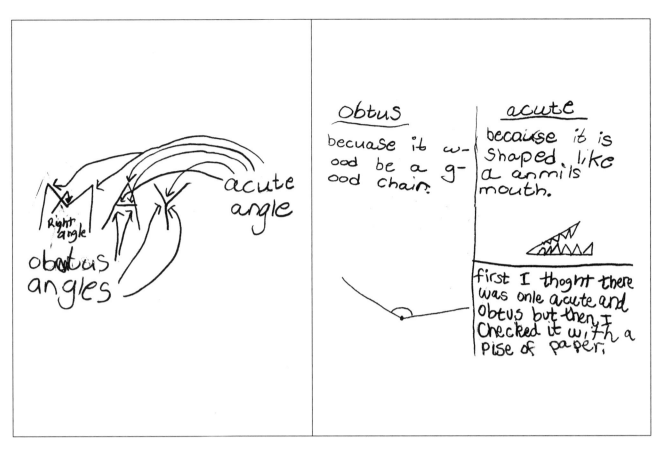

Figure 8–5: Daisy found examples of all three sizes of angles in the word MAY.

actually a right angle, but it's lying on its side." She described her discovery on the back of her paper. (See Figure 8–5.)

After about fifteen minutes, we picked up our materials and headed outside. Most of the children were immediately drawn to the white lines of the wall-ball court. I said, "I'd like four or five of you to run out to the fence and look for angles in the park."

"I'll go!" offered Frederick. He and two others ran off to investigate the park area that lies just beyond our grassy field.

"Oh, look!" I exclaimed. "There are probably lots of angles over by the baseball diamond."

"Let's go out there!" suggested Julias.

"Don't just look down," I advised. "Look in all directions to see what you can find."

Ashton sat down on the cement surface where our ball courts are and began scanning the area. His eyes halted when he noticed the branches of a tree and he began to draw. He wrote, *I could tell it was a obtuse angle because it did not make a letter "L," and the letter "L" is a right angle. It was wider than a "L."* (See Figure 8–6.)

Javier noticed and drew a dent in a pole that's part of one of the fences that surround the trees on our playground. He wrote, *This is a dent in a tree fence I found this in the black top. The bare was going*

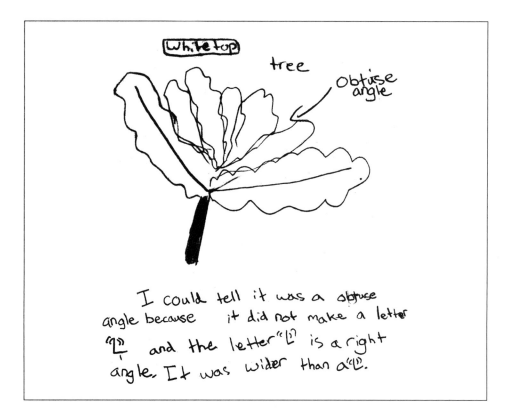

tree

Obtuse angle

White top

I could tell it was a obtuse angle because it did not make a letter "L" and the letter "L" is a right angle. It was wider than a "L".

parrell until it went in. I think someone kicked it or maybe a car banged into it. (See Figure 8–7.)

"You mean the bar was straight and parallel to the other bars, but this one is dented in, and the dent forms the angle," I clarified when he showed me his work.

It was interesting to watch the children connect the vocabulary of angles to the objects they see every day—the roofs of buildings, the spaces between their fingers, the monkey bars, the ramps that lead to the classroom doors, a lunch bag with its top neatly folded down, a flag, the hands of a clock, and the lines for games that are painted on the ground.

Madeline struggled to verbalize her thinking when describing her items, but her pictures demonstrated her understanding. She noticed the acute angle at the top of a cone, the right angle that a blade of grass forms where it shoots out of the ground, and the obtuse angle formed by the power lines overhead. (See Figure 8–8.)

After about fifteen more minutes, we headed back to the classroom to share our findings. The students taped their drawings into the appropriate columns on a piece of chart paper I had ruled into three columns and titled "Three Kinds of Angles." We analyzed the results.

"Hey, the wall-ball court is in all three columns," exclaimed Paul. Indeed it was. There was some disagreement about where the right angle was. Kristin had identified a corner at the front of the court as 90 degrees, but Billy disagreed. (See Figure 8–9.)

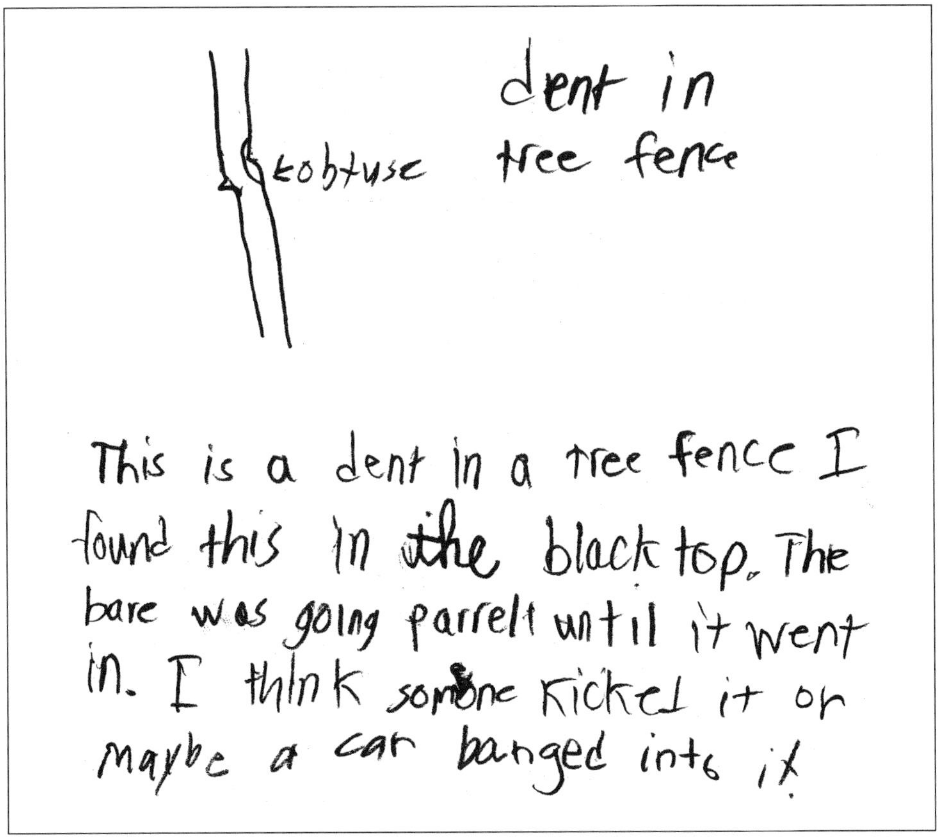

Figure 8–7: Javier discovered an obtuse angle in a dented fencepost.

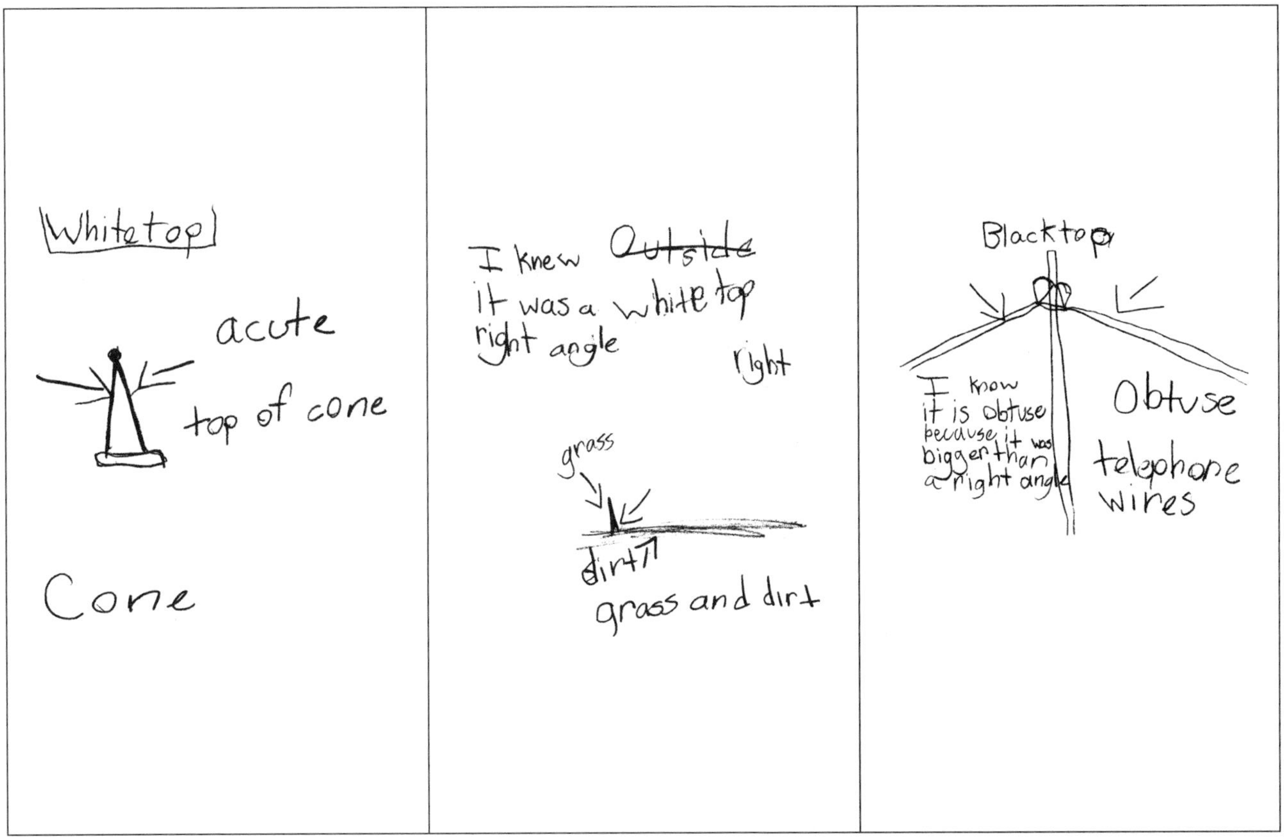

dent in tree fence

to obtuse

This is a dent in a tree fence I found this in the black top. The bare was going parrell until it went in. I think somone kicked it or maybe a car banged into it.

Whitetop

acute
top of cone

Cone

I knew Outside it was a white top right angle

Right

grass

dirt
grass and dirt

Blacktop

I know it is obtuse because it was bigger than a right angle

Obtuse telephone wires

Figure 8–8: Madeline demonstrated her understanding of angles through her drawings.

Figure 8–9: Kristin incorrectly identified a corner of the wall-ball court as a right angle, but one of its sides was curved.

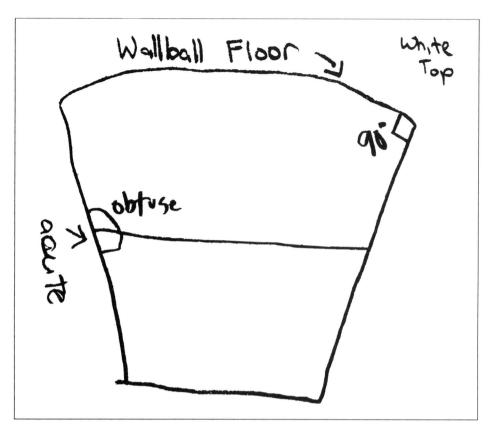

"Is it an angle if one of the lines is curved?" he asked.

We looked back at the book and I read, "Where two lines come together, they make an opening called an angle."

"See," said Billy, "that one is a line, but that other one isn't a line, 'cause it's curved like a circle."

"Yes, it is," objected Kristin. "Even though it's a curved line, it still makes an angle—look at the point."

"Let's look in the dictionary and see," I suggested.

Billy looked up the word *angle* and read the definition out loud: "A figure formed by two line segments or rays that share the same endpoint."

Kristin looked up *line segment* and read, "'A part of a line that contains two points called endpoints and all of the lines in between.' Let's see what it says for *line*. . . . , 'A straight . . .' Oh. It does have to be straight."

"Finish the definition, Kristin," I said.

"A straight path in a plane extending in both directions with no endpoints."

"So I wonder what this space is called if it's not an angle," I contemplated aloud. "I'll have to look into that." I added *ray* and *line* to our first chart.

"But there's still a wall-ball in the right-angle column," Paul pointed out. "Look at the one that Lilly did." (See Figure 8–10.)

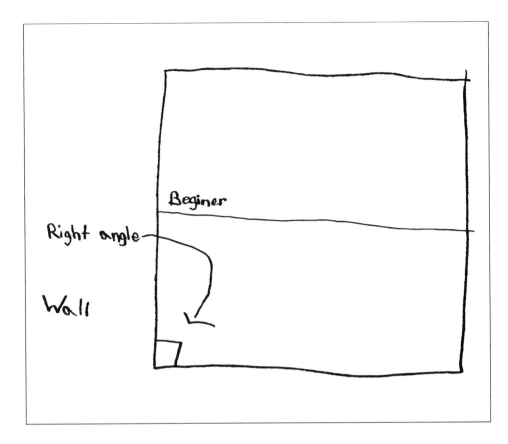

"Yeah, it goes straight up and all of the corners make a square," Lilly said confidently. "I found all three of my angles at the wall-ball court, but I did them separate. The wooden part has a whole bunch of right angles, 'cause it's like a huge skinny box standing up on its side."

Frederick commented on the letter U that Otto had drawn to represent an obtuse angle: "I don't think Otto's is really an angle. 'Cause it's not two straight lines like the dictionary said." (See Figure 8–11.)

"I know," Otto agreed. "I should have wrote a *V* instead of a *U*." This satisfied Frederick.

I looked at all of the pictures the children had drawn and asked the class, "I wonder if you could estimate the measurement of any of these angles," pointing to the ones in the *acute* column. "What do we know about them?"

"They're less than ninety degrees," said Javier.

"I think those are like forty-five degrees," said Julia, pointing to her own drawing of monkey bars. (See Figure 8–12.)

"Why do you think that?" I asked.

"'Cause it's like half-way to the bar," she answered.

"Yeah, but the line going down isn't ninety," said Paul. "It looks like maybe a hundred or maybe more."

"Point to the part you're talking about, Paul," I suggested so the rest of the students could follow his reasoning.

Figure 8–11: Otto decided he should have drawn the letter V instead of U to illustrate an obtuse angle.

Letter U

obtuse

Figure 8–12: Julia estimated an angle on the monkey bars at about 45 degrees.

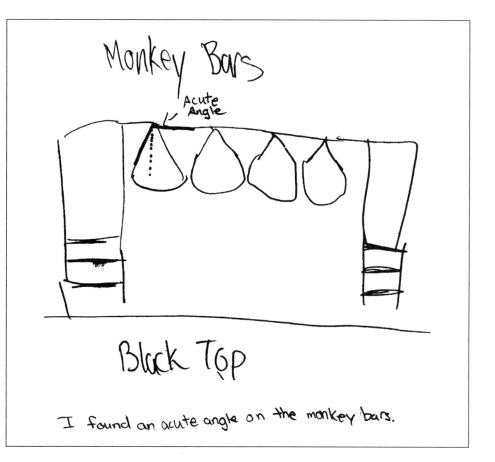

Monkey Bars

Acute Angle

Black Top

I found an acute angle on the monkey bars.

He pointed to the angle formed by the top bar and the outer bar of the first triangle. "It looks like a little less than half, but maybe it is forty-five."

"Forty-five what?" I reminded.

"Forty-five degrees."

"Does anybody know what we could do to find the exact measurement?"

"A compass," suggested Julias. "No, a protractor I mean," he corrected.

I turned back to the book and showed the children the page where two mice are talking about measuring the angle on a piece of cheese. I reminded them that if they ever need to know the *exact* measurement of an angle, they should use a protractor. But I encouraged them to practice estimating angle measurements, because if they can learn to do that fairly accurately, they will have a valuable tool to use in the future.

Hottest, Coldest, Highest, Deepest

Taught by Kathleen Gallagher

In *Hottest, Coldest, Highest, Deepest* (1998), Steve Jenkins presents some of the grandest wonders of the natural world—the longest river, deepest lake, highest mountain, and so on. The book brings meaning to numbers and measurement through engaging artwork, charts, maps, and comparative drawings. In this lesson, fifth graders engage in math discussions that foster deeper understanding of multiplication, measurement, and proportional reasoning. The work they do helps them make sense of estimation and rounding in a meaningful and relevant context.

MATERIALS

interlocking cubes, about 50 per pair of students

chart paper, 3 sheets

overhead transparency of instructions for Day 2 (see Blackline Masters)

Day 1

"I wonder what this book is about?" I asked as I showed the fifth-grade class a copy of *Hottest, Coldest, Highest, Deepest.*

"I think the hottest, coldest, highest, and deepest places," replied Jenny.

"Mount Everest is the highest place," added LaDree.

"The coldest place is probably the North Pole," said Beatrice

"Does anyone have ideas about the hottest place?" I asked.

"I think Death Valley," replied Edward.

"What about the deepest place?" I wondered. "Talk to your partner about that one."

I heard many children predicting the Pacific Ocean or the Atlantic Ocean. Jason thought it would be the Indian Ocean. Mariah was trying to remember the name of a trench she had heard something about. "Is anybody absolutely sure about the answer?" I asked.

Since nobody was a hundred percent sure, I reassured them that Steve Jenkins, the book's author, would clear it up for us. "We're going to learn lots of facts about the most extreme places in the world," I told them. "In order to keep track of everything we learn, I'd like you to make a chart before you come up to the rug to hear the book."

As I wrote the title of the book and the author's name at the top of a piece of chart paper, the children did the same on their own blank pieces of paper. I asked them to fold their papers into four columns. I modeled using LaDree's paper and they all did the same while I drew in the lines of my chart. When the children were finished, I asked them to come to the rug to listen to the book, bringing their papers, a pencil, and a hard surface to write on.

After reading the first page, which is about the Nile River, I asked the students questions to elicit the information needed for the chart. First I asked, "What extreme thing is being discussed on this page?"

The students answered, "The Nile River." I labeled the first column on the chart *Extreme Thing's Name,* then wrote *Nile* on the first row of that column.

"Where is the Nile River?" I asked. As the class responded with "Africa," I titled the second column *Where It Is* and wrote *Africa* in that column.

"What measurement is given for the Nile River?" I queried.

Jeffrey answered, "Four thousand, one hundred forty-five miles." I labeled the third column *Measurement* and recorded *4,145 miles.*

Finally I asked, "Why is the extreme thing famous?"

"I know," Katherine said, "it's the longest river in the world." I nodded and wrote the column heading *Extreme Thing's Claim to Fame,* and added *Longest River* under that heading.

Hottest, Coldest, Highest, Deepest

Extreme Thing's Name	Where It Is	Measurement	Extreme Thing's Claim to Fame
Nile	Africa	4,145 miles	longest river

I turned the page and we looked at a picture of Lake Baikal. The author uses the Empire State Building as a reference to illustrate the depth of the lake. I asked, "What is this?" pointing to the building in the bottom of the lake.

"That's the Empire State Building!" shouted the class.

"What's the Empire State Building doing at the bottom of Lake Baikal?" I asked.

"So we could see how deep it is," many students replied.

"Why do you think the author would use the Empire State Building to show us the depth of a lake?" I asked.

"Probably because lots of people know about that building," Michelle suggested.

"I think you're right," I agreed. "The author is using the Empire State Building because it is a landmark that many people know about. So how deep is Lake Baikal?"

"I think it's like five," replied Chris.

"Five what, Chris?" I asked.

"Five Empire State Buildings."

I laid my pencil next to the drawing of the Empire State Building marking the height with my finger. The children counted the number of Empire State Buildings that could be stacked in Lake Baikal as I moved the marked pencil up. After the second one, Christina said, "I think it's only four, because that looks like half."

"Yeah, I think it will be four too," Jenny agreed.

"It says here in the illustration that the Empire State Building is one thousand, two hundred fifty feet tall," I said, writing *1,250 feet* on the board. "Can we use that information to figure out the depth of Lake Baikal? Try to figure it out in your head and raise your hand when you have an answer." On the board I wrote *1,250 × 4*.

Many of the children in this class relied on the standard multiplication algorithm rather than using other strategies to figure mentally. Because holding all of the calculations in their heads was difficult, those children took the longest to get answers.

After giving the class some time to figure, I asked for their attention. "For some of you this problem seemed sort of easy. Others were struggling to hold a lot of different numbers in your head, and many of you got frustrated. So that we can learn from one another, I'd like someone to share your strategy for multiplying in your head. I'll record your thinking on the board. Everyone listen carefully, because I'm going to ask you to explain in your own words what the person who shared did. Who would like to share?"

Several hands shot up. I called on Jason because I thought he would be able to explain his steps clearly.

Jason said, "I did one thousand times four and got four thousand. Then I knew that two hundred fifty times four is one thousand, so I added it to four thousand and got five thousand." I recorded as Jason explained:

Jason's Way

$$1,000 \times 4 = 4,000$$
$$250 \times 4 = 1,000$$
$$4,000 + 1,000 = 5,000$$

"Why did you multiply one thousand times four?" I asked.

"I was doing one thousand two hundred fifty times four, so I just did one thousand times four first," he replied.

"So you sort of changed one thousand two hundred fifty into two friendlier numbers, right? If we wanted to write that step down," I asked the class, "what do you think I should write?" Their blank stares told me that I needed to rephrase the question.

I asked, "If we take one thousand out of one thousand two hundred fifty, how much would we have left?"

"Two hundred fifty," the children agreed.

"So Jason split one thousand two hundred fifty into two smaller parts so he could multiply easier numbers." Below Jason's name, I added two lines:

Jason's Way

$$1,250 = 1,000 + 250$$
$$(1,000 + 250) \times 4$$
$$1,000 \times 4 = 4,000$$
$$250 \times 4 = 1,000$$
$$4,000 + 1,000 = 5,000$$

I said to the class, "Explain to your partner the notation I wrote on the board." I pointed to $(1,000 + 250) \times 4$.

After a few minutes I asked, "So after Jason thought about one thousand two hundred fifty as one thousand and two hundred fifty, then what did he do?"

"He did one thousand times four," Jeffrey said, "and then two hundred fifty times four."

"Then he plussed the one thousand and the four thousand," Edward reported.

"Where was the four thousand from?" I asked, pointing to the *4,000* in the last number sentence.

"From the one thousand times four," many children replied.

"And where did the one thousand come from?" I asked.

"From the two hundred fifty times four."

"So Jason showed us a different way to think about multiplication than you usually do with paper and pencil," I said. "Now use the steps on the board to try to explain to your partner how Jason solved the problem. Both of you take a turn at explaining." Some students don't learn strategies only by listening. When they are expected to repeat what somebody else did, however, it helps them bring meaning to a new idea. It also makes them question why the person made certain decisions during the problem solving.

To end this part of the discussion, I told the class that mathematicians have special terminology for describing the way Jason solved this multiplication problem: "Actually, there are two names. One of them is *partial products* and the other is the *distributive property*." I wrote both terms on the board and made a mental note to refer back to them in future number talks. I then returned to the book.

"Do you think Lake Baikal is exactly five thousand feet deep?" I asked the class.

"It's probably a little deeper, 'cause I don't think it would be exactly four Empire State Buildings," said Chris. I read from the book that in one spot Lake Baikal is 5,134 feet, confirming Chris's conjecture.

"So what is the extreme thing's name?" I asked the students.

"Lake Baikal," they answered, recording on their charts as I recorded on the class chart.

"Where is it?" I continued.

"In Russia," they answered, adding to their charts.

"What is Lake Baikal's measurement?"

"Five thousand, one hundred, thirty-four."

"Was that inches, feet, miles?"

"It was feet," they agreed, adding the unit to their papers.

"And why is Lake Baikal famous?"

"Because it's the deepest lake!" they answered, writing in the fourth column.

Hottest, Coldest, Highest, Deepest

Extreme Thing's Name	Where It Is	Measurement	Extreme Thing's Claim to Fame
Nile	Africa	4,145 miles	longest river
Baikal	Russia	5,134 feet	deepest lake

As I continued reading, the children were intrigued by the book's comparative drawing and other illustrations. They laughed at how small the Empire State Building is compared to Mount Everest, and they noted that the hottest spot in the world is less than 2 degrees hotter than our own Death Valley. The students enjoyed the paper-cut illustrations of penguins in Antarctica and couldn't believe that any place could actually be minus 58 degree Fahrenheit in the summer. They loved the cloud drawings used to show relative wind speed.

When I read about Angel Falls, LaDree said, "Look how big the Empire State Building is now," and Keith commented, "That means it must be shorter than the deepest lake." Although we weren't talking about ratio and proportion, the children were informally thinking about these concepts.

When I read the page about the Marianas Trench, the deepest spot in the world, Katharine asked, "What do those little words say?" referring to a diagram that shows a tiny Empire State Building on top of a line that represents sea level. It was good that the children were gathered close to the book—otherwise they may not have noticed the tiny illustration of the Empire State Building compared to the Marianas Trench. A line further down in the diagram indicates the shore of the Dead Sea, which is 1,100 feet below sea level. Further down another line shows the average depth of the world's oceans at 16,000 feet, and even further down a line marks the depth of the Marianas Trench at 36,202 feet. We added the information about the Marianas Trench to our charts.

Hottest, Coldest, Highest, Deepest

Extreme Thing's Name	Where It Is	Measurement	Extreme Thing's Claim to Fame
Nile	Africa	4,145 mi	longest river
Baikal	Russia	5,134 ft.	deepest lake
Everest	Nepal	29,028 ft.	highest mountain
Al Aziziyah	Libya	136 degrees	hottest spot
Vostok	Antarctica	−129 degrees	coldest place
Mt. Washington	New Hampshire, USA	231 mi/hr.	windiest place
Angel Falls	Venezuela	3,212 ft.	highest waterfall
Marianas Trench	Philippines	36,202 ft.	deepest spot in the ocean
Sangay	Ecuador	Average of once every 24 hrs since 1937	most active volcano
Bay of Fundy	Canada	50 ft./6 hrs.	most extreme tides
Mt. Ranier	Washington, USA	1,200 in./yr.	snowiest place

Each time we added a measurement to the chart, I made sure to emphasize the unit of measurement used. For the most active volcano, we recorded *Average of once every 24 hours since 1937*. For the most extreme tides, we recorded *50 ft./6 hrs*. And for the snowiest place, we recorded *1,200 in./yr*. We talked about how to read the slash as "every," "per," or "each," which was good practice for the children.

When we finished reading the book, I asked the children to look over their charts to see if there were two measurements we could compare. I wanted to focus the discussion on comparing things that were measured in the same units. "Since the coldest place is measured in degrees and the windiest place is measured in miles per hour, we can't really compare them. What are two extreme places we could compare that are measured in the same units?" The children looked carefully at their charts.

Edward said, "The Marianas Trench is deeper than Mount Everest."

"That's a good one," I said, "but is Mount Everest deep?"

"No," the class agreed.

"How could we restate what Edward said to include the idea that we are talking about both depth and height?"

"Mount Everest is higher than the deepness of the Marianas Trench," said Keith.

I posted a new piece of chart paper and titled it *Extreme Places: What can we compare?* Underneath I wrote *The Marianas Trench is deeper than Mt. Everest is high*, then added the number sentence *36,202 ft. > 29,028 ft.*

Extreme Places
What Can We Compare?

The Marianas Trench is deeper than Mt. Everest is high.
36,202 ft. > 29,028 ft.

"What else could we compare?" I asked. As the children thought of examples, I excused them to return to their seats to record their thoughts and brainstorm as many other examples as they could from their charts. Having each child give an example first let me make sure that everyone understood exactly what to do.

When Katherine wanted to compare the length of the Nile River (4,145 miles) to the height of Mount Everest (29,028 feet), she ran into a problem: To compare, she had to find out how many feet are in a mile (5,290) and then multiply that number by the number of miles the Nile is long (4,145). Finally she wrote:

The Nile River is a lot longer than Mt. Everest is tall.
21,885,600 ft. > 29,028 ft.

I collected the children's papers as they walked out of the room to lunch so I could compile their ideas for the next day's class. On another sheet of chart paper, I recorded the following comparisons to share the next day.

Extreme Places
What Can We Compare?

The Marianas Trench is deeper than Mt. Everest is high.
36,202 ft. > 29,028 ft.

The Nile River is a lot longer than Mt. Everest is tall.
21,885,600 > 29,028 ft

The Marianas Trench is deeper than Angel Falls is high.
36,202 ft. > 3,212 ft.

Mt. Everest is taller than Angel Falls.
29,028 > 3,212 ft.

Lake Baikal is deeper than the height of Angel Falls.
5,134 ft. > 3,212 ft.

Day 2

When the children returned to the classroom after recess the next day, I asked them to read the statements I had written on the chart. Working with partners, they made sure they agreed with the statements and could read them aloud. Some of the fifth graders were confused about the Nile River statement and Katherine had to explain how she changed miles into feet. Then I displayed the instructions for the day's work on the overhead projector.

Hottest, Coldest, Highest, Deepest

1. Use cubes to build a representation of the two places you are comparing.

2. Draw a picture of your model. Try to make your drawing to scale.

3. Label your drawing with numbers to show how it relates to the actual measurements.

4. Explain in words how you know your drawing makes sense.

We read the instructions together to make sure everyone understood each of the four parts of the task. For step one, I showed them the interlocking cubes and explained how they were to use the cubes to build a model of the two things on the chart they were comparing. We talked about some of the decisions they would have to make in order to start building, such as deciding how much each cube would represent. After building their model they were to draw a picture of it (step two), label the drawing with numbers (step three), and write about how they knew that their model was an accurate representation of the two places (step four).

Jenny decided to build models of Mount Everest (29,028 feet) and Angel Falls (3,212 feet), with each cube representing 1,000 feet. She connected twenty-nine cubes for Mount Everest and three cubes for Angel Falls. When she drew her picture, she made each cube about half its actual size so it would fit on her paper. As she went to add the numbers to her paper, she was a little bit confused about what had happened to the extra 28 feet of Mount Everest. It was as if she knew instinctively to round, but didn't quite know how to articulate her thinking.

"Was there enough left to justify adding another cube?" I asked.

"No," Jenny replied.

"How come?" I probed.

"'Cause this is a thousand," she said, referring to the cube, "and I only need twenty-eight feet."

"What part of a cube do you think twenty-eight would be?" I asked, pointing to a cube. "How big would each foot be if this cube represents one thousand feet?" Jenny thought about this for a while and realized that one foot would be very thin.

"I think you rounded here, which was a really smart thing to do," I said. "Measurements are never really exact. Since you're working with thousands, is Mount Everest closer to twenty-nine thousand feet or thirty thousand feet?"

"Twenty-nine," Jenny said.

"OK, so go ahead and draw it with twenty-nine. It would be too hard to draw twenty-nine thousandths of a cube, especially because your cubes are already half the size of the actual ones. You can write *about twenty-nine thousand feet* on your paper when you label it. Now how will you draw your model of Angel Falls?"

Jenny continued working on her own. She decided to draw a little sliver of a cube to represent the 28 extra feet of Mount Everest and a slightly bigger sliver to represent the 212 extra feet of Angel Falls. (See Figure 9–1.)

Many children ended up building more than two models. After Edward finished his drawings of Lake Baikal and Mount Everest, he built Angel Falls, the Marianas Trench, and the Empire State Building, all with cubes that represented 1,000 feet. (See Figure 9–2.) He summed up his understanding, saying, "Lake Baikal is five Empire State buildings, Mount Everest is twenty-nine Empire State Buildings,

Angel Falls is three Empire State Buildings, and the Marianas Trench is thirty-six Empire State Buildings." Kimberly reminded Edward that only four Empire State buildings fit into Lake Baikal.

The lesson ended, but I looked forward to future conversations with the class about the purposes and challenges of rounding.

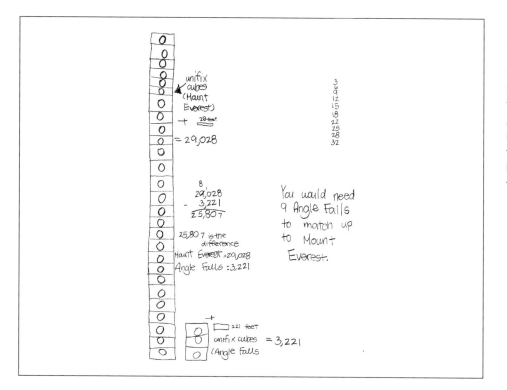

Figure 9–1: Each of her cubes represented 1,000 feet, so Jenny used slivers of cubes to represent the 28 extra feet for Mt. Everest and the 212 extra feet for Angel Falls. Jenny used 3,221 feet for the height of Angel Falls because she copied it from the chart incorrectly.

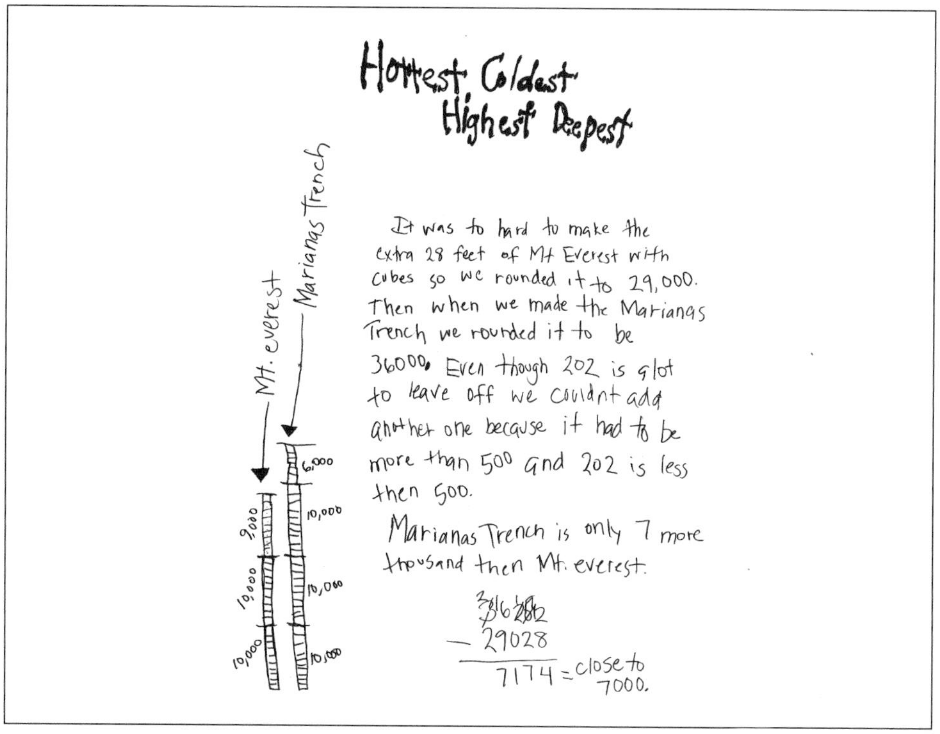

Figure 9–2: Representing each measurement with cubes provided students with a real context for rounding.

How Much, How Many, How Far, How Heavy, How Long, How Tall Is 1000?

Taught by Stephanie Sheffield

Just how big is one thousand? Helen Nolan's *How Much, How Many, How Far, How Heavy, How Long, How Tall Is 1000?* (1997) shows students that, depending on context, one thousand can be big or small. For example, in the case of acorns, one thousand would be only a small pile, but the one thousand trees those acorns might grow into would create an entire forest. On the first day of this three-day lesson, third graders are introduced to the cover of the book, then discuss ways to explore the number one hundred using the questions from the book's title—how much, how many, how far, how heavy, how long, and how tall. Working in pairs, the children choose one way to investigate one hundred, and they continue their exploration on the second day. On the third day, they listen to the book read aloud and discuss the examples provided, solving problems using patterns, multiplication, and division.

MATERIALS

Day 1

The third graders were waiting on the rug when I arrived. They greeted me enthusiastically and looked to see what book I had brought. The cover depicts the cartoon-like characters of a boy, a girl, a bear, and a dog gazing into a star-filled night sky. As I read the title of the book aloud, the class joined in. *"How Much, How Many,*

How Far, How Heavy, How Long, How Tall Is 1000?" we read together.

"I brought this book to read to you," I said, "but I'm not going to read it just yet." I heard sounds of disappointment from several students. "That's because I have an activity for you to do first," I explained. The groaners perked up. "Before we find out how much, how many, how far, how heavy, how long, and how tall one thousand is, we are going to explore another large number, one hundred. Let's think about each question in the title and brainstorm ways we could find the answer to that question. We'll start with the question *How much?* If we want to find out *How much is 100?* what kinds of things could we explore?"

After a few students raised their hands, I called on Bria. "We could find out how much you could buy for one hundred dollars," she suggested. I recorded Bria's idea on the board, and continued recording ideas as students suggested them.

Jake picked up on the money theme. "We could find out how much a hundred pennies is," he said. He quickly added, grinning, "Oh yeah, it's a dollar!"

Kaitlyn had another idea; "How much popcorn do you get if you pop one hundred popcorns," she said. Judging from the appreciative noises in the group, that idea was very popular.

I said, "Let's move on to the *How many* question.

Mikayla suggested, "How many cafeteria tables would we need for one hundred kids to eat lunch?"

Devin asked, "How many computers do we have in the school? Is it one hundred?"

Jake asked, "How many fingers do one hundred kids have?"

Sitting next to me, Cliff quietly responded to Jake's question, "One thousand." I asked him to explain how he figured that out, and he immediately lost confidence in his answer. "Uh, I mean two hundred." After a couple of moments he said, "I don't really know." It's interesting to watch students have sudden flashes of insight that they can't explain. This was something I had seen Cliff do before. He is a child with a very good intuitive sense of number, but sometimes struggles to express his thinking verbally. I decided not to push for an explanation at that point but to continue with the brainstorming.

"What about *How far?*" I asked. "Who has an idea for exploring *how far* for one hundred?"

Lorenzo had been quiet, so when he raised his hand, I called on him. "How far is one hundred steps?" he asked. Lorenzo is an English as a second language student. He finds mathematics easy and interesting, but sometimes has difficulty expressing himself.

"Lorenzo, do you mean, how far would you go if you walked one hundred steps?" I asked. He nodded, smiling. "That would be interesting," I agreed. "Who has another idea?"

Bailey raised her hand. "How far would one hundred kids stretch if they stood on the playground and held hands?"

Rufus said, "Yuck, I don't want to hold anybody's hand!"

I sighed, and thought to myself, "Yep, this is third grade!" Out loud I said, "We're only thinking up ideas, Rufus. Nobody has to do anything yet."

For *How heavy,* children made several suggestions: How heavy are one hundred third graders? How heavy are one hundred pattern blocks? How heavy are one hundred dice? How heavy are one hundred math books?

When we got to *How long,* the class generated many more ideas than they had for the previous questions. Julia suggested, "How long is one hundred paper clips?" Malina followed with, "How long would it be if you put one hundred math books on the floor and measured?" Kei said, "How long does it take to do one hundred jumping jacks?" I had been thinking that the *How long* questions would all have to do with linear measurement, but Kei made me realize it could refer to length of time, as well. There were several other suggestions for how long various things might take to do, or for how long a row of one hundred various things might reach. I recorded these and moved on to the next question. I wanted to be sure we had plenty of time to do the exploration.

For the last question, *How tall?* Devin suggested, "How tall would it be if you stacked one hundred dice?" Malina asked, "What if you had a hundred kids and they stood on each other's shoulders. How tall would that be?" I added those suggestions to the board.

I began to give directions for the activity: I said, "Mrs. Reid is going to help you find partners by choosing sticks out of the cup, two at a time." Each child's name was written on the end of a popsicle stick, and the sticks were placed in the cup with the names down so that they didn't show. This method worked well for choosing random pairs.

"Please sit together and talk about what you'd like to explore about one hundred. You can choose one of the questions on the board, or make one up yourselves. When you have chosen a question to explore, please come tell me about it before you begin work. Be sure to choose something that you and your partner can explore here at school and that will help you learn more about the number one hundred."

Before she started calling out the names, Maralyn reminded the students to be polite when the names were called out, even if someone got a partner who wasn't their first choice. "We're all friends in this class," she said. As Maralyn called out the names, the students excitedly stood and found new seats together. There were a few reluctant pairs, which happens sometimes when third grade boys and girls are paired to work together. Julia was clearly not happy to have Adrian as a partner, but after a few minutes of gentle encouragement from Maralyn, the two got to work on choosing a question to explore.

The students started coming up with their questions as soon as they paired up. I wanted to be sure that they chose questions that could be answered within a couple of class periods, and that they had a plan for how to go about answering the question. I made a mental note of which questions were chosen so that two pairs didn't explore the same thing. I wanted to have some variety in the ways of looking at one hundred when we came back together for discussion. One of my goals for the activity was to have students realize that the number one hundred could be large or small, depending on context. I thought that idea would be clearer to them if they investigated a wide range of questions.

After I had approved all the pairs' questions, I told the students to write a brief description of how they were going to explore their problem. Many asked if they should estimate as part of their plan, and I encouraged them to do so. There is always a kind of flurry of motion when a class begins a new activity like this. Most of it is purposeful, but sometimes a group needs some settling down before they really get to work. I find that the more often children are involved in explorations of this type, the easier it is for them to get down to the task at hand, without a lot of extra talk. Within a few minutes, all the students were working on their plans and bringing them to me to check out.

Rufus and Lorenzo asked for the dice to begin stacking them, while Devin and Kaitlyn started stacking math books. I dug into my wallet for nickels for Shameka and Kaitlyn. Malina and Gracie brought me their paper and asked if they could go to the gym to jump between the basketball hoops. They predicted that one hundred jumps would get them halfway across the court. Because there was a class in the gym at the time, I asked them to choose an exploration they could do in the classroom or outside. They walked over to the board to consider another option. Julia and Adrian had some trouble getting started. They knew they wanted to explore one hundred skips, but they didn't know if they wanted to skip one hundred times or for one hundred minutes. I told them they needed to sit together and talk about it until they both agreed what to do.

Before long it was time to get the students ready for their next class. I asked them to put their work in their folders so they could return to it the next day. "You'll have time to complete your explorations tomorrow," I told them. As I looked over their work later that day, I checked to see if they were clear about how they would conduct the exploration. Figures 10–1, 10–2, and 10–3 show three of their plans.

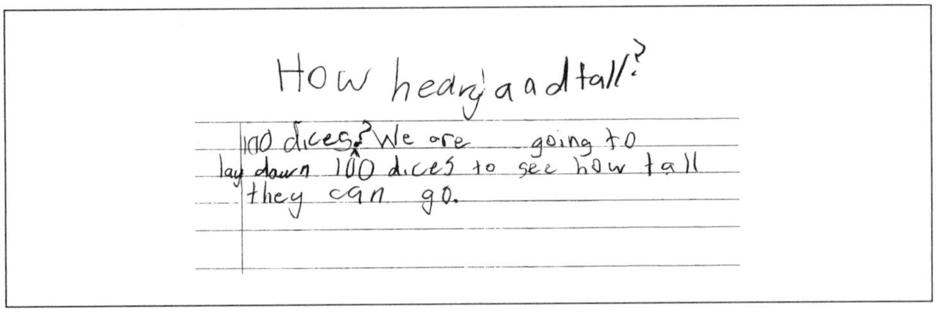

Figure 10–1: Lorenzo and Rufus described how they would find the height of one hundred dice.

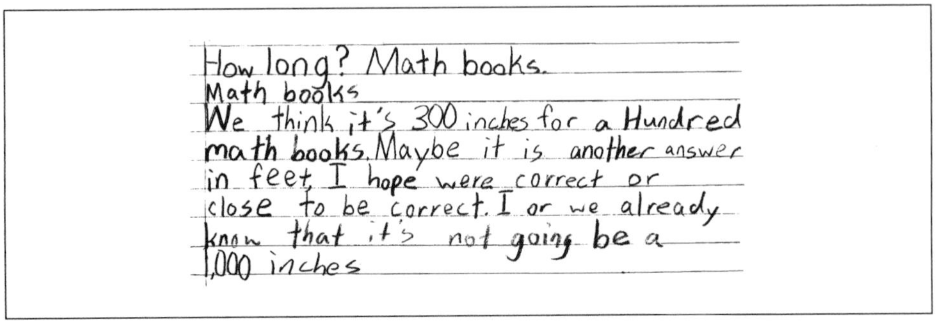

> How heavy and tall?
>
> 100 dices. We are going to lay down 100 dices to see how tall they can go.

Figure 10–2: Kei and her partner estimated before they explored how long one hundred math books would be.

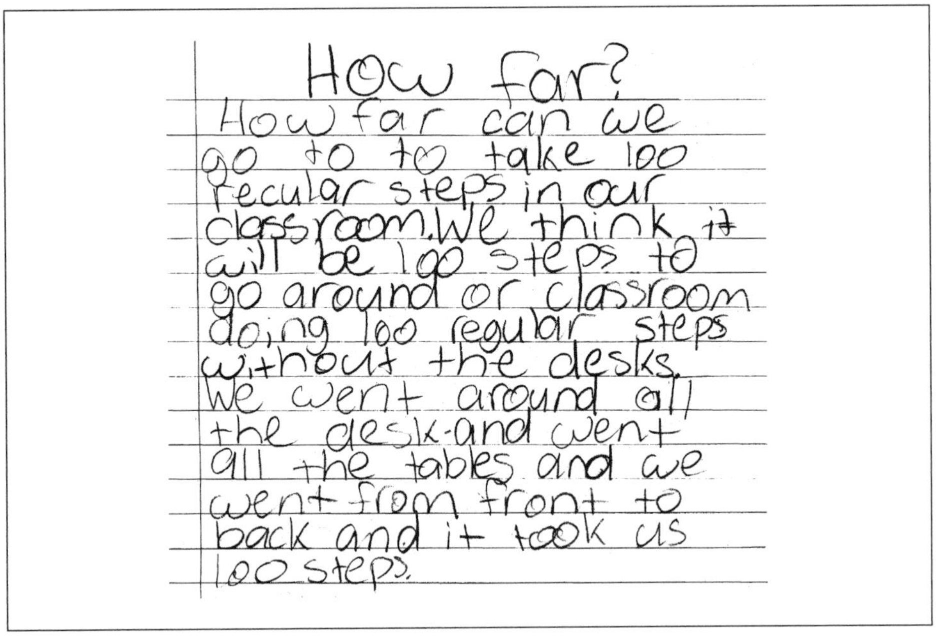

> How long? Math books.
> Math books
> We think it's 300 inches for a Hundred math books. Maybe it is another answer in feet, I hope were correct or close to be correct. I or we already know that it's not going be a 1,000 inches

Figure 10–3: Ariel explained how she and her partner walked around the room counting their steps.

> How far?
> How far can we go to to take 100 recular steps in our classroom. We think it will be 100 steps to go around or classroom doing 100 regular steps without the desks. We went around all the desk-and went all the tables and we went from front to back and it took us 100 steps.

Day 2

The next day the children were anxious to get right to work on their explorations, but I called them to the front of the room with their papers to check on their progress so far. I asked each pair of children to report the question they were exploring and explain their plan for answering it. I invited the rest of the class to give suggestions or ask questions. First I called on Lorenzo and Rufus.

Math and Nonfiction, Grades 3–5

"We're going to stack dice and find how tall one hundred of them goes," Lorenzo explained.

"But they keep falling down," Rufus added.

"What did you learn yesterday when you were working with the dice?" I asked.

"Well," Rufus said, "the dice kept falling down, so we put them in a line on the desk and measured them, then we got ten stacked up and you helped us hold them up while we measured them too. It was the same. So if we put the dice in a long line on the desk we'll get the same as if we stack them up." He added, "Kei gave us the idea."

I brought up another aspect of the investigation: "I gave you my tub of dice to use. Do you think there are one hundred dice in it?" I asked.

"Definitely not," Rufus said.

"How do you think you will complete the investigation if you don't have one hundred dice?"

"We could borrow some from another teacher," Lorenzo suggested.

"Any other ideas?" I asked, opening it up to the rest of the class.

Gracie raised her hand right away and started talking before I called on her. Using her hands to demonstrate, she said "You could tape them together and just flip them over and over until you have one hundred."

"How many dice do you think they should tape together?" I asked.

Gracie said, "I think ten, and then flip it ten times to make a hundred."

Lorenzo and Rufus both seemed to understand the suggestions they got, so I moved on to another pair of children.

"Ariel and Mikayla, tell us about your investigation," I said.

Mikayla explained, "We were going to walk one hundred steps all around the room, but we had to walk around the desks."

"Did you actually walk one hundred steps?" I asked.

"Yes," Ariel replied.

"How many times did you walk around the room?" I asked.

"I don't know. We didn't count that," she answered.

"Which question are you trying to answer?" I asked.

Mikayla said, "Our question is, *How far is one hundred steps?*"

"Do you have an answer yet?" I prompted.

"Not really," Ariel said.

"What if you start at the door to the third-grade hall and walk first in one direction, then in another," Kei suggested. "Then you'd know how far you went."

The discussion continued, with students describing how they were planning to find the answers to their questions. Some of the plans seemed to be working well, and the rest of the class made no suggestions. I reminded the students to include their question as part of the title of the paper, and to check with me before leaving the room.

> How far
> We are doing how far are one
>
> hundred nickles are when
> you stack them.
>
> We are going to see
> how far 100 inickles are.
>
> 1
> 21
> 21
> 21
> 21
> 21
> 21
> 21
> 21
> 21
> 21
> 210

The students got to work again. Shameka and Kaitlyn again asked for nickels to stack. They measured a stack of ten nickels, then added their result ten times. (See Figure 10–4.) Mikayla and Ariel went into the hall and together walked straight in one direction, counting steps as they went. Malina and Gracie went to the end of the third-grade hall and Malina started jumping while Gracie walked beside her counting the jumps. Julia and Adrian were also in the hall, with Julia skipping and Adrian holding my watch, timing one hundred seconds and counting Julia's laps from one end of the hall to the other.

When the class got back together, each pair of students reported about what they did and what they learned about one hundred. It's important for students to share their thinking about an activity like this, but they learn the most from the exploration they do themselves. In this lesson, they got a better sense of the number one hundred by exploring one question in depth, and their work built their curiosity about what the book would say about one thousand.

Day 3

The class knew when I walked in the next day that they were finally going to get to hear the book, and they were excited. "I wonder if it will be like the stuff we did," Kei remarked. I reread the title, and they all read it along with me. The first page of the book talks about the stars in the sky, asking, "How many do you think there are?"

"A million," someone called out.

"No, infinity," Jake said.

I didn't want to leave Jake's comment unchallenged, so I thought for a moment about how to respond. I said, "Jake, at any particular moment in time, there is an exact number of stars that could be counted, if we had a way to count them all. *Infinity* is a word we use to describe something without end, something with no exact number. So while it may seem that there is an infinite number of stars in the sky, there is actually a finite number, a *countable* number of stars." This wasn't a very satisfactory way to explain the concept of infinity, but in the interest of time I moved on.

As I read aloud, we discussed the scenarios it presents. Each page provides an opportunity to view one thousand as something small, as in a pile of one thousand acorns, or something large, as in the forest of trees those acorns could grow into. The children were fascinated by whether you could eat one thousand french fries. The book suggests that you could share one thousand fries with friends, each with a serving of forty fries. With that size serving, how many friends could share one thousand fries? Discussion started as soon as I read the question. Malina said, without stopping to think about it, "Each person could get two fries!" But Gracie contradicted her just as quickly, "Each person would get two french fries if five hundred people shared one thousand!"

"How did you figure that out, Gracie?" I asked.

She answered, "I know that five hundred plus five hundred equals one thousand."

Kei suggested, "It must be less than 200."

"I think we could try 126 friends," said Kaitlyn.

I decided to try to focus the discussion rather than use the guess-and-check strategy. "Let's think about this," I said. I wrote *1000* on the board and asked, "If you shared the fries with one person, how many would be left?" As I spoke I wrote,

$$
\begin{array}{r}
1000 \\
-40 \\
\hline
\end{array}
$$

"I know the answer. It's nine hundred sixty," Jake said.

"How did you figure that out so quickly?" I asked.

He replied, "I know that six plus four is ten, so sixty plus forty is one hundred, and one hundred plus nine hundred is one thousand."

I recorded the answer, and out to the side I wrote a *1* to indicate that one person had fries.

$$
\begin{array}{r}
1000 \\
-40 \quad 1 \\
\hline
960
\end{array}
$$

We continued to subtract by forty. When we had subtracted five times our subtraction problem looked like this:

$$
\begin{array}{rl}
1000 & \\
-40 & \quad 1 \\
\hline
960 & \\
-40 & \quad 1 \\
\hline
920 & \\
-40 & \quad 1 \\
\hline
880 & \\
-40 & \quad 1 \\
\hline
840 & \\
-40 & \quad 1 \\
\hline
800 & \\
\end{array}
$$

"So by now we've shared fries with five people. How many fries have we given away?" I asked.

"I think we've given away two hundred fries," Devin said. "We gave away forty five times. Five times four is twenty, so add a zero and it's two hundred."

"I don't get that," Malina said, frowning.

"I do," Cliff said. "You're not just multiplying one number by one number, like five times four. It's really five times forty, so you add a zero, like one is just a one, but ten is a one and a zero."

"I have another way for us to record the information in this problem that may help us make sense of it." I drew a T-chart on the side of the easel. In the first column I wrote *1* and in the second column I wrote *40*. "How do you think I should label these columns? What does the number forty tell us?"

Ariel answered, "That's the number of fries someone eats." I labeled the column with the word *Fries*. "So what about the other column? What should the label be?" I asked.

"That side is how many people eat the fries," Shameka said. I labeled it *People*.

I continued the left side of the chart with the numbers *2* through *5*, and asked the students to help me record the number of fries for the right side of the chart. They knew that the number of fries increased by forty each time and used the skip counting sequence to continue the pattern. I continued the pattern up to ten people. "Wow," I said, "I already have a long list for this T-chart, and we're only up to ten people. Let's see if we can make a leap. Watch the marks I'm making on the *People* side of the chart." I made three small dots under the 10 and wrote *15*, saying, "Dot, dot, dot, fifteen."

"What do you think those dots might mean?" I asked.

Jake replied, "It's like in a book when they do that. It means 'and so on.'"

"It is similar to that, Jake," I said. "In this case it means that I'm leaving some numbers off the chart. Which ones am I leaving off?"

The students responded together: "Eleven, twelve, thirteen, fourteen."

On the *Fries* side of the chart, I wrote three dots under the number 400. "What number do you think belongs here?" I asked.

People	Fries
1	40
2	80
3	120
4	160
5	200
6	240
7	280
8	320
9	360
10	400
.	.
.	.
.	.
15	

"I see a pattern!" Gracie said excitedly. "For five people it was two hundred fries, and for ten people it was four hundred fries, so for fifteen people it could be six hundred fries. See! It's just counting by twos!"

Cliff interjected, "You mean by two hundreds."

Gracie nodded, "Yeah, that's what I meant." Most of the class seemed to accept Gracie's idea, but before I wrote it down I called on Rufus, who seemed uneasy.

"I think it could also be eight hundred," he said.

"Can you explain how it could be eight hundred, Rufus?" I asked.

"If you double two hundred you get four hundred and if you double four hundred you get eight hundred," he replied.

Other students were nodding at this idea, and now seemed unsure what the pattern was. "How could we figure out which pattern is correct?" I asked. "Talk to the person next to you about this." After a minute or two, I called for the students' attention again, and asked for someone to share what they had come up with.

Mikayla spoke for herself and Ariel: "We think you just have to add forty five times and you'll get the answer. The answer will be six hundred. We think."

The rest of the class seemed to think that was a good idea, but Rufus suggested a short cut. He said, "I think we can just do five times forty. It's like five times four is twenty, because," he counted on his fingers, "four, eight, twelve, sixteen, twenty, and so if you add a zero it's two hundred. And two hundred plus four hundred is six hundred." I knew there were some children in the class who didn't follow Rufus's line of reasoning, so along with recording his method, I recorded the addition method suggested by Ariel and Mikayla.

Rufus's Method	Ariel and Mikayla's Method
$5 \times 4 = 20$	$400 + 40 = 440$
$5 \times 40 = 200$	$440 + 40 = 480$
$200 + 400 = 600$	$480 + 40 = 520$
	$520 + 40 = 560$
	$560 + 40 = 600$

Next, we continued filling in the T-chart in increments of five people, until we reached one thousand fries.

People	Fries
1	40
2	80
3	120
4	160
5	200
6	240
7	280
8	320
9	360
10	400
.	.
.	.
.	.
15	600
.	.
.	.
.	.
20	800
.	.
.	.
.	.
25	1,000

"So we could share the fries with twenty-five people," Jake said, summing up the work we had done. On the board I wrote:

25 people   40 fries each = 1,000 fries

"I could write this as a multiplication sentence," I said, and wrote:

25 × 40 = 1,000

I went on reading aloud. One page describes how far you could walk if you walked one thousand steps, and says that one thousand steps would take you around a baseball diamond about four times. "How many steps would it take to go around once?" I asked.

"That depends," Devin said thoughtfully. "If it was Mr. Burton," the assistant principal, "walking around, he would take less steps than Mrs. Liska," the principal, "because he takes bigger steps. His legs are longer."

"Let's assume that the person who is walking around once is the same person who walked around four times with one thousand steps," I offered.

"That's like division," Shenai said. "One thousand divided into four parts."

I wrote on the board:

1000 ÷ 4 =

Gracie jumped up and exclaimed, "I know. Last time we said that two five hundreds make a thousand. So just cut five hundred in half. That makes two hundred fifty! So it would take two hundred fifty steps to go around once." I thought of asking the class how many steps there were between bases, but they had been sitting a long time and I knew they wouldn't last much longer. I wanted to be sure to get to the end of the book.

The last few pages of the book present other interesting topics for mathematical discussion. I made a mental note to return to the book and have students think about some of these other ideas in more depth. This book offers a wealth of opportunities for exploring large numbers and gives students the chance to communicate their mathematical thinking in group discussions.

Icebergs and Glaciers
Taught by Stephanie Sheffield

Seymour Simon's *Icebergs and Glaciers* (1999) explains how glaciers are formed, how they move, and how chunks break off to form icebergs. The text is illustrated with photographs and diagrams. The five pages that focus on icebergs provide background for exploring fractions. In this lesson, fourth-grade students are given a piece of clay that represents the one-eighth of an iceberg that floats above the water, then use more clay to construct the missing seven-eighths.

MATERIALS

clay or play dough, about 1 cup per group of two or three students

a 7-inch piece of yarn, 1 piece per group

half-inch grid paper (see Blackline Masters)

I began by showing the fourth graders the photograph on the cover of *Icebergs and Glaciers*. "What genre do you think this book is?" I asked.

"What does 'genre' mean?" Marfa asked.

"You know," Billy explained, "It's like what kind of book is it—fiction, biography, like that."

"Oh, yeah," Marfa said.

Christina raised her hand. "I think it's going to be nonfiction," she said.

"Why do you think that?" I asked.

"Well, it has a real picture on the cover, and icebergs and glaciers are real things," she explained.

"I don't think that would make a very good title for a fiction book," Nelson commented. "It doesn't sound like a story book."

"Well, you're right, it is a nonfiction book. That means that it will help us learn more about icebergs and glaciers. Does anybody know anything about them already?" I asked.

"I do!" Jose called out excitedly. "The *Titanic* was sunk by an iceberg! I saw a show about it on the Discovery Channel."

"What else do you know about glaciers or icebergs?" I asked the class. I waited until several hands were up before calling on Demarque.

"Last year we did an experiment with ice cubes, and we found out that glaciers drag stuff with them when they move," he explained.

"What kind of stuff?" asked Angie.

"Stuff like rocks and sticks that are on the ground under the glacier. They move real slow and drag stuff."

I held the book up as I said, "Let's read now to find out how glaciers move, and how icebergs and glaciers are related."

When I read a nonfiction book aloud, I stop often to check in with the class and make sure they understand the facts presented. I might ask them to repeat an idea in their own words, or just ask if they have any questions.

After I finished reading *Icebergs and Glaciers*, I returned to the pages about icebergs. I reread the line that explains that seven-eighths of an iceberg is under water. I asked, "If seven-eighths of an iceberg is under water, how much is above water?" Almost the whole class raised their hands.

"One-eighth," Tali responded when I called on her. I sketched a pie slice on the board and labeled it $\frac{1}{8}$.

$$\frac{1}{8}$$

"Let's think about that fraction for a minute," I said. "If this is one-eighth, what does the whole thing look like?" I called on Sharra to come to the board. She drew a circle that incorporated the wedge shape I had drawn.

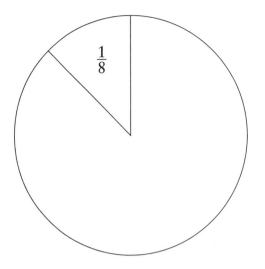

"What fraction of the circle is this part?" I asked, indicating the portion Sharra had drawn.

"If the little slice is one-eighth, then the rest is seven-eighths," Sharra said. I labeled the large section of the circle $\frac{7}{8}$.

"Can anyone else explain how you know that the part Sharra drew is seven-eighths of the circle?" I asked.

Billy raised his hand. "Can I come up there?" he asked. I nodded and handed him the marker as he came to the board.

"If this is one-eighth, that means the other parts have to be seven," he said. He drew lines to divide the circle into eight slices.

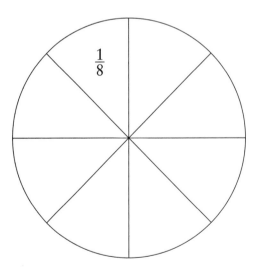

"What can you tell me about the pieces of a fraction?" I asked.

"That they are equal," Angie replied.

"Is that important?" I probed.

"Yes," she said, "Because if you were dividing a pie to share with your friends they would get mad if they weren't equal."

Next I drew a small rectangle on the board and labeled it $\frac{1}{8}$. "If this is one brownie, who would like to draw what you think the whole pan of brownies looks like?" I asked. Many hands went up, and I called on Linus. He came to the board and drew other rectangles connected to the one I had drawn, but his were not all the same size as mine.

"Hey wait!" Lamar interjected. "Don't they all have to be equal?"

"What needs to be equal, Lamar?" I asked.

"All the brownies have to be the same if each one is one-eighth." He erased the part of the rectangle Linus had drawn and redrew it. He started by drawing one more brownie just like mine right next to it, then he drew three more rows of two brownies to make the complete pan of brownies. I took a different color marker and wrote $\frac{7}{8}$ across Lamar's entire section.

I said, "Now we have two models of fractions showing one-eighth and seven-eighths. Why don't both of the one-eighth pieces look the same?"

Nelson answered, "That's easy. One is a piece of pizza and one is a brownie. They just don't look alike. They don't have to."

"And they are still both one-eighth?" I probed.

"Sure," Sharra said. "One-eighth of a pizza and one-eighth of a bunch of brownies aren't going to look alike." I saw heads nodding around the group, so I decided to move on to the next part of the lesson.

An Independent Activity

"I have another activity that involves fractions and icebergs. You will work in groups today. I'm going to give each group one piece of clay that represents the tip of an iceberg." I broke off a small chunk of clay and held it in my hand. "If this is the tip of the iceberg, what fraction of the whole iceberg am I holding?" I asked.

"One-eighth," the students said together.

"So," I said, "what does the seven-eighths look like? That's your group's job. You'll use this large lump of clay to create the part of the iceberg that is under water. And you'll use yarn to represent the water line." I held up a 7-inch piece of yarn. "Who can repeat the directions?"

Paula explained, "You're going to give us some clay and it's the part of the iceberg that is above the water. We have to figure out what the part under water looks like. But I have a question. Can we pick our own partners?"

"Not this time," I said. "I will tell you who will be in each group. When I call your name, please find a place to sit where you can work together. When your whole group is seated I'll call two of you up to get your clay."

The students were eager to begin. When they were seated I called two students from each group up to get their clay and a 7-inch piece of yarn. I deliberately gave each group a different amount of clay for the tip of the iceberg, so that when the groups shared at the end, we could focus on how the one-eighth they started with defined the size of the whole iceberg.

As they worked, I walked around and observed that the groups were starting with several different strategies. I listened in on Cort and Amy. Amy said, "I'm making the little piece into a cube. Then we can make eight more like it,"

"Seven more," Cort corrected her.

Linus, Lamar, and Christina were working together. They took their large hunk of clay and flattened it into a round disc about $\frac{1}{4}$ inch high. Then they used a pencil point to score the circle into eighths. They removed one of the eighths by pressing a scissors into the clay, then shaped that part to make something they thought looked like the tip of an iceberg.

Christina picked up the larger part of clay and announced, "That's it. That's the one-eighth and this is the other seven-eighths." After creating a "flat" iceberg, the group put the yarn between the two parts of clay to mark the water line, then raised their hands.

"We're finished," Linus declared.

"Could you write down how you created your whole iceberg, and include a sketch of the final iceberg?" I asked.

I gave the students two minutes to complete their work, then asked for their attention. "I want you all to have the opportunity to see the work of the other groups, and to explain to the class how you made your own icebergs. We'll start with Sharra and Nelson. Why don't you tell us how you made your complete iceberg?"

Nelson explained: "First we rolled up the clay into a little ball. Then we made more little balls the same size."

"We started with the tip of the iceberg that you gave us," Sharra added. "We knew we needed eight balls all together, and one was the tip. We smooched them together to make the whole iceberg."

Tali and Demetric had an interesting spread-out iceberg on their desk. I asked them how they made it. Demetric said, "We made chunks of two-eighths and put three of them together to make six-eighths, then we added one more to make seven-eighths. So seven-eighths is under the water and one-eighth is above."

We walked to Billy's desk next. He and Paula talked about how they made their iceberg. "We measured the tip piece with our hands," Paula said. "Then we measured chunks with our fingers to make them all the same. Then we squished them all together and put our water line down."

This lesson gave these fourth graders the opportunity to think about fractions using a three-dimensional model rather than the two-dimensional models we usually use. And because the students began with only a portion of the model iceberg, they had to think about how that fraction related to the whole in order to create the entire iceberg. (See Figures 11–1 through 11–4.)

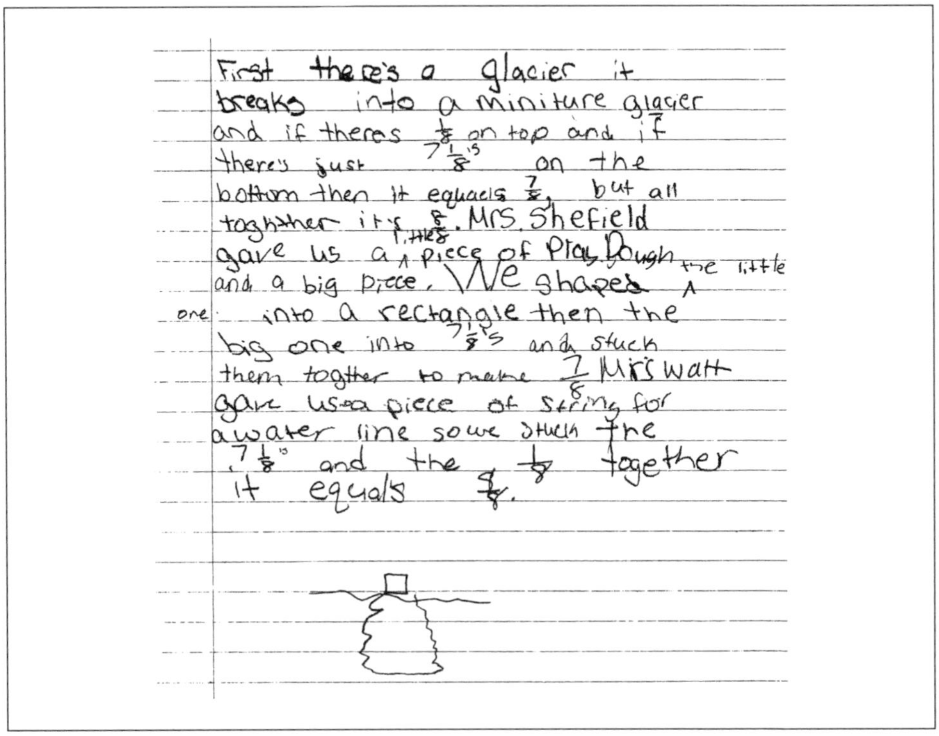
First there's a glacier it
breaks into a miniture glacier
and if theres 1/8 on top and if
there's just 7 1/8's on the
bottom then it equals 7/8, but all
toghther it's 8/8. Mrs. Shefield
gave us a 1/8 piece of Play Dough
and a big piece. We shaped the little
one into a rectangle then the
big one into 7 1/8's and stuck
them togther to make 7/8 Mrs watt
gave us a piece of string for
a water line so we stuck the
7 1/8's and the 1/8 together
it equals 8/8.

Figure 11–1: Marfa and Jose explain how they shaped their small piece of play dough into a rectangle and duplicated it to make seven more equivalent pieces.

Figure 11–2: Angie and Cristian drew a picture to illustrate what they did with the play dough.

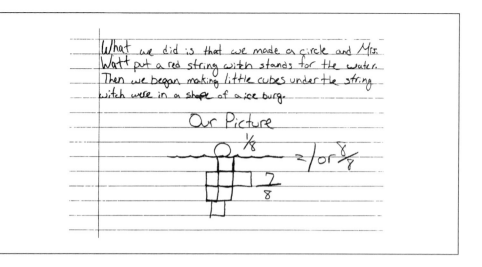

Figure 11–3: Linus and Christina's picture shows their interpretation of an iceberg.

Figure 11–4: Demarque and Tali used groups of two-eighths to form their total iceberg, which was eight-eighths.

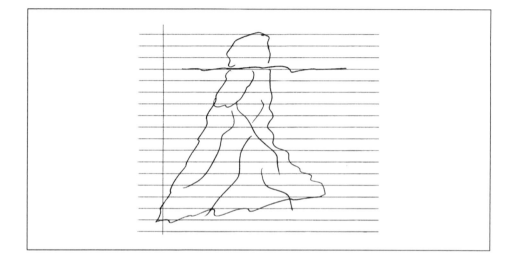

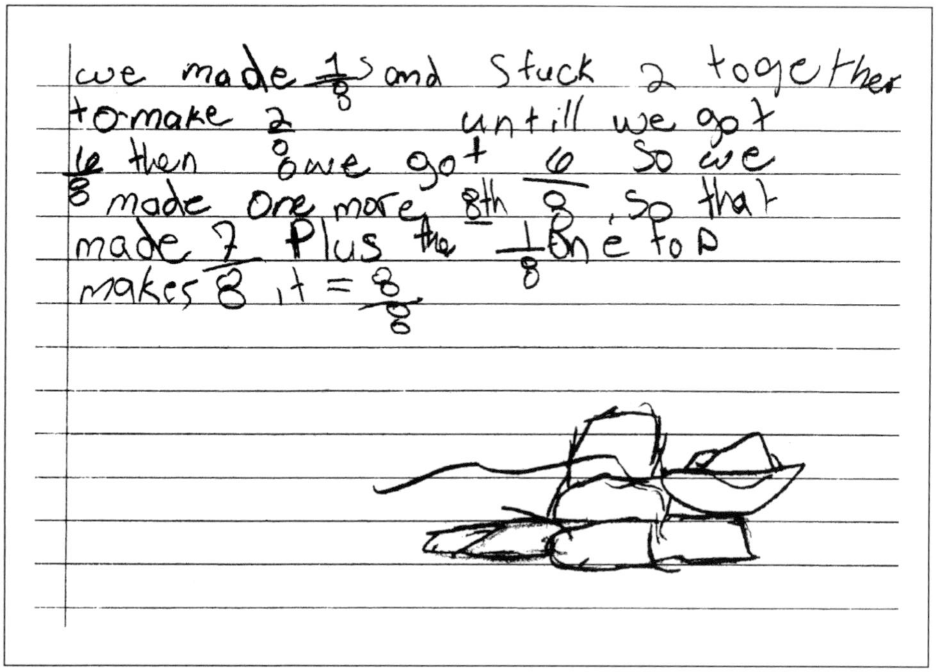

If the World Were a Village

Taught by Kathleen Gallagher

There are currently more than six billion people on the planet! In *If the World Were a Village: A Book About the World's People* (2002), David J. Smith helps children make sense of this enormous number by asking them to imagine the whole world as a village of just one hundred people. He presents data on various topics—nationalities, languages, ages, religions, and education—to describe the population in a compressed global village. In this lesson, fifth graders create circle graphs to depict the population information they've learned.

MATERIALS

Grid and Circle Worksheet, 2 or 3 per student
  (see Blackline Masters)
chart paper, 1 sheet

When I sat down in front of the fifth-grade class, I showed the students the cover of *If the World Were a Village.* "I'm excited about the book I have to share with you today," I told them. "It gives us a way to think about really large numbers." After reading the first paragraph, which is full of numbers about the world's population that are hard for the children to fathom, I stopped and read it again, this time having the children repeat the numbers as I recorded them on the board.

Large numbers in the book are written with spaces instead of commas. For example, the book explains that twenty-three countries in the world have more than fifty million people, and the numeral appears as 50 000 000. I recorded the number both that way and with commas—50,000,000—as the students had learned. I said, "Both of these representations mean the same thing, and even though we usually use commas, both are correct."

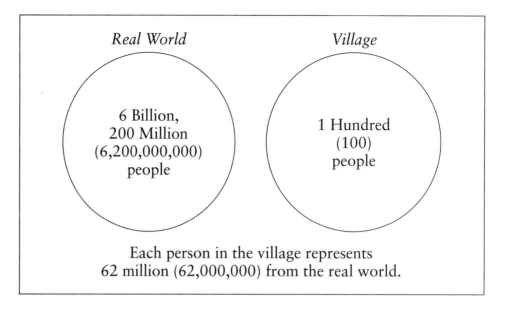

Real World   Village

6 Billion, 200 Million (6,200,000,000) people

1 Hundred (100) people

Each person in the village represents 62 million (62,000,000) from the real world.

I drew two circles on the board and labeled one *Real World* and the other *Village*. (See Figure 12–1.) As I read the second paragraph, which suggests that we imagine the entire population of the world as a village of just one hundred people, I wrote the actual world population, *6,200,000,000*, in the first circle and the equivalent village population, *100*, in the second circle.

As I read the next page, I listed on the board how the world's nationalities would be reflected in our global village of one hundred people:

61 are from Asia
13 are from Africa
12 are from Europe
8 are from South America, Central America (including Mexico), and the Caribbean
5 are from Canada and the United States
1 is from Oceania

I explained that Oceania includes Australia, New Zealand, and the islands of the south, west, and central Pacific. Also, as I wrote each line, we identified that area on our world map with a sticky note so we could refer to the places as we talked about them throughout the lesson. I showed the students a *Grid and Circle* worksheet. (See Figure 12–2.)

Pointing to the hundreds chart portion of the worksheet, I said, "Imagine that this grid represents the one hundred people in our global village. I'd like you to use your colored pencils to show how much of the grid represents the people from each continent." I distributed the worksheets and the children colored in squares to match the numbers in the global village. (See Figure 12–3.) They had used hundreds charts before to model decimals, but they hadn't done any real work with percents.

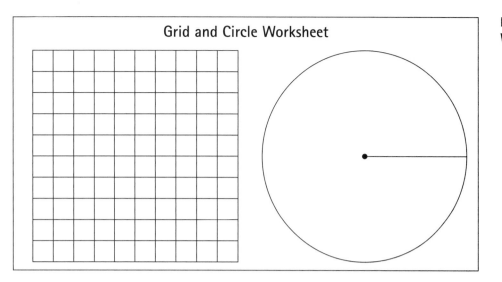

Figure 12–2: Grid and Circle Worksheet.

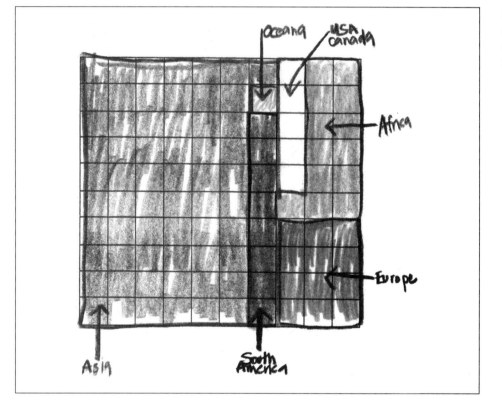
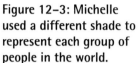

Figure 12–3: Michelle used a different shade to represent each group of people in the world.

"Can you guess what the circle next to your hundreds grid is for?" I asked the class.

"It looks like a pie chart," said Edwin.

"And what is a pie chart?"

"It's like a circle that's divided into pieces," said Jeffrey.

"We had so many of those in our science book last year. I remember one that showed that almost all of the animals in the whole world don't have bones," said Jack excitedly.

"Yeah, I remember that," said Jason.

"Well, mathematicians like to use circles to show how numbers relate to each other. It's called a percent circle, or circle graph, or pie chart, like Edwin said. We can use the percent circle to show how the number of people in each group in the global village relates to the number of people in each other group. The circle represents the whole. For the global village, the whole circle represents all one hundred people in the village."

"Do you want us to divide the circle up to show the same numbers as the square one?" asked Michelle.

"Yes, I'd like you to try to do that. I thought it would be easy since we've done so much work with number lines. This percent circle is like a number line in the shape of a circle." I drew a circle on the board with a dot in the middle and a line going straight up. "If the whole circle represents one hundred and I start here at zero and go halfway around, what number would go here?"

"Fifty," the class answered. I marked the half-way point and wrote the number *50* and the word *half*.

"If this is fifty, what would this point be?" I asked, making a mark half-way between 0 and 50.

"Twenty-five," they responded.

"Then what would this point represent?" I marked, half-way between 50 and 100.

"Seventy-five," they answered. I wrote in the benchmark numbers to show how the whole circle represented 100.

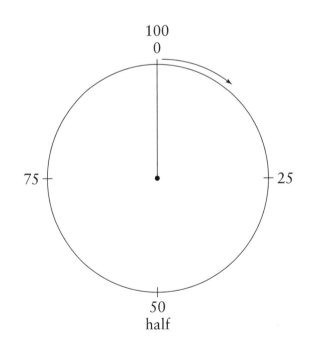

"Some people call it a pie chart because when it's divided up, the sections look like the pieces of a pie. If there were a line going from here to here, "I drew a line from the middle to 25," how much would this piece represent?" I asked, as I shaded in one-fourth of the circle.

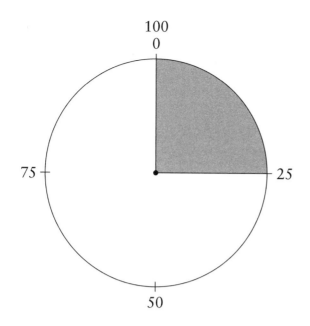

"It would be twenty-five percent," LaDree called out.

"Do you know what 'percent' means?" I asked.

"It's like how much you get right," answered Sandra.

"Can you give an example, Sandra?" I asked.

"Like on a math test I got eighty percent," she said.

I looked at the diagram on the board and said, "Right now our circle graph shows twenty-five percent. How can I make it show eighty percent? Talk to your partner and see what he or she thinks."

After several seconds, I called on Javier. "We think it's past the seventy-five, but not in the middle."

"How much past the seventy-five, do you think?" I asked.

Javier came up to the board. As he counted up from seventy-five by fives, he marked approximately equal sections of the circle: *75, 80, 85, 90, 95, 100.*

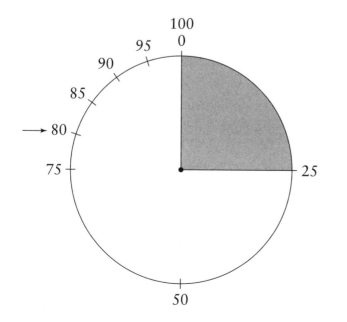

"So you think eighty percent is here?" I asked, drawing a line from the middle of the circle out to the 80. "Do the rest of you agree?"

I heard many children say, "I do," and I shaded 80 percent of the circle.

"Do you know how we write *percent*?" I asked.

"It's like that little line with the two little circles," Jeffrey responded. I drew the percent sign and wrote the words *eighty percent* on the board.

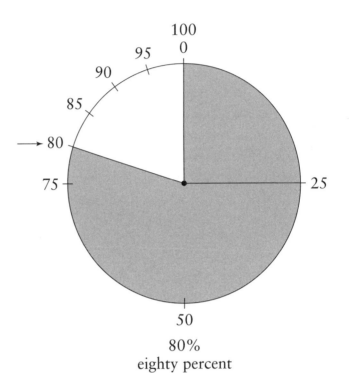

80%
eighty percent

"Let's look carefully at the word *percent* for a minute." I covered up the *per* part of the word so the children could focus on the *cent* and asked, "What does this remind you of?"

"Cent like a penny!" Jason called out.

"Yeah, like ten cents," agreed Edwin.

"What other words do you know that have this word part?"

"Centimeter," said Michelle.

"Centipede," said Edward.

I said, "A penny is called a cent because it's one one-hundredth of a dollar. A centimeter is called a centimeter because it's one one-hundredth of a meter."

"I think a centipede is called a centipede because it has one hundred legs," Jack interrupted.

"And do you know what *per* means?" I asked.

"I don't," said Sandra.

"It means 'for every.' Percent means 'for every hundred' or 'out of every hundred.' In the global village, if sixty-one out of one hundred people are from Asia, that means sixty-one percent are from Asia." I held up the worksheet again, showing both the grid and the circle. I said, "You already shaded in squares on the grid to show where the people in the global village come from. Now try to divide and shade the circle to show the same information."

The children got right to work. Nobody had had any trouble filling in the grid to match the numbers in the global village, but when they moved to the circle it was a little trickier. Some of them divided their circle into one hundred tiny pieces, forgetting to check to see if the benchmark numbers were lining up and consequently putting the numbers too close together or too far apart. Jack didn't write any numbers on his circle. He tried to make each piece the appropriate size. If it didn't work, he erased and tried again. Other children used a combination of approaches. (See Figures 12–4, 12–5, and 12–6.)

As students finished, I asked them to compare the size of each pie-chart piece with a partner's to see if they were similar. If they agreed that each piece made sense, I asked them to work on a list of generalizations: What do the diagrams tell us about the people in the global village? When most of the students had finished their diagrams and had begun to talk about what they meant, I called the group back together.

"What do your hundred-grid and pie-chart diagrams tell us about the people of the global village?" I asked. I posted a piece of chart paper to record the students' statements, titling it *The Global Village Represents the People of the World.*

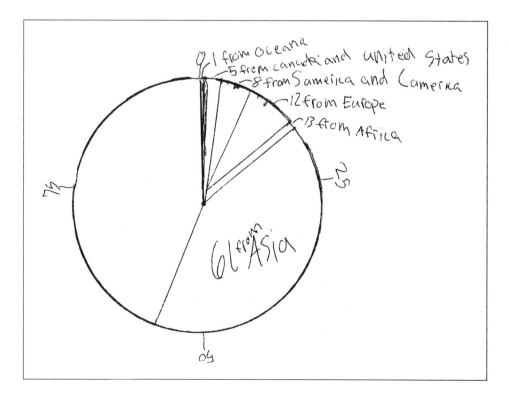

Figure 12–4: Keith estimated all his pieces but still had a large portion of his circle left over.

Figure 12–5: Jack erased
and started over four or
five times before he
came up with an accurate
representation.

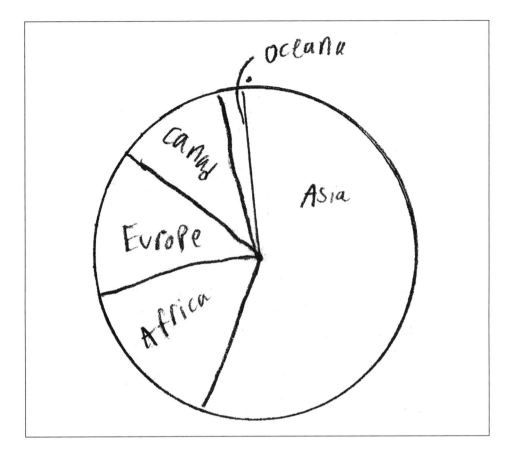

Figure 12–6: Jeffrey
chunked twelve and
thirteen to make twenty-
five and he made sixty-
one by going to seventy-
five and adding eleven more.
The last little bit of the
circle he divided into single
segments to show South
America, Canada, and
Oceania.

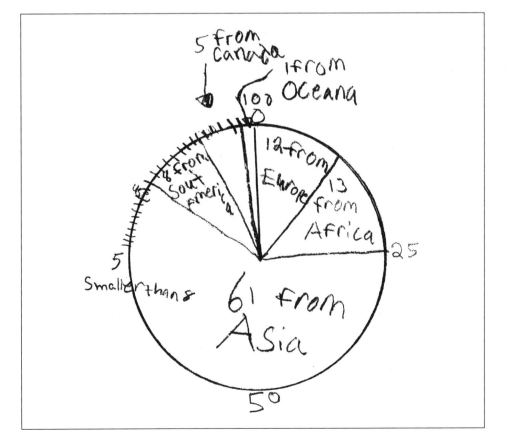

Math and Nonfiction, Grades 3–5

"More than half of the people are from Asia," said Chris.

"Check both of your diagrams to see if you agree with Chris's statement," I said as I recorded his statement on the chart. "How do you know it's more than half?" I asked.

"You can see it's more than half of the square and the circle," answered Carla.

"So what percent of the village is from Asia?" I asked.

"Sixty-one!" the children answered.

"Can you say that in a complete sentence?" I asked, wanting to give them experience using the language appropriately.

"Sixty-one percent of the people are from Asia," said Christina.

"What percent would be half?" I asked.

"Fifty percent is half, right?" asked Jason.

"That's right," I said, "so is sixty-one percent really more than half?"

"Yes, because sixty-one is more than fifty," Chris confirmed. I wrote on the chart: *More than half of the people are from Asia.*

"What else do you notice?" I asked.

"The United States and Canada both together have less people than everywhere else except Oceania," said Jeffrey.

"Check and see if your partner understood what Jeffrey just said," I challenged the class.

"Say it again, Jeffrey," asked Jessica. "I didn't hear."

Jeffrey repeated his statement and the children re-told it to their partners, checking to see if the words matched their own diagrams. As they talked, I recorded Jeffrey's statement.

"It has the second lowest," said Jack.

"What else?" I asked.

"Oceania has the lowest," Kimberly said quietly.

"The lowest what?" I questioned.

"The lowest number of people are from there," she answered.

"Is that what your diagrams show?" I asked as I wrote Kimberly's revised statement on the chart.

"Yes," the children agreed.

"My Oceania piece is such a skinny little sliver," said Sandra.

"So is mine," agreed many children.

"Europe and Africa are almost the same," added Beatrice.

"What's almost the same about them?" I asked.

"Africa just has one more than Europe," she stated.

"One more what?" I asked.

"One more person?" questioned Beatrice.

"Do you remember what the author said about each person in the global village?" I pointed to the board and the two circles representing the real world and the global village. As I pointed to the words, the children read, "Each person in the village represents sixty-two million from the real world."

"So in the real world, how many more people does Africa have than Europe?" I asked.

"It would be sixty-two million, because each person is the same as that number," reasoned LaDree.

I wanted the children to appreciate the mathematics the author had to do in order to create the global village. I said, "The author created the global village based on the real populations of the places we're learning about. So when we look at our circle graph that shows thirteen out of one hundred people from Africa, we know that for every one hundred people in the world, thirteen of them are from Africa. That's what percent means. It's not just 'out of one hundred,' but out of *every* one hundred."

"Can I say another one?" asked Christina.

"Sure," I said.

"South America added to the United States and Canada equals Africa," Christina offered proudly.

"What are we really adding?" I asked Christina.

"People, right?" Moving toward the map, she said, "If you count all the people from here [pointing to Canada], here [the United States], and here [South America], it would be the same as the people here [Africa]."

"Yes, and we can point to the real places in the world because the numbers in the global village are related to the real populations of the places we're learning about," I clarified.

"I have another one," said Carla. "Europe and Africa together equal twenty-five."

"Twenty-five what?" I asked.

"Twenty-five people of the village are from those two places," she said.

"And that means that twenty-five percent of the world's population is from Europe and Africa. That's twenty-five hundredths." I wrote $\frac{25}{100}$ on the board. "Does that number remind you of another fraction?" I asked.

"One-fourth?" asked Candace.

"Yes, that means one out of every four people are from Europe or Africa." I wanted to emphasize again that the one hundred people in the author's global village represent all of the people in the real world.

As I completed our chart (see below), I said. "I want you to go back to your seats and think about everything that we wrote here on our chart. I want you to decide on one of these statements to write on your paper. Use arrows to show what parts of your diagrams go with the statement you chose." (See Figure 12–7.)

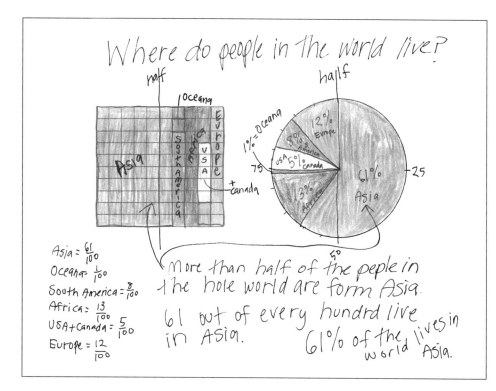

Figure 12–7: Carla used arrows to indicate the portions of the hundred grid and circle graph that supported her statement.

The Global Village Represents the People of the World

- More than half of the people are from Asia.

- The United States and Canada together have fewer people than everywhere else except Oceania.

- The least number of people are from Oceania.

- In the village, one more person is from Africa than there are people from Europe. In the real world, that's 62,000,000.

- The number of people from the USA plus the people from Canada and South America equals the number of people from Africa.

- Europe and Africa together = 25 percent of the population.

The period was over, but I planned to return to this book and provide many more opportunities for the students to explore large numbers, circle graph ratios, and percents.

If You Hopped Like a Frog

Taught by Stephanie Sheffield

If You Hopped Like a Frog, by David M. Schwartz (1999), is a picture book that compares the physical capabilities of animals and humans. It allows children to imagine, for example, how far they could hop, how much they could lift, and how fast they could run if they had the abilities of the animals that excel at those activities. Ratio and proportion are the key mathematical ideas explored in the book, which provides as much as a week's worth of activities that involve students in measuring in a variety of units, as well as computing using whole numbers, fractions, and large numbers. In this lesson, fifth graders find out how far they could hop if they hopped like a frog, then relate that measurement to their own lives. Then they explore another example from the book.

MATERIALS

measuring sticks (meter or yard), 1 per pair of students

rulers, 1 per pair of students

clock

Day 1

When I showed the cover of *If You Hopped Like a Frog* to the fifth graders, they were interested immediately. Although they were used to being read to in language arts, they were surprised to see a picture book in their math class. They sat on the floor in front of the rocking chair and I waited for them to quiet down so I could begin reading.

The book begins with a letter to the reader in which the author describes his childhood dreams of hopping like a frog and eating like a snake. He wasn't sure how far he would be able to hop if he could hop like a frog, or how much he could eat if he could eat like a snake, and swallow prey wider than his head. But he then explains that once you understand the mathematics behind those questions, it's easy to figure out the answers.

As I read the first page, "If you hopped like a frog . . . ," the class was interested to see the outcome. The next page shows a boy hopping from home plate to first base as the rest of his team looks on in awe. The children found the illustrations comical. They chuckled and commented throughout the book. The format of the book, with the leading part of the sentence, "If you _____ like a _____," gave the class the opportunity to make predictions before hearing the text on the following page.

When I read, "If you had the brain of a brachiosaurus . . . ," James jumped up from where he was sitting and said, "I know this! Dinosaurs had little, bitty brains."

"That's right!" John agreed. The students were amused when I read that their brains would be smaller than a pea.

When I had finished reading, the fifth graders were interested to find out why I had read this book to them. I showed them the last two pages and explained what we would do next. "David M. Schwartz, the author, wanted you to have a chance to think about the mathematics behind these statements, so he included some information and questions to help start your thinking. I'm going to read you some mathematical information about the frog, then we'll try to figure out how far you could hop if you hopped like a frog."

I read the information about the frog and then said, "A three-inch frog can hop sixty inches. Think about that: How many times its length can a frog hop?"

Denae spoke out right away: "Three times six is eighteen, so that's. . . ." She looked at the ceiling and tried to figure out the multiplication in her head. "It's a hundred eighty," she said after a moment.

"Wait a minute!" Cheryl interjected. "That can't be right! A frog can't hop one hundred eighty times its length. That's too much."

Darrell raised his hand. "Three times sixty is one hundred eighty, but I don't think that was the question. What was the question again? I forgot."

"If a three-inch frog can hop sixty inches, how many times its length can it hop?" I repeated.

"This is a trick question!" James exclaimed. "It says *times,* but you really have to divide. I think it's like, sixty *divided* by three, not *times.*"

Denae responded, "So that would be twenty, not a hundred eighty."

I looked around the group to see if other students agreed. "Can anyone else explain James's thinking?"

I called on Casey. "OK," she said, "this is what I think. See, a frog is three inches. That's like this much," using her fingers to approximate three inches. "If it hops twenty times its length, that would be twenty threes." She moved her fingers in a hopping motion forward. "So he would end up on sixty. So James is right. But I think you could multiply to find the answer, too."

James and Casey were seeing the problem in two different ways, and I wanted the class to have a chance to see how the two were connected. I called James to the board. "Can you write a number sentence to show how you thought about the problem?" I asked.

James thought for a minute before writing $60 \div 3 = 20$.

"Now Casey, can you write a number sentence to show what you are thinking?" Casey walked slowly to the board and wrote $3 \times$.

She stopped after this, and I could tell she was stuck.

"What did you know from the beginning, and which number did you have to find out?" I asked.

"Oh yeah," she said, and continued to write: $3 \times \_\_\_ = 60$.

She said, "I know three times two is six, so three times twenty is sixty."

"It's like a fact family," Sonny commented. Three times twenty is sixty, and sixty divided by three is twenty."

"So that means *what* about the frog?" I asked.

"It means a frog can jump twenty times its length," Sonny said.

"OK, so now we know that a frog can hop twenty times its own length," I began. "Now let's figure out how far *you* could hop if you hopped like a frog. I'd like a volunteer who already knows how tall he or she is."

Only a couple of hands went up. I called on James. "I know I'm five foot three," he said.

"If we want to know how far James could hop if he could hop like a frog, what do we need to do first?" I asked.

Lacey answered, "We have to multiply five feet three inches by twenty." She paused, then said, "But I don't think we can multiply feet and inches together. I think we have to change it to all feet or all inches."

"Who has an idea about that?" I asked.

Ernie responded, "I think he's five feet and then three twelfths of a foot, because there are twelve inches in a foot, but he's only three inches taller than a foot."

"I get what Ernie is saying," Denae chimed in. "But I think it would be easier to do it in inches."

"How should we do that, Denae?" I asked.

"Do five times twelve, then add the three inches," she replied.

I looked at Rhelea. "Do you understand what Denae did?" I asked. Rhelea nodded. "Can you explain it?"

Rhelea said, "She multiplied feet times twelve inches because there are twelve inches in a foot, then she added the other three inches because James is five feet three."

"What's next?" I asked. Several students raised their hands and I called on Allie.

"Now we have to multiply his height by twenty because frogs jump twenty times their length," she said. I wrote $63 \times 20 = \_\_\_\_$ on the board and let the students look at it for a few moments.

"Does anyone have an idea what the answer is?" I asked. Two children responded, with two different answers—1,260 and 1,200.

"Can either of you explain how you got your answer?" I asked.

Allie replied, "First I wrote it up and down."

"Like this?" I asked as I wrote:

$$\begin{array}{r} 63 \\ \times\ 20 \\ \hline \end{array}$$

"Yeah, like that. First you do sixty-three times two is one hundred twenty-six, then you add a zero because it's not two, it's twenty. So the answer is one thousand two hundred sixty."

"Oh, yeah," said Ernie, who had offered the answer 1,200. "That's right."

Sonny said, "That means James can jump one thousand two hundred sixty inches."

"How far is that?" I asked. "Does anyone have an idea? Is it farther than across the classroom? Could he jump from one end of the fifth-grade hall to the other? Could he jump across the school?" No one in the room could picture how far 1,260 inches would be.

"I think we have to find out how many feet it is," Casey mused. "We'll have to divide by twelve this time, because we multiplied by twelve when we turned the feet into inches."

I wrote $1,260 \div 12 = \_\_\_\_$ on the board.

"That's not how our teacher writes division problems," Darrell commented. "I don't know how to do it that way."

"How would you write this problem?" I asked. Darrell came to the board and wrote $12\overline{)1,260}$.

"I agree—that's another way to write a division problem. There is one more way this problem could be written. Does anybody know what that is?" I asked. This last symbolic form was more difficult for the children to come up with. At first Ashley thought she knew. She came to the board and wrote $12 \div 1,260 = \_\_\_\_$. Quickly, many hands went into the air. Children called out comments like, "That's not right!" "You've got it backwards!" I asked Lanie to explain her remark.

"Well, that means dividing twelve into one thousand two hundred sixty parts. That's too small!" she said.

I gave the class a hint: "Think about fractions."

Denae jumped up as if a lightbulb had turned on in her head. She came to the board and wrote $\frac{1,260}{12}$.

Many students are less familiar with writing a division problem as a fraction, but the understanding that every fraction actually represents a division problem is valuable when students work with fractions and decimals.

Working at their tables, the students solved the division problem and checked their answers with each other. They were excited to know that James could hop 105 feet. But did they really know how far 105 feet was? At first there was some confusion about the question, but then Casey raised her hand and said, "I know it's longer than my house. My dad measured our house the other day and it was twenty-five feet from the front door to the back door. So if there were four houses together that would be one hundred, like four quarters make a dollar. But then you have to add, like a person more, because there would be five feet left. So one person would be like five feet."

On the board I drew four houses and one stick figure.

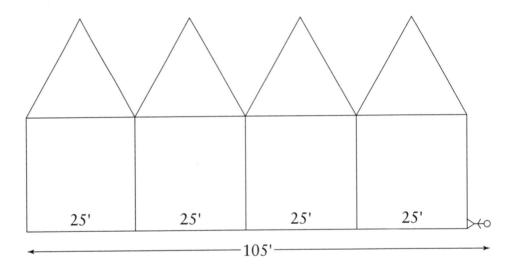

Before class was over, I gave a homework assignment. "I want you to find out how tall you are and then figure how far you could jump if you could hop like a frog. Let's go over the steps we just went through to be sure that you understand what to do at home. Who can tell us the first thing you'll need to do at home?" As the students suggested steps, I recorded them on the overhead projector. Some students took notes as I wrote.

1. *Find your height.*

2. *Convert your height to inches.*

3. *Multiply your height in inches by 20.*

4. *Convert the length you could hop back into feet and inches.*

Day 2

When I arrived the next day, the class was excited about continuing the problem. I asked who had done the homework assignment and I immediately heard about all the problems the students had encountered.

Ernie had done some work on his assignment, but on his paper he had recorded that he was 6 feet 3 inches tall, which I knew he wasn't.

Denae said, "I couldn't do it because I didn't know how tall I was. My mom was at work so I couldn't ask her."

"My mom said she didn't know how tall I was," Suzanne commented.

Kareem said, "We didn't have a ruler at home."

"I tried to do it but I got confused," John added.

"I did mine!" James announced. The other students were not impressed. They groaned and hollered and waved their arms in his direction.

"That's not fair! We did his together yesterday," Lacey complained.

I moved on to address the new issue at hand. I knew that all the children would need to find their heights before they could figure their frog-hopping length. Before they got started, I wanted to be sure they were clear about how to measure each other. "Since we already knew James's height, let's use him as a guinea pig," I said.

"I'll measure him," Casey offered.

"I'll help," added Pristina.

I asked James to come up to the board and I handed Casey a measuring stick with inches on one side and centimeters on the other. Casey and Pristina turned the stick over a few times before deciding to use the side with inches. They positioned James with his back to the board, then put the measuring stick on the very bottom of the board, which extends to the floor, right next to James. First they made a mark on the board at the top of the stick. Then they moved the stick up so that the bottom of the stick touched the mark they had made, and tried to make a mark where the top of James's head was. This required some squashing down of his hair and putting a ruler on his head perpendicular to the measuring stick. They found that James was as tall as one measuring stick plus $22\frac{1}{2}$ inches. The girls recorded on the board that the length of one measuring stick was approximately $39\frac{1}{2}$ inches. They added $39\frac{1}{2}$ to $22\frac{1}{2}$ and got 63 inches for his height.

After we reviewed the important steps, I was ready to have the students measure each other. "I want you to work with a partner and find your height," I directed. "Then I want you to figure out how far you could hop if you could hop like a frog."

The students jumped up and quickly found partners. Pairs of children came to me to get measuring sticks, then looked for places at the board to stand to be measured. I suggested that some of them lie on the floor, because it wouldn't hurt the carpet to mark it with chalk. As the children finished measuring each other, they went to their desks to calculate how far they could hop if they were frogs. There wasn't enough time left to discuss their work, so we continued the lesson the following day.

Day 3

"I looked over your papers yesterday, and I see that everyone now knows how far you could hop if you could hop like a frog," I began. "But I'm wondering if you really understand how far that is?"

"I think I could jump a little farther than four houses," Ernie said.

"Whose house are you thinking of?" I asked.

"Well, I guess Casey's house," he answered.

"Have you ever been to Casey's house?" I went on. Ernie was quick to deny having ever even seen her house. "So can you really imagine how long four houses and a little more is?"

"Not really," he allowed.

"It doesn't make sense to me for you to think about how far you could hop in relation to a house you've never seen or been to. You need to have a picture in your mind about how long that hop would be, but it needs to be a picture of something you know well. Today you'll have the chance to find something here at school to help you think about that length. We're going to brainstorm some things in the classroom and around school that you might want to measure. Any ideas?" I asked.

"We could measure the classroom," Lacey suggested.

"How about the hall?" Sonny asked.

"Both of those are good ideas," I responded. "Who else has an idea about what to measure?"

"I want to measure the sofa near the front office," Lanie said.

"I know," Cheryl interrupted, "the boards!"

"OK. You've got lots of good ideas here. Now you need to find one or two partners and pick one thing in the school to measure. This will be your reference point in describing how far you could hop if you could hop like a frog. When you know what you and your partners want to measure, come tell me. You'll also need to tell me what measurement tool you are planning to use."

The children sprang up and moved quickly around the room negotiating who would be partners with whom. In just a few minutes all the groups were formed and students had come to me for yardsticks or meter sticks. I asked each group of students to choose a wooden yardstick, a flexible plastic meter stick, or a 12-inch ruler. I wanted them to think about which measurement tool would best serve them for their task. Groups of students spread out around the room, some squatting down to measure the floor, some marking the bulletin board as they moved the measurement tool. Three girls went to the front hall of the school to measure the sofa. Denae and Paul used a 12-inch ruler to measure the board at the front of the room. They placed the ruler at the end of the board, marked where the far end of the ruler was, moved the ruler so that the first end was at the mark, then repeating the procedure.

In about thirty minutes the students had finished making their measurements and were settling in to do their write-ups. I called for their attention. "I want to talk to you about your papers as you begin to record your findings. Think about what you should include in this paper," I said and paused to let them think. "What would you expect to be included in a really good write-up of this measurement experience? I'll make a list on the overhead as you give me ideas."

Sonny raised his hand with a mischievous smile on his face. "What do you think Sonny?" I asked.

"Your name!" he crowed, laughing.

"Absolutely," I agreed. "A really good paper will have your name on it. Any other ideas?"

I called on Denae next. "I think it should tell what you measured, and how long it was," she suggested. I wrote on the overhead:

Write your name.
Tell what you measured.
Record the measurement.

There were several hands up now, and I called on James.

"I'll bet you want to us to show our work, don't you," he said.

"Yes, I do," I replied. "What work do you think you should show?"

"How we multiplied and divided, that kind of thing," he answered.

"OK, anything else?"

"Maybe you could draw a picture," Casey suggested.

"Write with pencil," Angela said, "in case you make a mistake."

John added, "Prove your answer." I added all of these ideas to the list.

Write your name.
Tell what you measured.
Record the measurement.
Show your computations.
Use pictures and diagrams.
Write in pencil.
Prove your answer.

"I'm going to leave this list up and I want you to look back at it as you work," I said. "Try to decide if your paper is complete before you turn

If You Hopped Like a Frog

it in. OK, now we're ready for the results of your measurement experiences. We'll put them all up so that you can describe your frog hopping in terms of any of these measurements."

As students called out their results I recorded on the board.

couch: 6 ft., 18 in.
length of classroom: 39 inches 10 times, and 10 inches more
length of 5th grade hallway: 23 yds., $20\frac{1}{2}$ in.
height of classroom door: 6'10"
board length: 24'6"

I asked the students to each use one of the things the class had measured to describe how far they could hop if they could hop like a frog. As they finished, they turned their papers in to me and quietly started on another assignment. I noticed that some students had used most of the criteria we listed to create a complete paper, while others turned in papers that were disorganized or less complete. I chose work that I thought exemplified the criteria we had established and put those papers aside. Later, I asked the students whose work I had chosen if I could use it in tomorrow's class, without using their names. They all agreed.

Day 4

The next day I took out the transparencies I had made of the students' work I had chosen the day before, without their names. Before we got started on the last part of this activity, I wanted to review these work samples so students could see what made a complete paper. Most of the students had compared the distance they could hop to one of the things they measured in the classroom, but Kareem had compared his hopping distance to the depth of a swimming pool. We reviewed Suzanne's, Paul's, and Kareem's papers, referring to the list of criteria from the day before. (See Figures 13–1, 13–2, and 13–3.)

I went back to *If You Hopped Like a Frog* to introduce the last part of the activity. "Remember this book?" I asked. The students laughed. "When we read this book at the beginning of the week we noticed these pages at the back that give more mathematical information about the animal-to-human comparisons. The author wrote a paragraph for each of the animal pages, and each little paragraph ends with a question. For instance, the paragraph titled 'If You Craned Your Neck Like a Crane . . .' ends with two questions: How tall are you? How long would your neck be if it were $\frac{1}{3}$ your height?

"Your job will be to choose a paragraph to investigate with your partner. Read the paragraph carefully and find the answer to the final question. Our investigation of the past few days should give you some

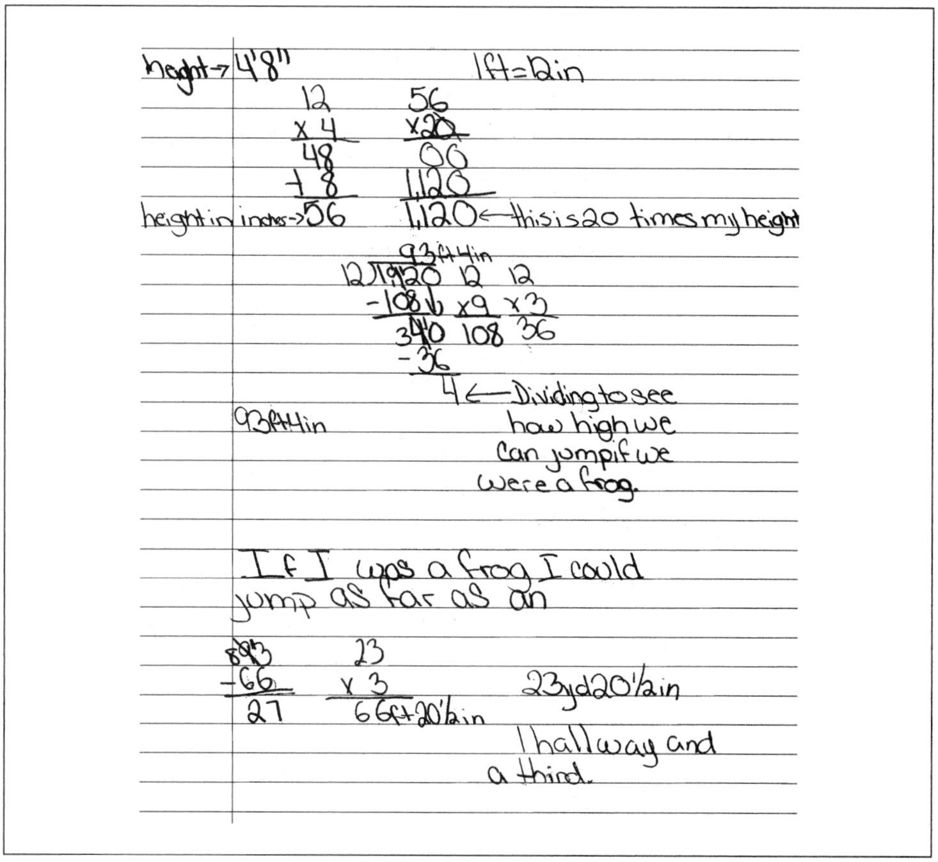

Figure 13–1: Suzanne labeled the numbers and operations she used.

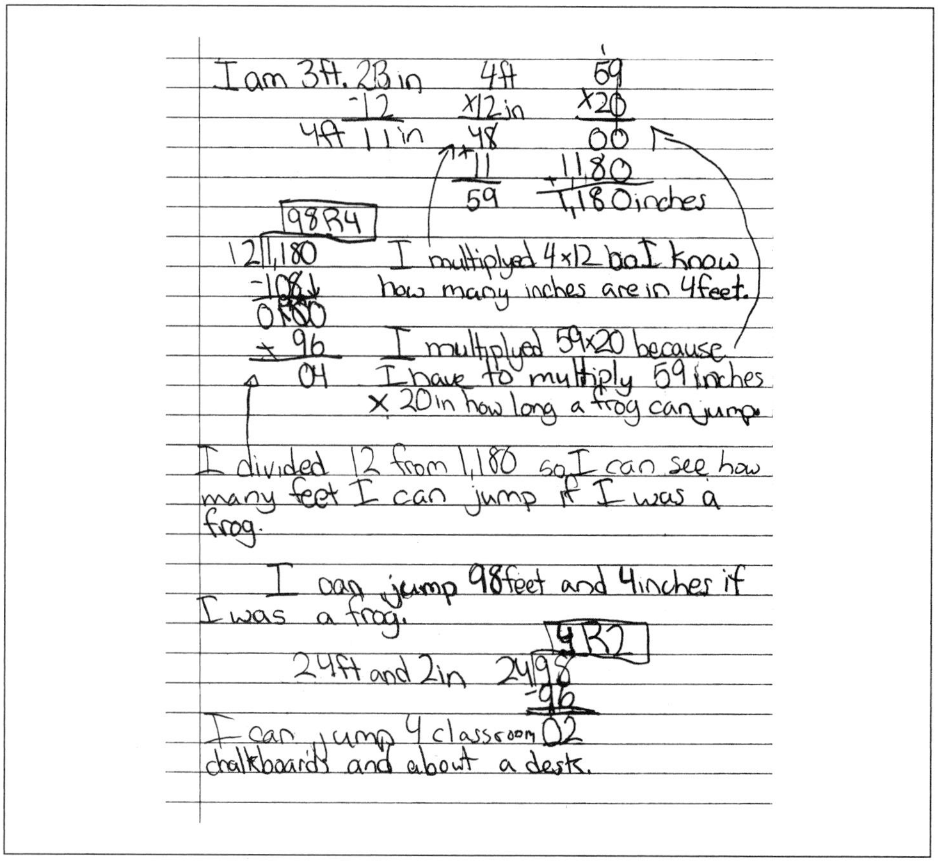

height→ 4'8"   1ft=12in

```
      12        56
     x 4       x20
     ---       ---
      48        00
     +8        1120
```
height in inches→56   1,120 ←this is 20 times my height

```
        9384/4in
    12)1120   12    12
      -108    x9    x3
       340   ---   ---
        -36  108    36
        ---
         4 ←Dividing to see
              how high we
              can jump if we
9384ftin     were a frog.
```

If I was a frog I could
jump as far as an

```
   893      23
   -66      x 3          23yd20½in
   ---     ------
    27     66ft+20½in
                        1 hallway and
                        a third.
```

Figure 13–2: Paul explained why he did each step in his calculations.

```
I am 3ft.23in     4ft      59
       -12       x12in    x20
      ------     ----     ----
      4ft 11in    48       00
                 +11      1180
                 ----    ------
                  59     1,180 inches
      98R4
   12)1,180      I multiplyed 4x12 ba I know
     -108        how many inches are in 4feet.
     ----
     0 00
     + 96        I multiplyed 59x20 because
     ----        I have to multiply 59 inches
       04        x 20 in how long a frog can jump.
```

I divided 12 from 1,180 so I can see how
many feet I can jump if I was a
frog.

   I can jump 98feet and 4inches if
I was a frog.

```
                        4R2
   24ft and 2in      24)98
                       -96
                       ----
                         02
```

I can jump 4 classroom
chalkboards and about a desk.

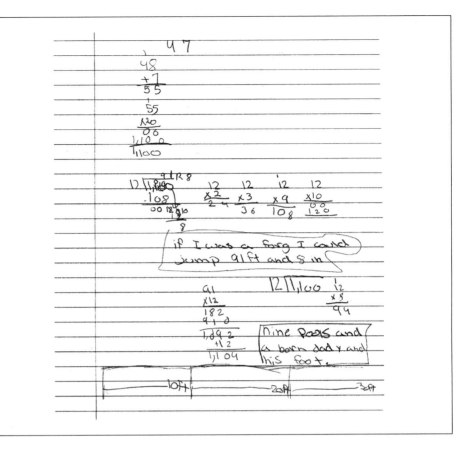

good background for getting started. I've made a copy of the paragraphs so that you don't all have to try read the book at the same time."

The class was eager to begin. Each pair chose a slip of paper with a paragraph describing the physical abilities of one animal, then got right to work answering the question. Their teacher, Tamara Barr, and I stayed busy checking in with the students. Ernie and Darrell were working to find out how far they could run if they scurried like a spider.

"It's just like the frog!" Ernie exclaimed. "You find your height in inches and then times it by thirty-three. Then we knew how far we could run if we ran like a spider. Because spiders can run thirty-three times their length in a second."

"So how far could you run in a second?" I asked.

"One hundred sixty-five feet!" he answered excitedly. "I divided that by three, and so it's fifty-five yards. In one second! That's fast!" (See Figure 13–4.)

Reanni and her partner Lacey were working on how long their necks would be if they could crane their necks like a crane. They called me over when they got stuck. "We don't know how to find what a third of our height is. That's how long our necks would be."

"What ideas do you have so far?" I asked. I wanted to get an idea of what they had already tried before I gave them any direction.

"We think maybe we have to subtract," Lacey said.

Figure 13-4: Ernie was excited to find that, if he scurried like a spider, he could run the length of a football field in a second and a half.

> **If you scurried like a spider** ①
>
> hieght 5'
>
> 1.3,300
>
> First I had to find out and write down my hieght. Then I multiply it by 33. Then I devide it by 3. Whild makes it 55 yds. The total seconds is 1sc 55 mlsc. Then I multiply the total yds by 60.
> ① The total yds I can run in 1 mn is 3,300.
>
> ② I can run a footballfield in 1sc and 55 nsc
>
> ③ ft per sc 1,980ft

"Or measure," Reanni said.

I decided to try to help them relate this task to something they had done before. "If I wanted you to find a third of this piece of paper, what would you do?" I asked.

"I would fold it into three parts," Reanni replied.

"What kind of parts?"

"Equal parts," Lacey said. "Oh, I get it. We have to divide ourselves into equal parts and then. . . ." Her voice trailed off. She had a slightly confused look on her face.

Reanni had an idea now: "I think we have to find out how tall we are and divide that in three pieces. So one piece is one third. And that's how long our neck would be."

I left Reanni and Lacey working hard and smiling. (See Figure 13–5.)

Near the end of the class period, the students were ready to share their work. They came to the front of the room and amazed their classmates with statistics on what they could eat, how far they could see, or how fast they could run if they behaved as the animals do. They were interested in each other's reports and eager to share their own. Although this lesson took four math class periods to finish, the students were engaged in meaningful mathematics during the entire time. They measured, computed, and made comparisons using references from their own lives. (See Figures 13–6, 13–7, and 13–8.)

Figure 13–5: Lacey drew a picture of Reanni with a 21-inch neck.

In the figure (handwritten notes):

5'2in 63 ← add my height to 18 inches

1ft = 12 in
6 in

+18
81 in
18 inches

5'2"

2'
3)63
6↓
03
3

divided by 3 and you get 21

If I cut my selfes in 1/3 pecies

If I craned your neck like a crane my neck would be 21in (1ft 9in)

12
+12
21

21
−12
9

a really long neck

Figure 13–6: Lawrence explained how long his tongue would be if he were a chameleon.

In the figure (handwritten notes):

If You Flicked Your Tongue like A Chameleon

My height: 5 Feet 0 inches   2)5 → 2.5 Feet 0 inches
My Chameleon tongue
My tongue: 2.5 Feet 0 inches

If I flicked my tongue like a chameleon my tongue would be 2.5 feet 0 inches (29 inches) long. If you wanted to know how long your tongue was you would have to find your height and divide it by 2.

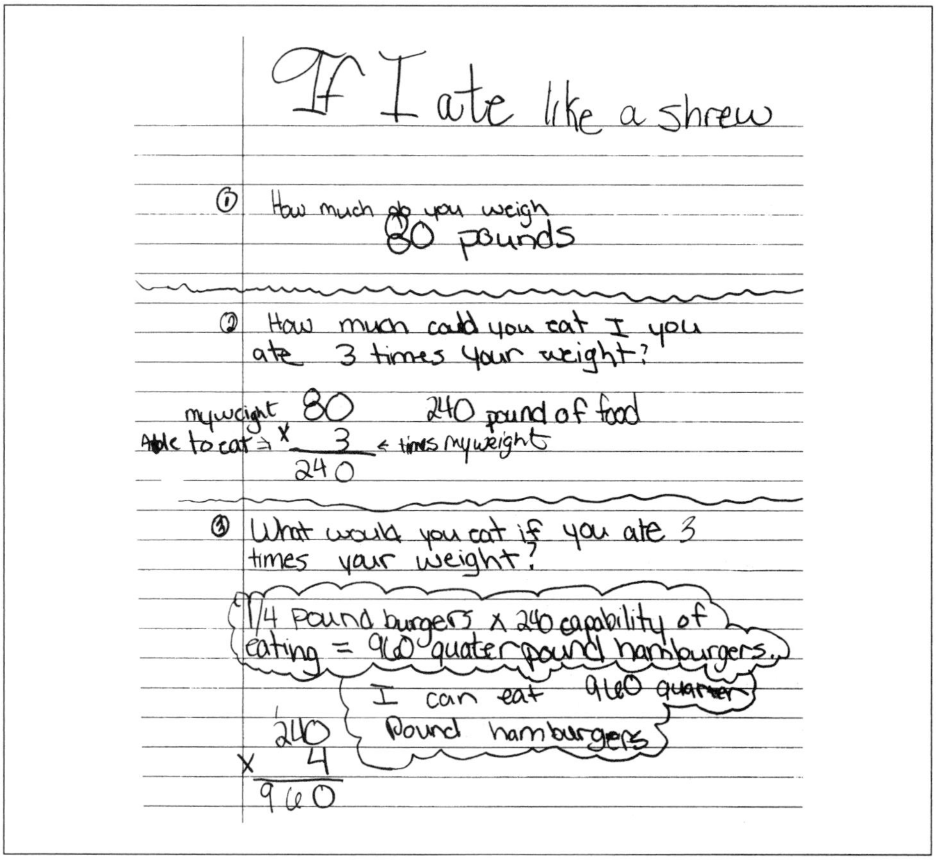

Figure 13–7: Victoria discovered that if she ate three times her weight, as a shrew does, she could eat 960 quarter-pound hamburgers.

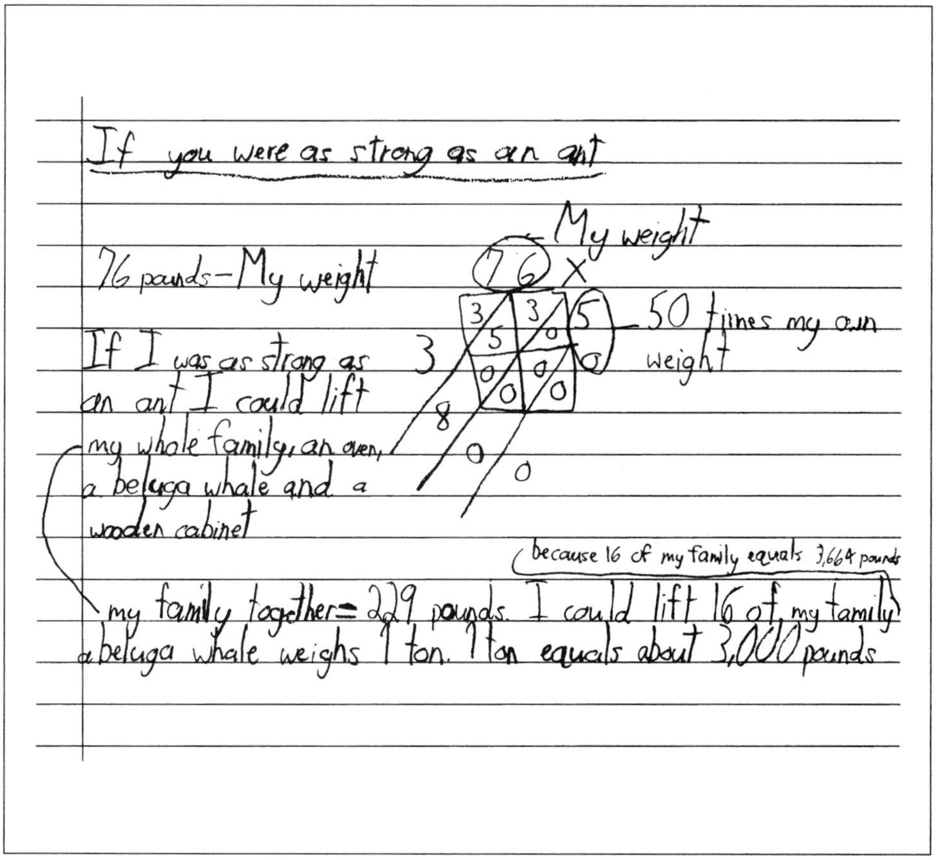

Figure 13–8: Kyle determined that he could lift his whole family and more if he had the lifting power of an ant.

In the Next Three Seconds . . .
Predictions for the Millennium

Taught by Stephanie Sheffield

Rowland Morgan's *In the Next Three Seconds . . . Predictions for the Millennium* (1997) is a collection of predictions about everyday and not-so-everyday events that will take place in the next three seconds, the next three minutes, the next three hours, days, weeks . . . all the way up to the next three million years. The book's wealth of words and pictures give students the opportunity to deal with large numbers, and to consider the consequences of our actions here on earth. In this lesson, taught in a fifth-grade class, students explore just one of the predictions made in the book and use estimation, multiplication, and division to make a prediction of their own.

MATERIALS

The front and back of this large-format book provide clues to its wonderful content. Sitting in the rocking chair in the meeting area of the classroom, I held the book so the fifth graders could see the cover as they came and sat down. The cover shows a large circle, which on careful inspection you can see is the outline of a pocket watch. Inside the circle are illustrations and words radiating from a central picture of the Statue of Liberty. There were excited exclamations as the students squinted to read the small print surrounding the picture of the Statue of Liberty, which tells what could happen in the next three seconds.

"That looks cool," Ace exclaimed.

"Read us the one about the Statue of Liberty," Roxanne suggested.

I read, "In the next three seconds, Italians will drink a stack of cases of mineral water as high as the Statue of Liberty."

"Wow, that's a lot of water," she sighed.

I read a few more entries from the cover of the book to give the class a taste of what the book is like. When I opened the book, I purposely skipped the introduction, which gives directions for making your own predictions. Each two-page spread after the introduction covers a specific period of time, but always in increments of three: three seconds, three minutes, three hours, three days, three nights, three weeks, three months, three years, three decades, three centuries, three thousand years, and three million years. On the first two-page spread, I read almost all the entries for what could happen in the next three seconds. We learned that in the next three seconds, Russians will mail more than four thousand letters or parcels and that Americans will buy fifty-six air-conditioning units. We stopped to discuss many of these interesting tidbits. Some of them were clearly trivia, for instance, that three teddy bears would be given as gifts. The students were interested to learn that "ninety-three trees will be cut down to make the liners for disposable diapers."

"Every three seconds they cut down that many trees?" Olivia asked, unbelieving.

"They don't cut down trees at night," Rick countered.

Cameron disagreed, saying, "It isn't night on the other side of the world and they could be cutting the trees down there." I thought this might be a good time to talk about how the author had made his predictions.

"Do you think people really cut down exactly ninety-three trees every three seconds?" I asked.

"Who would time them to know when three seconds was over?" Rachel asked.

"Yeah," Burton continued, "who could count all the trees being cut down all over the world at exactly the same three seconds? They must be guessing in this book."

I turned back and read the introduction, which explains the role of counting throughout history, from caterers counting for imperial banquets in ancient China to the sophisticated counting we do today with computers. The author describes how vast bits of information are fed into computers constantly. "The facts in this book are worked out from this great new wealth of information," I told the class.

"Do you think the author's predictions are meant to be exact or estimates?" I asked. The children agreed that the predictions must be estimates, and I moved on to read the next page, which is about what will happen in the next three minutes. I read fewer entries from this page, following the students' interests as they suggested "Read the one about the dinosaurs!" or "I bet that one with the cows on the bun with lettuce is about hamburgers." There is more to this book than could possibly be read in one sitting, so I read just enough to give the students the flavor of each section. Some entries were easier for the class to understand than others, depending on the context. Because many of the entries led to conversations about important world issues, the book would fit nicely into a social studies curriculum, but I was focused on using this book as a springboard for a math problem, so I read just a bit from each two-page spread.

After promising to leave the book in the classroom for their perusal during reader's workshop, I moved on to presenting the problem I wanted the students to solve. "If you wanted to make a prediction about things that take three minutes or three hours, what is something you could easily count without leaving this room?" I asked. I gave the students a few minutes to think, and suggested that they talk to someone sitting near them about their ideas. "Together, see if you can come up with something you could count in the room that would help you make a prediction about that same event in the future."

The students buzzed and gesticulated as they talked together and raised their hands excitedly to report on their ideas. "We think you could do something like write your name over and over and do it for three minutes," Antonia said. "Then you could figure out how many times you could write your name in three minutes or three hours."

Cameron challenged this idea. "Yeah, but it's not like in the book where you know that people are always doing that. We think we could count how many times someone blinks their eyes in a minute and figure it out for three minutes or three hours." Anthony nodded enthusiastically.

"That sounds workable," I said. "Any other ideas?"

"I think we could count how many times the classroom door opens in three minutes," Andre said.

Victoria raised her hand. "Could we find out how many times your heart beats in three minutes?"

"I know!" Ranna exclaimed. "We could count how many times you breathe. That would be easy!" We talked together as a class and decided to choose just two options, breathing and blinking. Then we discussed how to gather the information we needed to make the predictions.

"We have to count how many times our partner breathes or blinks in three minutes," Anthony explained. "Then we can figure out how many times they could breathe or blink in three hours."

"I think it will be boring counting someone blinking for three minutes," Andres mused. "Can't we just count for one minute and multiply by three?"

"Great idea, Andres," Cameron agreed. "Can we do that?"

"Absolutely," I said. "You and your partner need to decide on the prediction you'd like to make, and then take turns counting each other's breathing or blinking. Then think about the calculations you'll have to do to make your predictions." The students went to sit at their seats with their partners.

Ethan and Cecelia got out paper and pencil and made a plan for timing. "I'll time one minute and you count me blink," Cecelia told Ethan. "Then we'll multiply that by three." Cecelia motioned to Ethan to start counting. He made a tally mark every time she blinked until she motioned again for him to stop. Cecelia counted up her blinks and found that she had blinked twenty times. Next they traded jobs and Cecelia made tally marks for Ethan's blinks—twenty-two times in one minute. To find their average number of blinks per minute they added twenty plus twenty-two and divided by two. Next they multiplied twenty-one by three to find out how many times, on average, they blinked in three minutes.

Cameron and Mason were much less enthusiastic blinkers. Their average blinks in a minute were five. They multiplied by three to get fifteen blinks in three minutes, then multiplied sixty by three. Confused, I asked, "Where did the sixty come from?" Cameron answered, "There's sixty minutes in an hour, so sixty minutes times three hours is one hundred eighty minutes. Then we multiplied that times five, because we blink five times every minute. That gives us nine hundred blinks in three hours." (See Figure 14–1.)

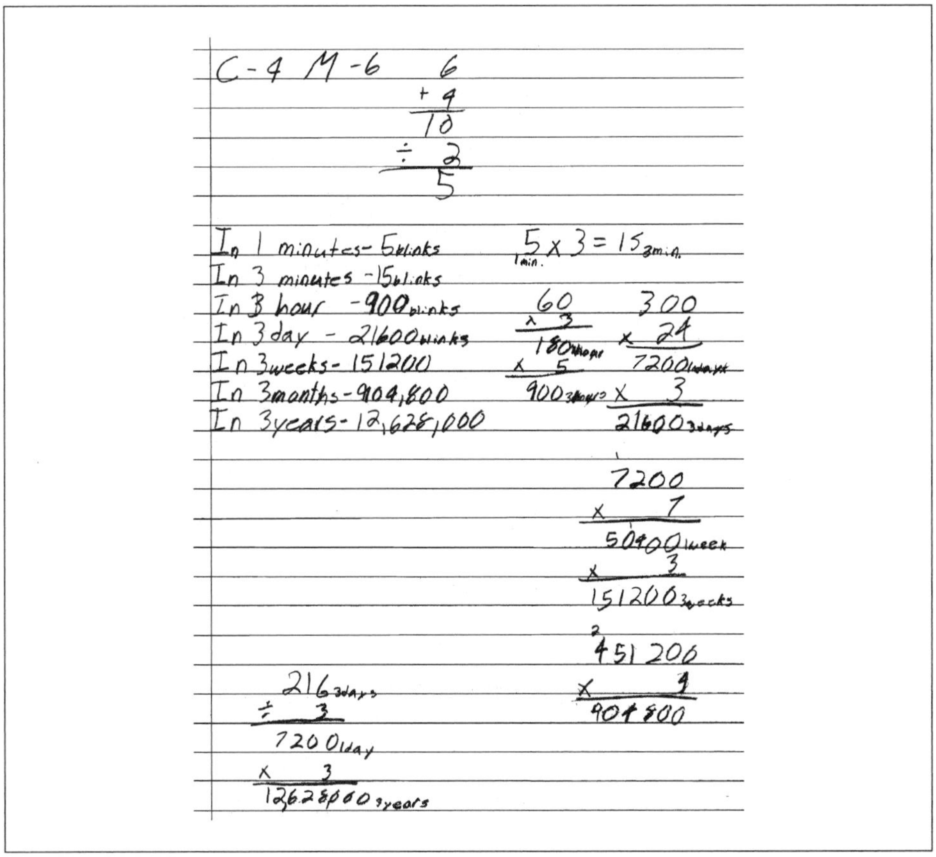

Figure 14–1: Cameron and Mason clearly understood how to calculate the number of times they could blink in three minutes, three hours, and so forth.

Figure 14–2: Ingrid, Douglas, and Ranna made a computation error in one of the early steps and had to recalculate.

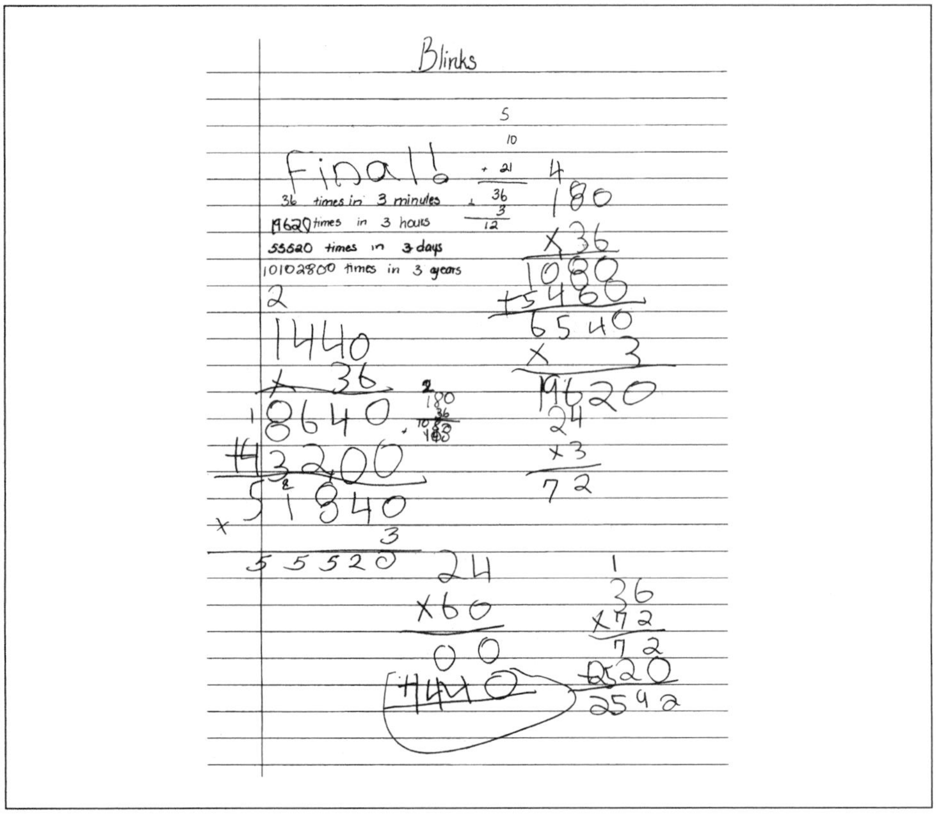

Ingrid, Douglas, and Ranna worked together. They took turns timing one minute and counting each other blinking. They used twelve blinks per minute as their average. Ranna explained what they did: "First we multiplied twelve by three and found out we blinked thirty-six times in three minutes. Then we knew that there are sixty minutes in an hour, so we timesed sixty by three and got one hundred eighty."

"That's how many minutes in three hours," Douglas cut in.

"Right," Ranna continued. "So we multiplied one hundred eighty times thirty-six and got six thousand five hundred forty." I noticed that they had made an error when adding partial products, incorrectly adding eighty plus sixty, because one of the zeroes in the tens place looked like a six. Because of this error, their other calculations were off. (See Figure 14–2 for their work and Figure 14–3 for Olivia's.)

Follow-up Activities

To follow up on this lesson, students could research other pieces of information, such as these:

- the number of cartons of milk drunk in the next three days or weeks
- the number of teeth lost by students in three days

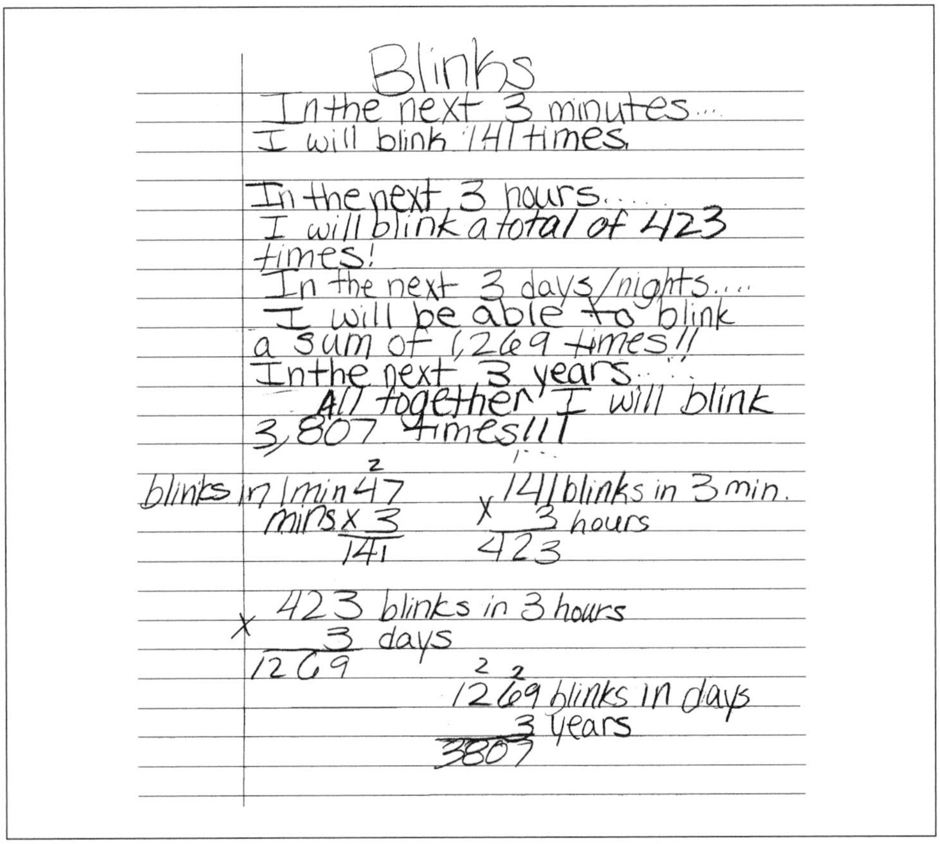

Figure 14–3: Olivia started off on the right track, but forgot to multiply by sixty to find the number of blinks in an hour.

- the number of pencils used by students in three weeks

- the number of bandages distributed by the school nurse in three days

- the number of "good" visits students make with the principal in three days

- the number of school lunches purchased by students in their grade level in three days

A More Perfect Union

Taught by Kathleen Gallagher

Betsy and Giulio Maestro's *A More Perfect Union* (1990) gives children a sense of how people can work together to create great things. In this lesson, fifth graders listen to the story, then use calculators and what they know about averages to try to figure out the age of each delegate to the Constitutional Convention. We did this lesson over two days, reading the book on the first and focusing on the concept of averaging on day two.

Note: This lesson is more effective if the children have had some real-world experience with averaging. The students in this class took a spelling test each week and kept track of their averages in their spelling binders. They had also participated in an activity in which they each tried ten shots on the basketball court, recorded the total number of baskets they made, and found their group and class averages.

MATERIALS

Day 1

When I walked into the fifth-grade class with a book about the Constitution, the class commented, "Hey, that's not a book about math."

"Don't you all know that math is everywhere?" I responded. "I'm going to read you a story today about the Constitution, which I know you've learned a little bit about, and then I have an interesting problem for you to solve. As I read, I want you to pay attention to the people in the book, because the problem we are going to do is about the people."

I introduced the book and read the foreword. We talked a little bit about the American Revolution so the children understood that this story took place after the United States won independence from

England. We discussed the imaginary example of all of the classes in our school deciding together that they wanted to rule themselves and becoming independent from the principal and the teachers and kept this analogy going as we read the book to help the students identify with the story.

On page fourteen, I paused and asked the class to look carefully at the illustrations, which depict the states' delegates to the Constitutional Convention in Philadelphia in 1787. "What do you notice?" I asked.

"Their clothes are old-fashioned," said Jeffrey.

"That guy has white hair," added Jessica.

"Lots of them have white hair," said Edwin.

"They're all men, right?" questioned Sandra.

"They are all men," I confirmed.

"They have ponytails," said Kimberly.

"And all of them are wearing those short pants and long white socks," added Jessica.

"How would the group look different today?" I asked the class.

"I think they would be dressed differently," said Jeffrey.

"There would probably be women and also more different kinds of people," added Sandra.

"I'm sure you're right Sandra," I agreed. "What do you think about their ages? How old do you think the men are?"

"That guy standing up is probably like thirty," said Carla.

"George Washington is maybe fifty or sixty, I think," said Jeffrey.

"That guy in the back looks kind of younger," said Candace. "Maybe he's like twenty-seven."

"Okay," I said, "Let's continue reading."

The children noticed immediately on the next page that the man standing had a peg leg. "He looks kind of old," said Christina. "Maybe he fought in the war and that's how he lost his leg."

"These are more close-up pictures," I said. "Can you estimate some of their ages?"

"That guy on the end looks older than the one with the red hair next to him," said Edwin. "I think the old one's, like, fifty and the other one is, like, twenty."

"Those two on the other side look kind of young. They both have ponytails," said Carla.

"OK, so it seems like the men are lots of different ages, right?" I asked.

"Yeah," said Jessica, "and some of them wore wigs back then so they might look older than they really are."

"That's true," I agreed.

As I continued to read, the children kept trying to guess the ages of the delegates. But they were also engaged in the story, clapping when New Hampshire became the ninth state to vote yes on the

Constitution. They noticed that the flags shown were different than our flag today. Edwin said, "It's because now we have fifty states and each state has a star."

"When I come back tomorrow, I'm going to share some of the special facts the authors include at the end of the book and we're going to do an interesting problem about averages. When you go home tonight, try to find out as much as you can about what the word *average* means," I directed.

Day 2

I called the class to the rug and there shared the fact pages at the back of the book. When we came to the section titled "Interesting Facts About the Convention and the Delegates," I said, "Listen to this," and read, "The average age of the delegates was forty-three. Benjamin Franklin, at eighty-one, was the oldest. Jonathon Dayton, the youngest, was twenty-six."

"What does the word *average* mean?" I asked the class. "Turn to your partner and discuss what you know about averages."

After several seconds I asked, "So what is an average?"

"I think it means like normal," said Jeffrey.

"Say more about that," I encouraged.

"Like if you're average you're just normal, like not too good and not too bad."

"Yeah, like not the best and not the worst," added Jessica.

"OK, what else?"

"I think it's like the middle, like rounding to the half," said Jessica.

"Can you give an example?" I asked.

"Like if you have a lot of things and you find the one in the middle, like half-way between the smallest and the biggest," she explained.

"What would be an example of that?" I asked.

"Like when we did the basketball shots, we had a lot of numbers and we put them in order and found the middle one."

"Oh, you mean the *median*. That is a kind of average. Did you learn the three kinds of averages?" I asked.

"Mean, median, and mode," said Keith.

"Jessica explained the median. Does anyone remember what the *mode* is?" I asked.

"Is it the one that's the most?" asked Carla.

"Well, let's look at an example," I suggested. I quickly wrote five numbers on the board:

Basketball Shots

4, 6, 6, 6, 8

"Let's say these are the scores of five kids who shot baskets. The first kid got four out of ten, three of the kids got six out of ten, and one kid got eight out of ten. What would be the mode? See what your partner thinks."

I knew there was disagreement. Some kids thought the mode was eight, because that was the highest number. Others thought it was six, because there were more sixes than any other number. I clarified, "In this example the mode is six because six was the score that occurred more often than any other. Does anyone remember what the *mean* is? Because when the authors say, 'The average age of the delegates was forty-three,' they are talking about the mean."

"I think you add all the numbers and divide by how many there are," said Edward.

"That's right," I confirmed. "So if we added up the ages of all of the delegates and divided by fifty-five (the total number of delegates), we would get forty-three. Forty-three was the average age of the delegates."

"So here's the problem," I continued. On the board, I drew a number line and marked the numbers zero and one hundred. Then I made a mark for 43 and labeled it. "How old was the youngest person?"

"Twenty-six!" the class answered. I marked and labeled *26* on the number line.

"And how old was the oldest?"

"Eighty-one!" they exclaimed. I marked *81*.

Average Age

"How many delegates were there all together?" I asked.

"Fifty-five," they answered.

"OK, let's think about an easier problem. Let's pretend there were only five delegates. Do you think you could figure out five ages that average forty-three?"

"We could just guess ages and test them out," said Sandra.

"What if one was twenty-six and one was eighty-one, and the rest were forty-three? Would that work?" asked Chris.

I answered, "I think it would be really good if all of you worked with a partner and tried to solve this problem." Before I modeled a strategy too explicitly, I wanted to find out what all of the children would do on their own. I added, "I'd like all of you to take a calculator and a piece of paper and see if you can figure out five ages between twenty-six and eighty-one that have an average of forty-three. I'm going to walk around and see what you do, and then we'll talk some more." I excused the class from the rug by table groups.

As I walked around, it became clear that many students were confused and were simply trying any operation that occurred to them and hoping for the best. Beatrice and Jenny were trying to figure out what numbers go into forty-three equally. Keith was trying to figure out what forty-three divided by four was. And Michael was multiplying forty-three times fifty-five and then subtracting random numbers between twenty-six and eighty-one, thinking he'd be done if he ended up at forty-three. Most of the other students were using Sandra's strategy of guess-and-check. It seemed as if they needed help thinking about how to use the wrong answers they were getting to inform their choice of numbers the next time they tried. So I brought them back together for a whole-group discussion at the board.

I asked Chris and Javier to share first. "So what did you guys find out?" I asked.

"We added twenty-six plus forty-three plus forty-three plus forty-three plus eighty-one and got two hundred thirty-six. Then we divided by five and got forty-seven point two, so we think it didn't work, right?"

"Hmm," I said, "if the average of those five numbers is forty-seven point two, what do you think you could do to lower the average?"

"I think if we use lower numbers we'll get a lower average," said Jeffrey. "When we did twenty-six plus twenty-eight plus thirty plus thirty-two plus eighty-one, it equaled one hundred ninety-seven. Then we divided by five and it was thirty-nine point four. We were gonna try some higher numbers to see if it would work."

"Let's do that example together and see what happens," I suggested. I marked the numbers *26*, *28*, *30*, *32*, and *81* and recorded on the board on the number line while the children punched in the numbers on their calculators.

Average Age

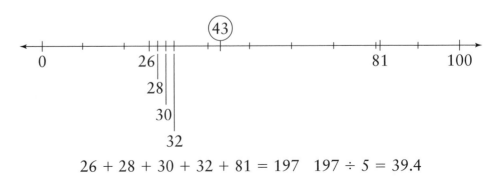

$$26 + 28 + 30 + 32 + 81 = 197 \quad 197 \div 5 = 39.4$$

"So if we want the average to go up, Jeffrey said we should add some higher numbers. What number do you think we should add?"

"I was going to add on seventy," said Jeffrey.

"Why seventy?" I asked.

"Because there's a lot of numbers on that side of the forty-three," pointing to the left side of the number line, "but not a lot on that side, so I thought it might work."

"Okay, let's add on seventy." I marked seventy on the number line. "We already know this total," I said, pointing to the first five numbers we added. "What was it?" I asked.

"One hundred ninety-seven," they said.

"So let's try one hundred ninety-seven plus seventy."

"Two hundred sixty-seven," the children called out.

"Now, what will we divide by?" I asked, checking to see if they would pick up the fact that now we had six ages in our collection.

"Divided by five," blurted several children at once.

"How many ages do we have all together now?" I asked. I pointed to each of the numbers on our number line and the children counted, "One, two, three, four, five, six!"

"It's two hundred sixty-seven divided by six!" said Keith excitedly.

"What is it?" I asked.

"Forty-four point five," the children answered.

I wrote the equation down underneath the previous one and asked, "Did the average go up as we predicted?"

Average Age

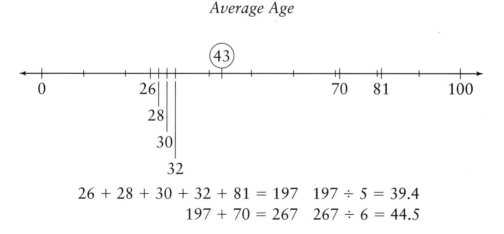

$$26 + 28 + 30 + 32 + 81 = 197 \quad 197 \div 5 = 39.4$$
$$197 + 70 = 267 \quad 267 \div 6 = 44.5$$

"Yeah, but now it's too high," said Christina, discouraged.

"But it's closer. Let's try another one. Talk to your partner to decide what would be a good number to try next," I said.

Jenny said, "We thought since when we added seventy it went past forty-three, maybe we should put a lower number than forty-three."

"Maybe thirty," Jessica added.

I said, "Why don't you experiment with some more numbers. But remember, each time you add in a new age, the number of ages you divide by also increases by one."

As I walked around the room I saw that most of the children were experimenting with the guess-and-check strategy with varied levels of sophistication.

Keith had an interesting strategy. When I asked him what he was doing, he said, "I'm finding two numbers that add up to eighty-six that are between twenty-six and eighty-one and then I keep on adding numbers until the average is forty-three."

"How come you're choosing two numbers at a time?" I asked.

"Because I know if I add them up and divide it by two it will be forty-three."

"How's it working?" I wondered.

"It's good. First the average turned out to be forty-eight point two five. Then, when I added two more numbers, it's forty-six point five. Now if I add two more maybe it will be closer." It was interesting that Keith was choosing pairs of numbers that averaged forty-three on their own.

Christina and her partner were still trying to come up with just five numbers whose average was forty-three. They kept adjusting the numbers, bringing the average to forty-four. They planned to make further adjustments to bring the average to forty-three. (See Figure 15–1.)

"How will you decide what number to change?" I asked.

"If the average is too high, then we change the low number, thirty-three, to a higher one."

Figure 15–1: Christina and her partner worked to find exactly five numbers with an average of forty-three.

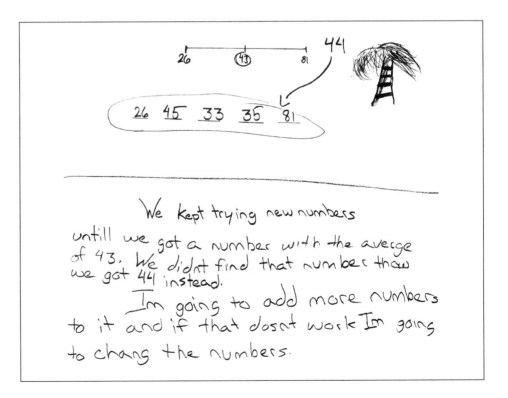

Math and Nonfiction, Grades 3–5

Candace and Casey were also trying different combinations of numbers, but they kept adding more numbers, dividing by a bigger number each time. By the eighth number they had achieved the average of forty-three. (See Figure 15–2.)

Jessica also understood the concept of the numbers having to balance out. Her paper shows how she added numbers down from eighty-one and up from twenty-six until she got to forty-three. With thirty-four numbers, her average came out to fifty-three point five. (See Figure 15–3.) When I asked what she thought her next step might be, she said, "Maybe I should finish the numbers on the eighty-one side."

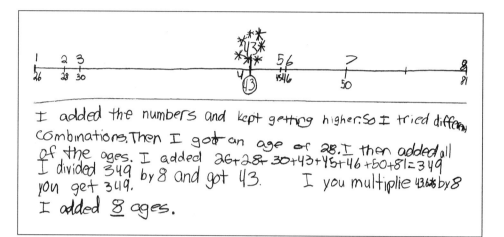

Figure 15–2: Candace and Casey found eight numbers that averaged forty-three.

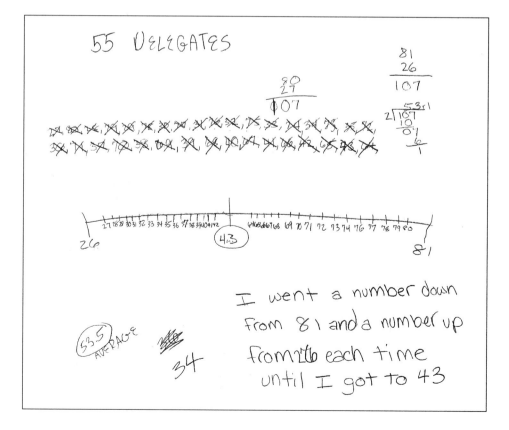

Figure 15–3: Jessica moved from the two ends of the number line toward the middle to find ages that averaged forty-three.

We talked about what each of the numbers stood for and what the average meant. Jessica said, "I probably need to add more young ones."

"Do you think there could have been more than one delegate that was thirty-five or thirty-six?" I asked, pointing to those numbers on her diagram.

"Probably," she said.

Jessica got so involved in the pattern she was using that she forgot that the numbers actually meant something. Bringing her back to the context helped her figure out what direction to move in next.

Javier and Chris were diligently working. They had begun with the idea of making each of the remaining delegates forty-three years old. They started simply with five ages and after finding the average was forty-seven point two, abandoned their original strategy and adopted a new one. To find the next age, they subtracted forty-three (the average) from eighty-one (the highest age) to get thirty-eight and made that the age of the next delegate. When they found their new average was thirty-nine point three, they subtracted thirty-eight (the age they had last added) from eighty-one, getting forty-three, then adding forty-three. They continued on with the same pattern and by the time they had added nine ages, they had achieved an average of forty-three point five. (See Figure 15–4.)

We were nearing the end of the period, so I asked the children to stop working and think for a minute about *how* they were working on the problem. "It's important that I understand your thinking," I said, "so please use the last few minutes of class to write down the strategies you've been using to find numbers that average to forty-three."

"But ours aren't at forty-three yet," said Javier.

"It's OK." I said. "I want to understand what you've been doing up to this point."

Figure 15–4: Javier and Chris assumed that four of the delegates were forty-three years old and found an average age of forty-three and a half.

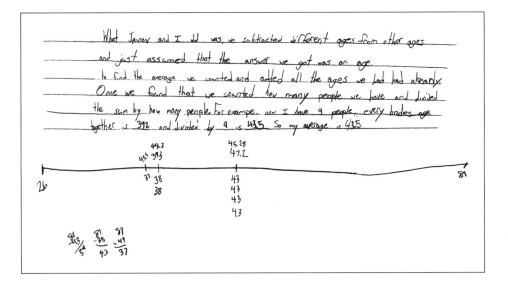

Math and Nonfiction, Grades 3–5

After Keith finished his writing, he told me excitedly that when he added two more numbers, twenty-nine and thirty-seven, his average came out to forty-three. I was confused, because Keith had reported earlier that he was adding pairs of numbers that added to eighty-six, and twenty-nine plus thirty-seven equals sixty-six, not eighty-six. When I asked about it he said, "Oh, I made a mistake, but I wonder why it worked?" Keith's mistake had gotten him to a correct combination of numbers. His strategy was sound, except that twenty-six and eighty-one, the ages of the youngest and the oldest delegate, don't add to eighty-six. He did show some intuitive understanding, however, that the numbers he added into the equation had to balance around forty-three.

One group of four students continued working after the rest of the class had turned in their papers. They decided to try the number twenty and ended up with an average of forty-one. "Could there have been a twenty-year-old delegate?" I asked.

They responded, "Oh no! We forgot. Maybe let's try thirty."

"But we already have a thirty," Bryan pointed out.

"Do you think there could have been more than one thirty-year-old delegate?" I asked.

"I guess," said Beatrice, and they added thirty into their equation, ending up with an average of forty-two point four.

Average Age

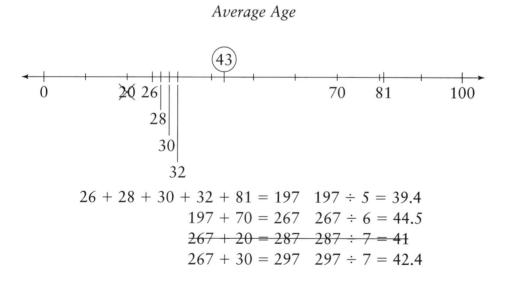

$$26 + 28 + 30 + 32 + 81 = 197 \quad 197 \div 5 = 39.4$$
$$197 + 70 = 267 \quad 267 \div 6 = 44.5$$
$$\cancel{267 + 20 = 287} \quad \cancel{287 \div 7 = 41}$$
$$267 + 30 = 297 \quad 297 \div 7 = 42.4$$

"That's pretty close to forty-three," I said.

"Yeah, maybe we could add another thirty-year-old," suggested Jack.

The children needed to get to lunch. Although they got a lot of practice figuring out averages, their understanding was still pretty fragile. They would need many more opportunities to make sense of the concept of average in meaningful contexts.

One Tiny Turtle

Taught by Kathleen Gallagher

One Tiny Turtle, by Nicola Davies (2001), chronicles the solitary life of one loggerhead turtle that makes its way to the sea despite overwhelming odds. The turtle grows, wanders thousands of miles, and, after thirty years, makes her way back to the very same beach where she hatched to lay eggs of her own. The beautiful illustrations make children fall in love with this amazing animal. Sections of wavy text provide answers to the questions children have as they listen to the story. In this lesson, third graders use a 1–100 chart to figure out the number of eggs the loggerhead turtle lays in her lifetime.

MATERIALS

1–100 chart, 1 per student (see Blackline Masters)

1–100 chart overhead transparency

additional information about loggerhead turtles from the Internet

centimeter cubes, about 25 per student

base 10 blocks, 1 set available for students who would like to use them

Before presenting this book to a class of third graders, I held up a 1–100 chart and asked, "Have any of you ever used this before?" Most of the children raised their hands as they informed me that they each had a chart in their math folders. "Great," I said. "Why don't you get your hundreds charts out, then give me your attention at the overhead."

I projected a transparency of the 1–100 chart and said, "Put your finger on the number twenty on your chart." I put my own finger on the overhead chart. "Now add three," I continued. I waited a minute to make sure everyone understood how to move a finger on the 1–100 chart to keep track of the total. When everybody's finger was on twenty-three, I said, "Subtract ten." As I looked around I saw that some children moved their finger directly to thirteen, while others counted back one square at a time. Once all the children were pointing to thirteen, I said, "Subtract twelve." Most of the class counted back twelve spaces, but a few children moved up one square to the three then moved two squares to the left. One child, Kiara, moved straight to the one.

"Raise your hand if you know the number your finger is on," I said. Everybody's hand shot up. I pointed to the children one-by-one and they told me what number their finger was pointing to. Not all the students said one, but most did, so the few who had landed on a different number realized that they had figured incorrectly.

"The number one is an important number in the book I'm going to read to you in a minute." I said. "But before I do, let's play again." We played a few more rounds on the hundred chart so I could see their level of facility with a variety of numbers.

When we were on the number seventy-three and I said to subtract forty, I watched Alex count four squares straight up to thirty-three.

"Alex, how did you subtract forty so fast?" I asked.

"I just counted up four," he said.

"How come you counted up four if I said to subtract forty?"

"'Cause if you just move up it's like taking away ten, so I just moved up four for forty," he responded.

"Does that work?" I asked the class. "Everybody put your finger back on seventy-three and subtract ten."

"It's sixty-three!" several students said quickly. Others were counting back by ones and verified the answer more slowly.

"Subtract ten more."

"Fifty-three!" a few more said quickly this time.

"Subtract ten more," I said.

"Forty-three!" more of the children chorused as they began to catch on to the idea that they could just move up one row of ten.

"Subtract ten more," I said again.

"Thirty-three!"

"Wow," I said. "That's a good trick, moving up a row to subtract ten, but why does it work?"

"It's a pattern!" Katy blurted out.

"What do you mean?" I asked.

"Seventy-three, sixty-three, fifty-three, forty-three," Katy said.

"What does that have to do with subtracting forty?" I asked.

"Every time you move up, it's taking away ten," Jessica reflected.

"But why?" I pushed.

They sat quietly for a minute, and finally Victoria said, "Maybe because there's ten in a row."

"Is it true for any number?" I asked. "What about for forty-seven minus ten? Put your finger on forty-seven and just move up one row. What number do you land on?"

"Thirty-seven!" they answered.

"That's right," Phillip said. "Forty-seven take away ten is thirty-seven."

"Try some other problems with your partner and see if it's always true that moving up a row results in subtracting ten. Then try to figure out why." I wanted to give Victoria a chance to solidify her idea and the rest of the class an opportunity to think more. After a minute or two, I asked, "What did you find out?"

Jean shared first. "Victoria's right. I think it's because there's ten in a row."

"All the numbers going down are adding ten," Diego added.

"We noticed that when you're on thirty-seven and you take away ten, you take away the seven first and then the other three are in the upper row," Anthony pointed out.

"Everybody try that one again and see if you can understand what Anthony just said," I directed. It is important to bring meaning to the *whys* that come up about the 1–100 chart. The chart is a powerful tool for understanding our base ten number system and I want students to be able to do more than just move their fingers around the grid.

"Today we are going to use the hundreds chart as a tool to help solve a problem about a turtle. But before I give you the problem, I want to read a book to you. I'd like you to come to the meeting area so you'll all be able to see the pictures."

As the children settled down on the rug, I held up the book and read the title aloud. We talked about the cover and how cute the little turtle looks. The children noticed that the eggs in the picture are almost as big as the turtle and they predicted that the turtle might have just hatched.

I read the introduction slowly so the children could appreciate each important piece of information the author provides. When I read nonfiction aloud, students have to listen in a different way than they do to fiction. They need time to assimilate the facts they hear into what they already know about the subject.

I turned the page and began reading the text. The children were immediately drawn to the book's beautiful language and the bright and lovely paintings that capture the mysterious life of the fascinating loggerhead. Throughout the story, the author compares the size of the growing turtle to various objects the children can relate to—a bottle top, a dinner plate, a barrel. Toward the end of the book, the author provides information about the turtle's eggs. I read slowly to help the children remember the facts. The story is a little bit startling for some children. As the baby turtles try to make their way toward the water, they get confused by the city lights behind them, and hungry birds attack from overhead. The story ends as just one tiny turtle makes her way to the same sea her mother discovered many years before.

I gave the class a quiet moment to consider the book before I began speaking. I said, "Wow. Only one turtle made it out of all of those eggs."

"That's why the book is called *One Tiny Turtle*," Anthony said thoughtfully.

"So for each nest of eggs, only one turtle makes it to the sea?" I questioned.

"Maybe not only one. Maybe sometimes two or three will make it," Phillip hypothesized.

"Maybe even ten could make it," Samantha said hopefully.

"I wonder if we could estimate how many eggs the loggerhead turtle lays in her lifetime," I asked the class. "How would we begin to do that?" As the children thought, I wrote on the board:

About how many eggs does the loggerhead turtle lay in her lifetime?

"Hmmm," thought Phillip.
"One hundred eggs were in each hole," Kiara remembered.
On the board I recorded:

100 eggs

I asked, "Does she make just one nest?"
"I think she makes three or four," Samantha replied.
"Let's look back and see." I turned back the pages and read aloud: "Females stay close to their nesting beach for several months. In that time they usually make at least four nests and sometimes as many as ten." I asked the children, "What number do you think we should record for the number of nests she makes?" (**Note:** If this were an older group, I would record the range rather than a single number, and the problem would be more complicated.)

The children responded with many different numbers and reasons. Together we decided that for this problem we would use the number four, because, in Alex's words, "Probably all the turtles do at least four but some do more, but not all of them do more, so we should use four." Alex is well respected by his peers as an animal expert so I recorded his idea on the board:

100 eggs
4 nests

"Let's figure out how many eggs she lays in a lifetime if she has four nests," I said. "Then, if we have time, we can figure it out for other numbers of nests. Do we have all we need to know to solve this problem?"

"That would be four hundred eggs," Samantha concluded.

"Four hundred eggs in her whole lifetime?" I questioned.

"I think so," Samantha answered.

The children needed more information in order to answer the question I had asked, but they didn't yet realize they did. I knew when I was planning the lesson that the book didn't provide all of the information needed, so I did some research on the Internet. I said to the class, "I found many websites about loggerhead turtles, and some of them provided information that is different from what's in the book. For example, in the book, the author tells us that females usually produce two to three clutches each season."

"What's a clutch? Is that like a nest?" wondered Jean.

"That's exactly what I wondered when I read it," I told the class. "I looked up the word *clutch* in the dictionary and it said, 'the number of eggs produced or incubated at one time.' So, yes, I think the word clutch means the same as the word nest."

"Part of the reason that this turtle is so difficult to study is that it moves around so much. But here are some things that I learned: Loggerhead turtles nest every second or third year and their lifespan is usually about fifty years." I added the last two facts to the board:

About how many eggs does the loggerhead turtle lay in her lifetime?

100 eggs in each clutch
4 clutches each season
They nest every second or third year.
Lifespan is usually about 50 years.

"I'd like you all to try to solve the problem of how many eggs a loggerhead turtle will lay in her lifetime on your hundreds chart before you start using your pencil," I explained. Directing their attention to the 1–100 chart on the overhead, I asked, "Does anybody remember what the book said about how old our turtle was when she began laying eggs?" I thumbed through the story until we found the description of the turtle returning to the beach to lay her eggs. I began reading, "For thirty years you might not find her. Then one summer night she arrives on the beach where she was born."

"She was thirty years old," Victoria said excitedly.

"What about the time when she was growing? I think she was about thirty-five," Diego speculated.

"The Internet site I visited said loggerhead turtles can begin laying eggs after only seven years, so maybe they could begin at any age between seven and thirty. Which number do you think we should use for our estimate?" I had the students talk to their partners about this. Most wanted to use the number thirty.

"How many nests did she make when she was thirty?" I asked.

"Four," the class responded.

I stacked four centimeter cubes on the number thirty on the overhead 1–100 chart. "How many eggs is that all together?" I asked.

"Four hundred," most replied.

"Then what happened?"

The class wasn't sure how to use the third piece of information on the chart we had made. I pointed to it and said, "Let's read this again."

The children read, "They nest every second or third year."

"What does that mean?" I asked.

"I think she doesn't lay eggs every year. She probably waits two years or maybe three," Victoria interpreted.

"That's right," I told the class. "Let's say she makes a nest every two years." I circled the word *second* on the board. "How could we show that on our hundred chart?"

"On thirty-two, put four more cubes," Alex suggested.

Following Alex's advice helped the others understand how they could use their own hundreds charts to keep track of all of the nests the turtle made. I said, "After you figure out your answer, explain on paper how you figured it out. When we put the charts and the cubes away, I want to be able to understand how you solved the problem. So try to show on your paper exactly what you did."

Many children told the story as they modeled the problem. Jessica used her finger to keep track of the number she and Kiara were on. As she pointed to thirty-six, she said, "Then she made four more," and Kiara placed four cubes in that box on their chart.

Many children kept the pattern going past fifty, so I interrupted the students and directed their attention to the last piece of information on the board. "Would you all please read this aloud for me?" I asked.

"Lifespan is usually about fifty years," they read in unison.

"Does she keep laying eggs until she dies?" Anthony wanted to know.

I responded, "Let's say, for this example, that by the time she turns fifty, she has stopped laying eggs. We would need to do more research to find out if that is a realistic assumption to make."

I looked down at Alex's 1–100 chart and saw that he had drawn four cubes inside the thirtieth square. He had done the same for thirty-two, thirty-four, and thirty-six. But on thirty-eight, he had written the number *4*, and he had continued writing *4* in every other square up to sixty-four, which was where he was when I stopped the class. He immediately began erasing his fours on all numbers higher than forty-eight. (See Figure 16–1.)

"So she didn't lay any eggs when she was fifty years old?" he questioned.

"No, by fifty she had stopped laying eggs," I confirmed.

It was interesting to see the children move so quickly from the concrete to the abstract. When I asked Alex why he stopped drawing cubes he replied, "It's easier just to write the number." On his paper he wrote: *The amount of clutches in her lifetime is 40.* He arrived at forty by adding sixteen, for the cubes on his paper, plus twenty-four for the six remaining fours he had written.

"What are we trying to figure out?" I asked.

Alex looked back on the board and read, "About how many eggs does the loggerhead turtle lay in her lifetime?"

"Each of these is one hundred eggs," he said pointing to one of the cubes on his hundred chart. "One hundred, two hundred, three hundred, four hundred." Alex continued counting by hundreds, pointing to each cube. When he got to where he had written the fours instead of stacking cubes, he tapped each numeral four times as he continued to count by hundreds. "Forty hundred," he said.

"Can you write down what you just did?" I challenged.

"I'll try," he said obediently.

When I came back about ten minutes later and looked at his paper, I was excited to see how Alex had connected his skip-counting by

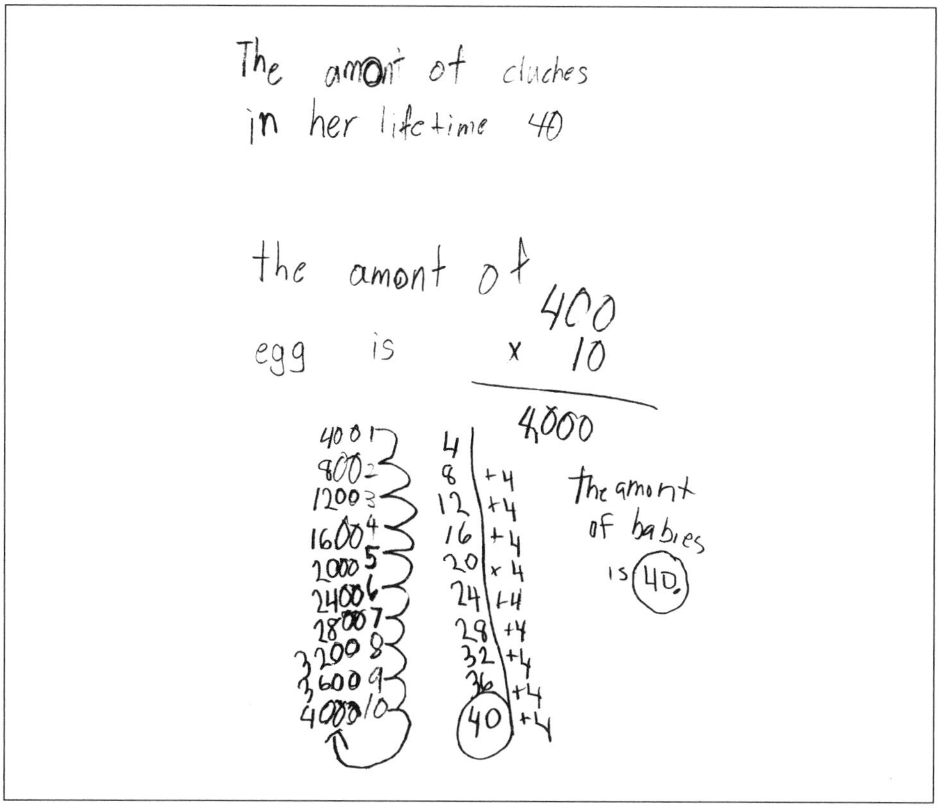

Figure 16–2: Alex con-
nected his skip-counting by
hundreds to the concept of
multiplying four hundred
times ten.

hundreds to the concept of multiplying four hundred by ten. He
had done a lot of erasing before he figured out how to show his skip-
counting on paper, but when Alex explained his process to me, I was
confident that he had internalized the connection. (See Figure 16–2.)

"I was making Xs for each of the cubes and writing four hundred
next to each of the four Xs," Alex said. "But then I changed my mind
and started adding four hundred each time. Then I knew that there
was four hundred ten times, so I wrote the numbers." He pointed to
where he had recorded *400 × 10 = 4,000*.

"What's this number?" I asked, pointing to the 4,000.

"It's forty hundred, but when I saw the three zeros, I knew I had to
put a comma, so I think it's four thousand. And I think this is two
thousand," Alex said, pointing to the 2,000 in his list of skip-counting.
"And this is one thousand, two hundred," he added, pointing to the
1,200 he had written in his list.

I congratulated Alex, "Wow, you made sense of a lot of big
numbers."

"Yeah, I did," he said sweetly.

"So what are these numbers?" I asked, pointing to the place where
he had skip-counted by four.

"That's the number of baby turtles that make it," he replied. "I did
the same thing, but each cube was just one so I counted by fours up to
forty."

Victoria and Samantha were spread out on the floor with two papers and four stacks of hundreds from the base 10 blocks. They explained their process a different way. They had figured out how many years the turtle laid eggs between the ages of thirty and fifty and then multiplied by four to represent the four clutches she lays in a year. When I asked how they figured out that the number was ten, they drew a box showing how they skip-counted by twos from thirty to fifty. They crossed off the fifty because the turtle didn't lay eggs that year and showed how they counted the numbers. (See Figure 16–3.)

"Why did you multiply by four?" I asked.

"Because each of these years there were four clutches of eggs," Victoria said.

"Why did you multiply forty times one hundred?" I continued.

"'Cause each of these cubes is one hundred eggs," Samantha explained.

"And how did you figure out forty times one hundred?" I asked.

Victoria explained, "We wrote four hundred in each box from thirty to forty-eight, and then we counted the four hundreds. We had to use the hundred blocks to know how much it was all together. It made four thousands, because there were ten hundreds in each stack." (See Figure 16–4.)

I asked Victoria and Samantha to place the 100 hundreds blocks they had arranged on a desk where everyone could see and then I walked over to Anthony.

1	2	3	4	5	6	7	8	9	10
11	12	13	14	15	16	17	18	19	20
21	22	23	24	25	26	27	28	29	30 (400)
31	32 (400)	33	34 (4)	35	36 (400)	37	38 (400)	39	40 (400)
41	42 (400)	43	44 (400)	45	46 (4)	47	48 (400)	49	50
51	52	53	54	55	56	57	58	59	60
61	62	63	64	65	66	67	68	69	70
71	72	73	74	75	76	77	78	79	80
81	82	83	84	85	86	87	88	89	90
91	92	93	94	95	96	97	98	99	100

Figure 16–4: Samantha and Victoria used both a hundred chart and hundred blocks to find the total number of eggs laid.

Anthony used a similar strategy but his paper looked very different. He used words to try to explain what he did. Earlier in the period when I had asked him to draw a picture to show how he got his answer, he drew a picture of the turtle and one clutch of eggs. In his mind, his explanation made sense, but he hadn't shown the answer to the problem I had posed. Nor had he shown where he began counting and where he stopped. On his 1–100 chart, he had placed four cubes on each of the numbers from thirty to forty-eight, but he hadn't communicated that on his paper. Still, I was proud of his attempt. It emphasized the importance of giving children many opportunities to communicate their process on paper. (See Figure 16–5.)

I wanted the children to see all of the different ways their classmates had represented their thinking on paper, so before I excused them for recess, I had them take a look. When Anthony saw Alex's paper he exclaimed, "Hey, he did it just like me!" He pointed at Alex's list that showed how he skip-counted by fours. I was reminded at this point how important it is for students to share their work with each other. Anthony was able to connect his own process to Alex's representation. Even though he couldn't communicate exactly what he had done on paper, he was able to recognize his method in somebody else's.

After a minute or so, I called the students to order and asked, "Tell me again what we were trying to figure out?"

"How many eggs the turtle lays in her lifetime," the students chorused.

"And how many eggs does she lay?" I asked.

Some children said forty. Some said forty hundred. And some said four thousand. I wrote each of the numbers on the board:

forty
forty hundred
four thousand

I pointed to *forty* and asked, "What does this number stand for?"

Phillip said, "That's the number of babies who live, 'cause out of each one hundred eggs, probably only one turtle makes it."

"What's this number?" I asked, pointing to *forty hundred*.

"That's four thousand, because forty hundreds is four thousands," Victoria explained. She shared the model she and Samantha had built.

I asked, "So is forty [I wrote *40* on the board] hundred [I wrote *00* next to the 40] the same as four thousand [I wrote *4,000*]?"

"Yes, because each ten hundred is one thousand," Samantha realized.

After letting Samantha's statement sink in for a few seconds, I thought it was important to remind the students that all of the calculating we had done was still only an estimate. I asked, "Do you think every loggerhead turtle lays four thousand eggs in her lifetime?"

Jean, who had been pretty quiet the whole period, spoke up first. "If we would have started at seven instead of thirty, it would have been a higher number, like probably twice as much."

"Plus, what if she made more nests than just four? The book said maybe she could make ten nests," Alex added.

"You're right," I told them. "This was just an estimate based on numbers we decided to use from the texts we read from. It would be interesting to use different numbers and see what the range of possibilities could be. I'll put the book out at a center and you can try out other numbers. Thanks for all of the hard work you did today."

As I reflected on the lesson, I realized that one reason the children were able to make sense of these big numbers was because they had a real-world context in which to work with them.

Roman Numerals I to MM

Taught by Stephanie Sheffield

In *Roman Numerals I to MM* (1996), Arthur Geisert introduces children to Roman numerals by asking them to count the pigs in the book's illustrations. The text is simple and easy to understand, and the pictures make thinking about Roman numerals fun and engaging. In this lesson with fifth graders, the book provides the springboard for an introduction to Roman numerals. After establishing the value of Roman numerals, students use Venn diagrams to compare them with our system of numeration.

MATERIALS

The fifth-grade class was waiting for me when I walked in. "Did you bring a book to read?" Cessily asked. In answer, I held up *Roman Numerals I to MM*, showing the back cover.

Alex leaned closer to see better. "Are those pigs in a swimming pool?" he asked incredulously.

"Yup," I answered. "Doesn't it make you curious to read the book?" The whole class signaled their agreement with excited exclamations.

I invited the children to sit on the floor in the open space near the board. When they were settled, I turned the book around and read the title. Next I read the subtitle, "*Numerabilia Romana Uno ad Duo Mila*. What do you think that means?" I asked.

"I heard *uno*. That means one in Spanish," Alfonso said. "But if the rest is Spanish, I don't know those words."

"I think the first part is Roman numerals," Ranna guessed.

Chloe spoke up: "I think *duo* means two. Like a singing duo."

"*Mila* might mean million," Cameron suggested.

"You've had a lot of good ideas about how to translate these words. Do you have any idea what language it may be?" I asked.

"Italian," was Alex's quick answer.

"Or Spanish," Cessily said.

"I think it's Roman," Mason said.

"Well, you're all close," I said. "There is no language called Roman, but the Roman people spoke *Latin,* and these words are written in Latin. And the Spanish and Italian languages are derived from Latin. That means they both came from Latin."

"Rome is in Italy," Darnell commented.

"That's right, Darnell. That's another connection. In ancient times, Rome was one of the major cultural centers of the world. This book is an introduction to the numerals they used then." I explained.

Andrew raised his hand. "Isn't Latin a dead language?" he asked.

There was some other conversation in the room when Andrew was speaking and I misheard him. "A dad language?" I asked. "I guess you could call it a Dad language, since several other languages came from Latin."

"No," Andrew said laughing, "I said 'dead' language, not 'dad' language." There were chuckles all around the classroom.

I read aloud the first page of the book, which identifies the seven letters that stand for numbers in the Roman numeral system. I wrote them on the board as I read:

$$I \quad V \quad X \quad L \quad C \quad D \quad M$$

Each of the three pictures on next page shows a different number of pigs. The text invites the reader to count the pigs to determine the meaning of the Roman numeral in each picture.

"I know that I means one," Alex offered.

"*V* must be five," Chloe added. "I see five pigs." I wrote *1* and *5* under the *I* and *V* on the board.

"The next picture is nine," Cameron shared.

"No, it's not," countered Mason. "There's a pig hiding behind the house. That makes ten." I wrote *10* under the *X*.

I turned the page to a picture of many pigs on a jungle gym, labeled *L*. "I think it's a hundred," Ranna suggested. "Or maybe fifty." Other children also made predictions. I began to count aloud, pointing to the pigs as I did so, using the grid of the jungle gym bars to help me keep track of which pigs I had counted. The class was pleased when I reached fifty.

"I knew it!" Darnell crowed.

The picture on the following page, of pigs on seesaws, was labeled *C*. "What do you think the *C* means?" I asked.

Cameron, who is a native Spanish speaker, answered, "*Cien* means one hundred in Spanish, so maybe *C* means one hundred in Roman."

"Yeah!" Huey said excitedly, "A cent is, like, one-hundredth of a dollar."

"Does anyone know any other words that start with *cent*?" I asked.

"Century!" Andrea called out.

"And centipede," Ellie said. "They have one hundred legs."

Alex added to the discussion: "It looks like there are twice as many pigs on the seesaws as on the monkey bars, so I think it has to be one hundred. Do we have to count them?"

"I think we can agree that *C* means one hundred without counting," I said. "Let's look at this another way." On the board I drew a T-chart, labeled the left column *Roman Numerals*, and listed the seven Roman numerals underneath. I labeled the right column *Our Numerals*:

Roman Numerals	Our Numerals
I	
V	
X	
L	
C	
D	
M	

Next to the *I*, I wrote *1*, and next to the *V*, I wrote *5*. "Help me fill out the rest of this chart," I said.

Andrea said, "Next comes ten, then fifty." I recorded them on the T-chart:

Roman Numerals	Our Numerals
I	1
V	5
X	10
L	50
C	100
D	
M	

"Then fifty and one hundred," Cameron added.

"OK," I said, "Let's see if this helps us see a pattern. Do you notice anything?" Several children raised their hands. I hadn't heard from Cessily yet, so I called on her. "It's like it goes one, five, one, five."

Cessily indicated the pattern on the right side of the chart, pointing to one and five, then to the one and the five in the numerals ten and fifty. "I think the next number, the *D*, has to be five hundred."

"Why do you think that, Cessily?" I asked.

"I'm not sure," she said. "I just think it follows the pattern. The next number needs to start with five."

"I have an idea!" Andrew exclaimed. "See, the five doubled and the next number is ten. And if the fifty doubles, the next number is one hundred." Others agreed. Andrew concluded, "So Cessily is right. If *D* is five hundred then the next number has to be double it, one thousand." I agreed and filled the numbers in on the T-chart:

Roman Numerals	Our Numerals
I	1
V	5
X	10
L	50
C	100
D	500
M	1000

Braden pointed to the chart. "I think I see the pattern. One times five is five," he said, "and five plus five is ten." I recorded this on the T-chart:

Roman Numerals	Our Numerals	
I	1	
V	5	× 5
X	10	+ 5
L	50	
C	100	
D	500	
M	1000	

"And then ten times five is fifty," Victoria observed, "and fifty plus fifty is one hundred." I added that to the chart:

Roman Numerals	Our Numerals	
I	1	
V	5	× 5
X	10	+ 5
L	50	× 5
C	100	+ 50
D	500	
M	1000	

"I know another way we could write it," Ethan said. "Instead of plus five and plus fifty, you could just put times two, because we're doubling. So *M* would be one thousand because you get one thousand when you double five hundred."

"Yeah!" Andrew exclaimed. "That's right! We said before it was doubling!" Andrew was up on his knees, excitedly gesturing toward the board. I reminded him to sit down so the students behind him could see. I quickly drew a second T-chart and labeled it the way Ethan suggested:

Roman Numerals	Our Numerals
I	1
V	5 ⟩ × 5
X	10 ⟩ × 2
L	50 ⟩ × 5
C	100 ⟩ × 2
D	500 ⟩ × 5
M	1000 ⟩ × 2

"We've gotten a bit ahead of the book here," I said. "Let's look at the pictures on the next few pages and see if they match what we think the pattern is telling us." To illustrate the numeral *D*, the author uses a two-page spread depicting pigs playing around in a pond. "Do you think this is five hundred pigs like we predicted?" I asked.

Andrea said, "It's definitely more than two hundred."

I turned to the two pages that show *M* pigs. "That looks like twice as many as the page before," Huey commented.

The book explains that Roman numerals are read from left to right, and that the numerals *I*, *X*, and *C* can be used two or three times in a row. "Why do you think that's not true for *D*, *V*, or *L*?" I asked, and waited a few moments to give the class time to think about the question.

When several children had raised their hands I called on Cameron. "If you had two *D*s, that would equal *M*, and it's easier to just use *M*," he explained.

"And two *V*s make an *X*," Ranna added.

"And two *L*s make a *C*," Alex chimed in.

"What about *C* then, can you put two or three of them together?" I asked.

"Sure, that would just be two hundred or three hundred," Ellie said.

I turned to that page that shows a total of *MM*, or two thousand, pigs. Cameron raised his hand. "Isn't there something about subtraction with Roman numerals?"

"You're right, Cameron, I think that's coming up," I said. The next two pages explain how Roman numeral are written with the largest numeral first, and numerals of equal or lesser value next. When they appear in this order, all the numerals are added to find the total. However, when a smaller numeral is placed before a larger numeral, the smaller gets subtracted from the larger. I stopped before reading the sentence that gives examples of this subtraction.

"Cameron, can you think of a numeral that works like that?" I asked.

"I think nine is like that. You write it *IX*, so it's like one less than ten," he explained. I wrote on the board: *1 = I*. Under it I wrote *2 = ____*.

"*I—I!*" the students called out together. I recorded their response.

Next I wrote *3 = ____*, and the students responded, "*I—I—I.*" I continued by writing *4 = ____*.

"*I—V!*" several children called out. I listed numerals up to twenty and recorded the Roman numeral equivalents as they gave them.

"How would you write the number thirty-four?" I asked. "Talk to the person next to you about that." I listened to be sure everyone had enough time to talk it through, then I had Andrea and Ellie record the Roman numeral on the board.

Mason raised his hand and asked a question: "What are our numbers called? Are they American numbers?"

"That's a good question, Mason," I responded. "Our numerals are considered Arabic numerals. The mathematician Fibonacci introduced them to the Western world. They were an improvement over Roman numerals in a number of ways." (**Note:** After class I looked up more information about the numerals we use today and found they are actually referred to as Hindu-Arabic numerals. I gave the class that information later that week.)

Comparing Roman Numerals with Our Number System

Mason's question was a nice transition to what I had planned to ask next. "Can you think of any ways that Roman numerals are different from our numerals?" I asked. I gave the students a few moments before I called on Darnell.

"Roman numerals are letters and our numerals are numbers," he observed.

Ellie spoke next. "Roman numerals are all made with seven letters. Our numbers have . . ." Ellie stopped to count on her fingers. "Oh yeah, ten numbers."

"In Roman numerals you have to subtract to make some numbers. We don't have to subtract," Ranna observed.

"How do our numerals work?" I asked her.

"You just write the biggest number first, and then the numbers get smaller and smaller," she said.

"But it's like adding," Cameron interjected. "You know how we do expanded form? Like five hundred plus forty plus two is five hundred forty two." I wrote on the board:

$$500 + 40 + 2 = 542$$

"I know another way they're different," Alfonso said, smiling. "Only Roman numerals are used for the Super Bowl." Since the Super Bowl had recently been held in our area, it was still on Alfonso's mind.

"You're right," I replied. "That's another difference between Roman numerals and our numerals. I want you all to spend some time thinking about how our number system is similar to and different from Roman numerals. I'd like you to work with a partner so you'll have someone to talk to, and I'd like you to record your ideas on a Venn diagram. Who remembers what that looks like?"

"It's like two circles that overlap," Chloe said.

"Right," I said, drawing two intersecting circles on the board. "You'll need to label each circle so I can understand your Venn diagram when I look at it later. And I have one last challenge for you. At the very end of the book the author tells how many pigs there are in the whole book. I'll write the number on the board using Roman numerals and you and your partner can try to figure out just how many pigs there are altogether. Remember to finish your Venn diagram first, though." As the students got organized to work, I wrote on the board:

This book contains MMMMDCCCLXIV pigs.

The students were clearly interested in the assignment. They talked animatedly about their ideas while carefully constructing their Venn diagrams. Ranna and Cessily were excited about something they had discovered, and they called me over.

"We just thought of something," Cessily said. "Roman numerals don't have a zero!"

"You're right," I agreed. "That is a major difference, and it was considered an improvement when Arabic numerals were first introduced in the West."

The class seemed to be divided about whether Roman numerals could be used in fractions, and they weren't sure about decimals, either. Most of the students got to the extra activity of figuring out how many pigs are in the book. Working with and thinking about Roman numerals made the whole class more aware of how our own Hindu-Arabic numerals work in our number system. (See Figures 17–1 through 17–4.)

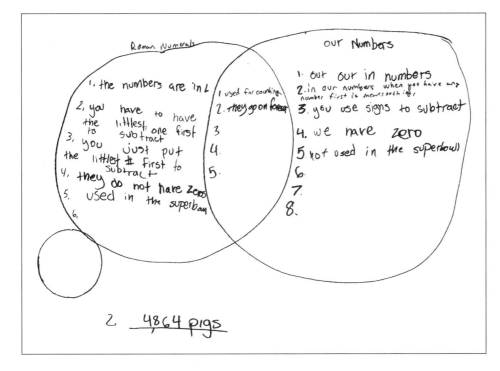

Figure 17-1: Mason and Alfonso had a hard time thinking of similarities between Roman numerals and our numerals.

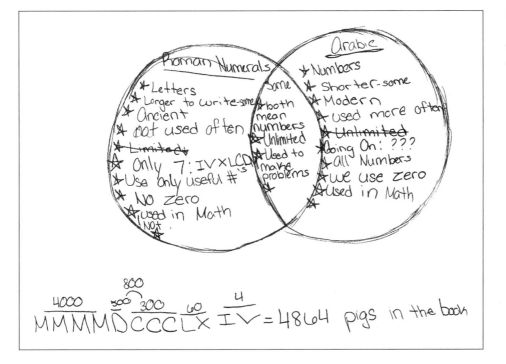

Figure 17-2: Andrea and Ellie showed how they figured out the number of pigs in the book.

Figure 17–3: Alex and Braden found many ways the number systems are alike and many ways they are different.

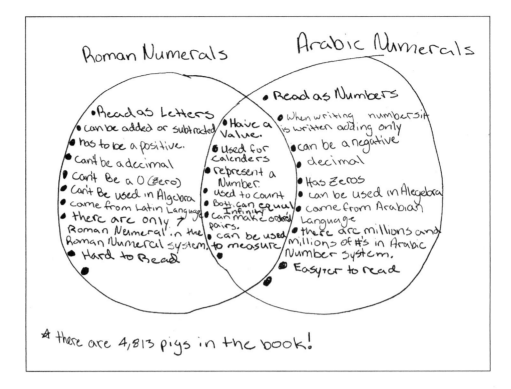

Figure 17–4: Ranna and Cessily dated their diagram using Roman numerals.

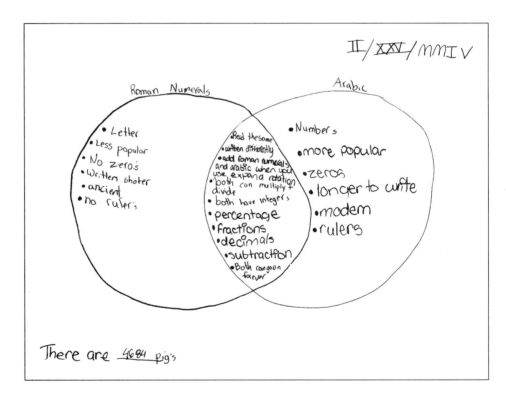

Ten Times Better

Taught by Stephanie Sheffield

In *Ten Times Better* (2000), Richard Michelson depicts animals boasting about their own favorite numbers to help young readers count and multiply by ten. The elephant, for example, is proud of the number one, which represents his one strong trunk, while the giant squid thinks ten is best because he has ten tentacles. After counting from one to ten and from ten to one hundred, the book provides more information about the animals. Each animal description ends with a question that students must multiply by ten to answer. The last page of the book presents the answers and a fact that relates each answer to something in a child's realm of experience. In this lesson, third graders use various strategies to solve problems involving multiples of ten.

MATERIALS

As soon as the third-grade class was settled in front of the rocking chair, I began reading *Ten Times Better*. I had positioned a white board on an easel next to the rocker so that I would have a place to record interesting things that came up in the reading.

"What's a 'schnoz'?" Sierra asked when I read the page about the elephant.

"Look at the picture, it must be his trunk," Jake retorted.

"It's a slang word for nose," I clarified.

After I read the next page, where the squid talks about being ten times better, Malina exclaimed, "This is a book about multiplying. We just learned that!"

I continued reading, with the class eagerly anticipating what the next page would describe. "Part of the book counts by ones and part of it counts by tens," Devin observed. The students were able to predict the numbers that were coming up and they were interested in the animal parts that represent each number. Some, like the insect legs for the number six, were easy to anticipate, but others, like the eyes on a peacock's feathers, were much harder. The children enjoyed the author's clever rhymes.

After reading the book through once, I returned to the first two pages and showed them to the class. On the board I wrote:

Elephant's trunk 1   *10 squid tentacles*

I drew an arrow from the one to the ten and asked, "What is the relationship between these two numbers?"

Lorenzo answered, "One times ten is ten."

I added a second line, again drawing an arrow:

Elephant's trunk   1 —→ *10 squid tentacles*
Camel's humps   2 —→ *20 feathers on sage grouse male*

"And what's the relationship between these two numbers?" I asked.

Many children raised their hands. "Two times ten is twenty," they said together.

I continued writing on the board and asking the students to recall, with the help of the illustrations, the numbers in the book and what animals they related to. The completed chart looked like this:

Elephant's trunk   1 —→   *10 squid tentacles*
Camel's humps   2 —→   *20 feathers on sage grouse male*
Sloth toes   3 —→   *30 feet on a centipede*
Warthog tusks   4 —→   *40 warts on frog*
Starfish legs   5 —→   *50 goldfish in school*
Ant legs   6 —→   *60 crocodile teeth*
Raccoon tail rings   7 —→   *70 spots on giraffe neck*
Tarantula legs   8 —→   *80 eyes on peacock tail*
Armadillo bands   9 —→   *90 zebra stripes*
Chimpanzee fingers   10 —→   *100 bees in a hive*

"I want you to think about the relationships between the numbers on the chart. What do you notice?" I asked.

Malina raised her hand and said, "It's like ten times one is ten, ten times two is twenty, ten times three is thirty, ten times four is forty. . . ."

I stopped her and asked, "Where do you see that pattern?"

Malina pointed to the right side of the chart. "These are the numbers you say when you count by tens," she explained. "They're all the ten timeses."

Jake jumped up to point to the chart and add an observation. "These numbers," he said, indicating the single digits on the left side, "are the same as these," pointing to the multiples of ten on the right, "except without the zeros. If you add a zero to these, you get these." He moved his finger across the rows to demonstrate.

After Jake sat down I asked, "Did you enjoy the book?" The class was unanimous in its approval. "Well, I'm glad you did, and I'm happy to tell you that it isn't finished. The author has included some interesting facts about each of the animals, and some math questions for you to solve as well. I'd like you to go back to your seats and get three things: a pencil, some paper, and something hard to write on. Then come back and sit in front of the easel and we'll work on some of these problems."

The class was ready for a break at this point, and getting up to get their writing materials provided an opportunity to stretch. When they were settled again, I showed them the information that starts on page thirty-five. "The animals are arranged on these pages, not in the order they appear in the book, but in alphabetical order."

"Oh, that's why the ant is first," Devin said.

I read, "If you were very strong, you could lift something that weighs about the same amount that you do. If you weighed fifty pounds you could lift a fifty-pound television set. Ants are *TEN TIMES STRONGER*. If an ant weighed fifty pounds, how many pounds could it lift?" I then said, "Think about that by yourself for a few minutes before we talk about it together."

After just a minute or so Mikayla said, "I don't get it." I asked for the attention of anyone who was confused, and those students scooted to the front of the group near the easel. On the board I drew a T-chart and labeled the two columns *your weight* and *you can lift*:

your weight	you can lift

"The author tells us that if you are strong, you can lift about the same amount that you weigh. So according to the book, if you weigh six pounds, how much can you lift?" I asked.

"Six pounds?" Daniella answered.

"That's right," I said, writing 6 in each column of the T-chart:

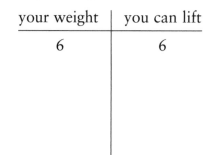

your weight	you can lift
6	6

"And if a child weighed twenty-nine pounds?" I asked, writing *29* on the chart, "How much could she lift?"

Adrian answered, "Twenty-nine. Now I get it." I quickly added two more sets of numbers to the chart:

your weight	you can lift
6	6
29	29
47	47
50	50

Then I drew a new T-chart, with the columns labeled *ant's weight* and *ant can lift*:

ant's weight	ant can lift

"The book says an ant can lift ten times its weight. So if an ant weighed one pound," I said, writing *1* in the first column, "how much could it lift?"

Kaitlyn answered. "Ten times one is ten, so it could lift ten pounds, couldn't it?" I nodded and recorded *10* on the T-chart:

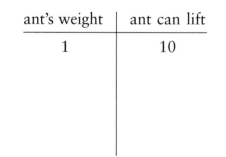

ant's weight	ant can lift
1	10

I wrote a *2* in the first column and asked what number should go in the second column. Kei said, "Twenty." She explained her thinking. "The line in the middle is kind of like a times line. Whatever number is in the first column you times it by ten to get the number in the second column."

"That's right, Kei," I said. "Here's another way of looking at the same thing. If I expanded the T-chart to show what's happening, it might look like this:

ant's weight	change	ant can lift
1	× 10	10

"We said that if an ant weighed one pound it could lift ten pounds. I've added the change column to show the relationship between the two numbers. An ant can lift ten times its weight. So if it weighed thirty pounds, what could it lift?"

Daniella answered, "Three hundred." I recorded that on the chart. Next I wrote *16* in the first column and invited Kei up to fill in how much the ant could lift:

ant's weight	change	ant can lift
1	× 10	10
30	× 10	300
16		

Finally, I wrote *50* in the first column. "This is the problem the book gave us. Do you think you can solve it now?" I asked. The students all nodded and started writing.

After a few minutes I asked for the class's attention and we discussed the problem. Rufus read his solution. "Five hundred, because fifty times ten equals five hundred and an ant is ten times stronger. And we are fifty pounds. So the problem is fifty times ten equals five hundred."

I asked Sara to read her answer. She read, "fifty times ten equals five hundred. Fifty pounds is the weight and the ten means ten times stronger." I decided the class was clear about this problem, so I moved on to the next one.

I chose the camel problem to read next. The book states that camels are ten times thirstier than most people, and can drink ten times more water in one minute than you drink all day. The question in the book is, "If you drink five glasses of water in one day, how many can a camel drink in one minute?" The children's heads went down as they started working on the problem. I reread the question once and waited while they worked. A few minutes later I asked, "Who would like to share your solution to the problem?"

Several children were eager to share. I called on Mikayla, who read, "five times ten equals fifty." She held up her paper and showed how she had written *kids drink* under the number five and *camels drink* under the fifty. Mikayla continued, "I solved this problem by if you drink five glasses of water and a camel drinks ten more cups of water, then you multiply and you get fifty." (See Figure 18–1.)

"I did it like Mikayla," Jake said, "only I made a T-chart, too." (See Figure 18–2.)

Next we read about the centipede. I explained the problem: "If a centipede were six feet long, it could run twelve feet in one second." I stopped to be sure everyone could picture this distance. I put a yard-stick on the floor.

"Look, the tiles on the floor are one foot each!" Devin announced.

"We don't need the yardstick, we can just count the tiles," Malina said.

I asked Malina to stand at the edge of one tile, and had Adrian count six tiles and stand at the other end of the six feet. "That's the length of this giant centipede we're imagining," I said. On the board I wrote:

<table>
<tr><td>10" centipede</td><td>20"/sec.</td></tr>
<tr><td>6' centipede</td><td>12'/sec.</td></tr>
</table>

Figure 18–1: Mikayla explained why she multiplied five times ten to find out how many cups of water a camel could drink.

Ten time better

2. 5 × 10 = 50   I solved
Kids Minute Camels this problem
drink   drink
by If you drink 5 glasses
of water and a camel drinks
ten more cups of water
the you. So multiply and you
get 50   camel

Math and Nonfiction, Grades 3–5

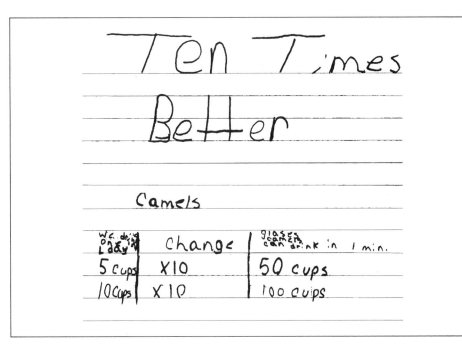

Figure 18–2: Jake used a T-chart to explain his thinking.

"This is what we know. Adrian, will you show us how far twelve feet is?" Adrian walked and counted tile squares, stopping with his feet on the edge of the twelfth square.

"If the centipede were six feet long, this is how far it could run in one second," I said.

"Wow! That would be scary!" Ariel commented. Others made exclamatory remarks before I asked for their attention again.

"The question is, how far could the six-foot centipede run in ten seconds?" I asked.

I had expected the students to solve this problem in roughly the same way they solved the other two. But one of the joys of teaching is being surprised by your students, and once again I was surprised. After the class had worked on the problem for a few minutes I asked for students to share their thinking. Adrian came to the board and wrote ten twelves in a vertical line, put a plus sign to the side and a line underneath. He wrote his answer at the bottom: *110*.

"That's not what I got. I think we should add that up again," Sierra said.

Adrian pointed to the twos as the class counted aloud together from two to twenty by twos. He wrote a zero in the ones column and put a two in the tens column. The students added the tens as Adrian pointed. When they finished with one hundred twenty, Adrian looked surprised and said, "Oh!" He seemed convinced that they now had the correct answer. (See Figure 18–3.)

"Did anyone solve this in a different way?" I asked.

Sara said, "I did." She stood up and showed the class her paper. "I drew twelve circles and put ten inside them," she said.

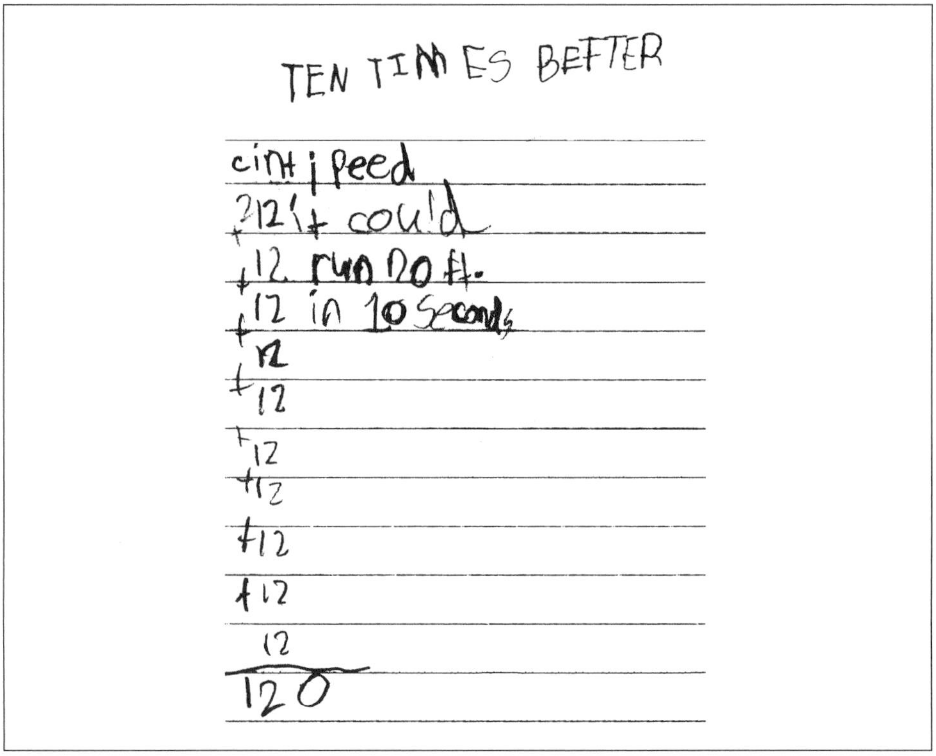

Figure 18–3: Adrian corrected his total after the class computed together.

Figure 18–3: Adrian corrected his total after the class computed together.

TEN TIMES BEFTER

cintipeed
212 could
12 run 120 ft.
12 in 10 seconds
12
12
12
12
12
12
12
120

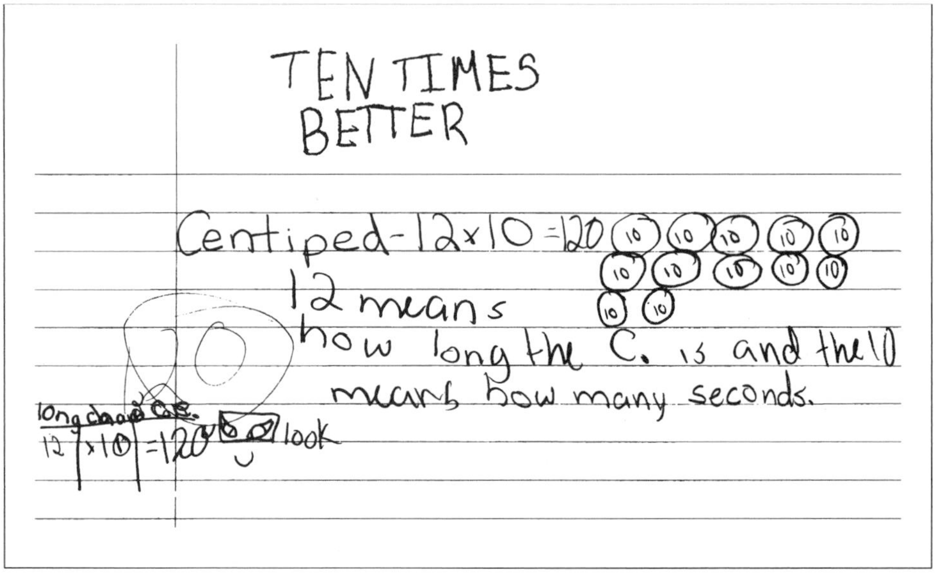

Figure 18–4: Sara used the commutative nature of multiplication to solve the centipede problem.

TEN TIMES BETTER

Centiped-12×10 =120

12 means
how long the C. is and the 10
means how many seconds.

long ch a pe.
12 ×10 =120 look

"Why did you do that Sara?" I asked, curious.

"I knew it was twelve times ten, but I can count by tens better than I can count by twelves. So I made twelve tens instead of ten twelves. I knew that three times two is the same as two times three, so I thought it might be the same for bigger numbers," she explained. (See Figure 18–4.)

Rufus raised his hand. "I did it sort of like Adrian, but I added different." He showed the class his paper and read, "I figured out if five

Math and Nonfiction, Grades 3–5

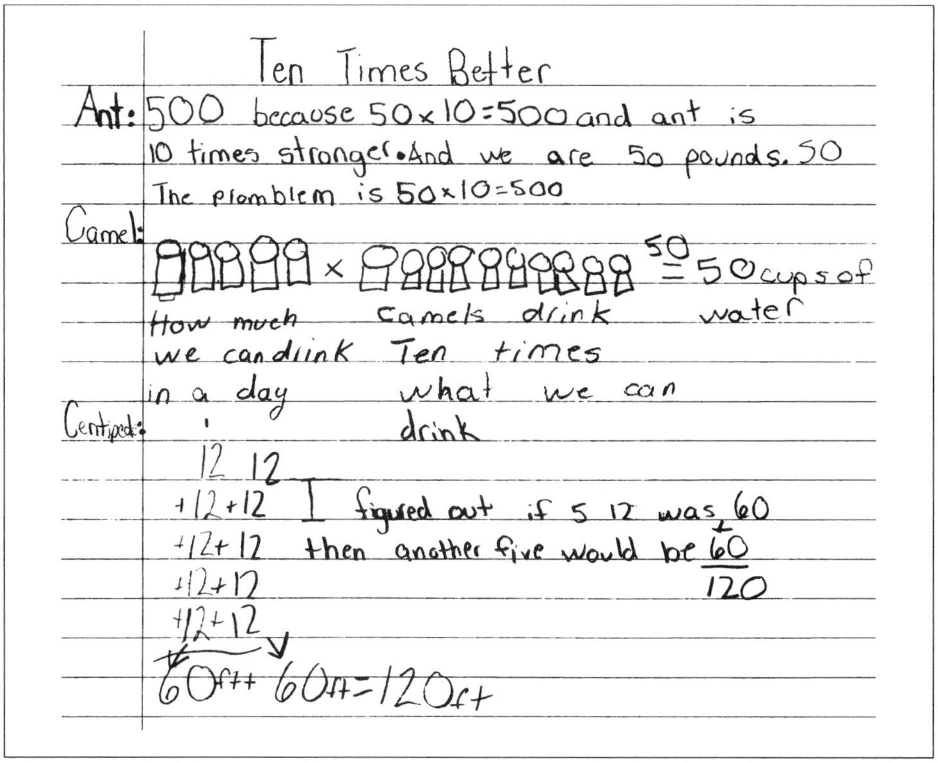
Ten Times Better
Ant: 500 because 50×10=500 and ant is
10 times stronger. And we are 50 pounds. 50
The plomblem is 50×10=500
Camel:
× 50 = 50 cups of
How much camels drink water
we can drink Ten times
in a day what we can
drink
Centipede:
12 12
+12+12 I figured out if 5 12 was 60
+12+12 then another five would be 60
+12+12 120
+12+12
60ft + 60ft = 120ft

Figure 18–5: Rufus added five twelves, then doubled the answer to get a sum of 120.

twelves was sixty, then another five would be sixty. And sixty plus sixty is one hundred twenty." (See Figure 18–5.)

Julia was waving her hand excitedly. "My way is different," she exclaimed. "I counted by twelves."

"Wow, Julia, how far can you count by twelves?" I asked.

She smiled. "Only to forty-eight," she admitted, "but then I just added twelve each time." (See Figure 18–6.)

Jake was the last to share. On the board he wrote, *12 – 10*. "First I split twelve into ten and two. Then I multiplied ten times ten and got one hundred, and ten times two and got twenty. One hundred plus twenty is one hundred twenty," he concluded.

The next set of problems we tackled was about the elephant. First we read that an elephant may weigh ten tons as an adult.

"How much is a ton?" Ariel asked.

Devin knew: "It's two thousand pounds."

"So how many pounds does an elephant weigh as an adult?" I asked. Kei and Bailey both got twenty thousand pounds as their answer, but Kei multiplied and Bailey added. (See Figures 18–7 and 18–8.)

In the next paragraph, we learned that an elephant eats as much in one day as a person eats in a month. The question is, "If you eat forty pounds of food a month, and an elephant is ten times hungrier than you are, how much would it eat in a month?" The class was really ready to work on this one, now that they had been exposed to so many strategies. (See Figure 18–9.)

Figure 18–6: Julia counted by twelves to forty-eight, then added twelves to get to 120.

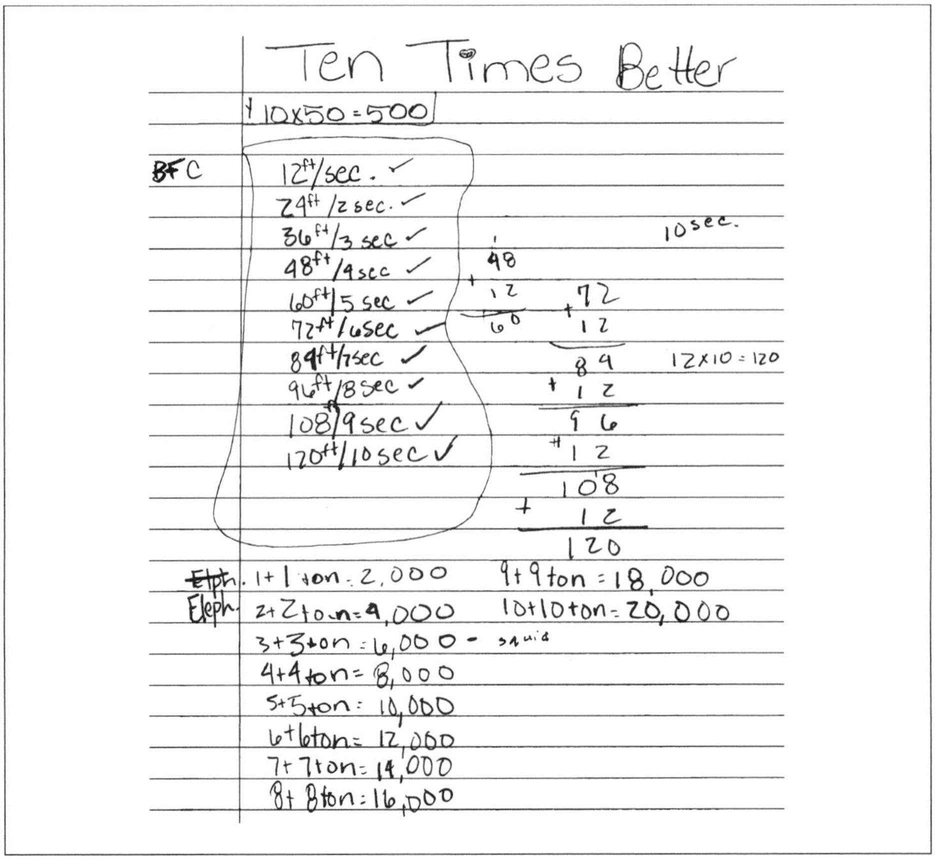

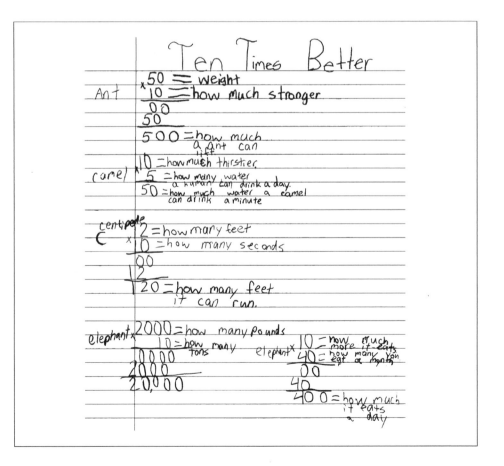

Figure 18–7: Kei multiplied the way her mother had taught her.

Math and Nonfiction, Grades 3–5

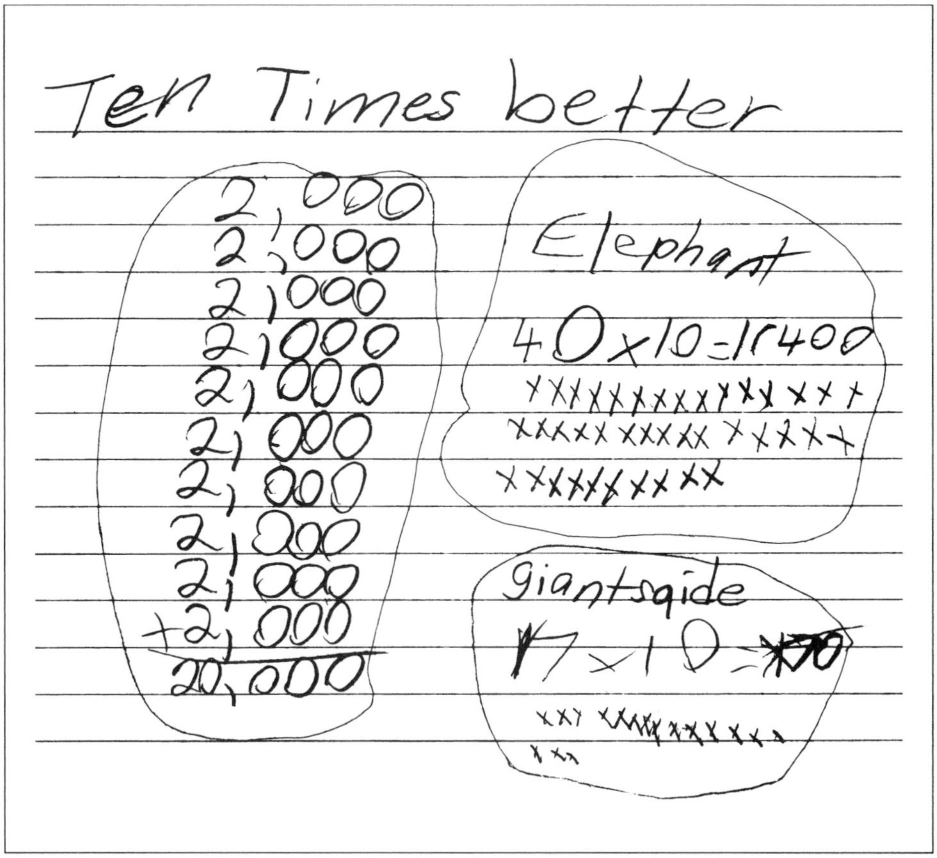

Figure 18–8: Bailey lined up ten 2,000s and added.

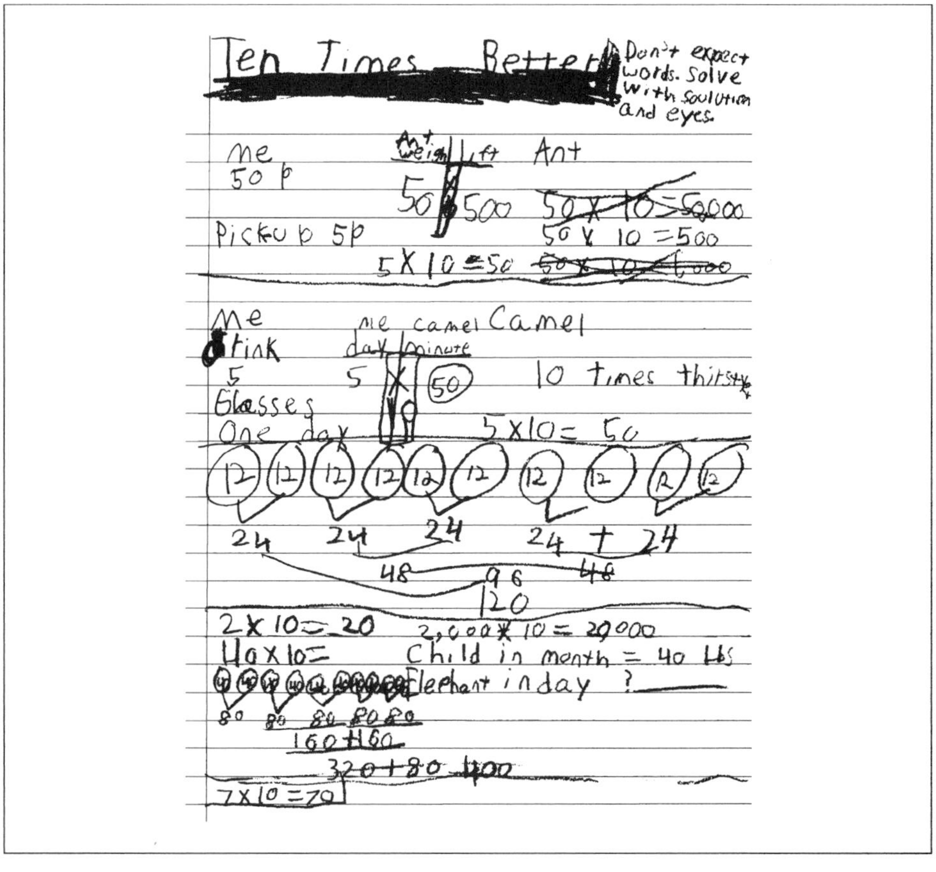

Figure 18–9: Devin used a variety of strategies, including T-charts, addition, and multiplication.

After solving this problem, they solved one more: If a giant squid is ten times longer than a seven-foot tall basketball player, how long is it? (See Figure 18–10.)

Although this class had just finished a multiplication unit, they weren't all ready to use multiplication in their problem solving. They were moving in and out of being comfortable with multiplication, using it at times and relying on addition at other times. I was confident that more experience would give them more comfort with and trust in the multiplication process.

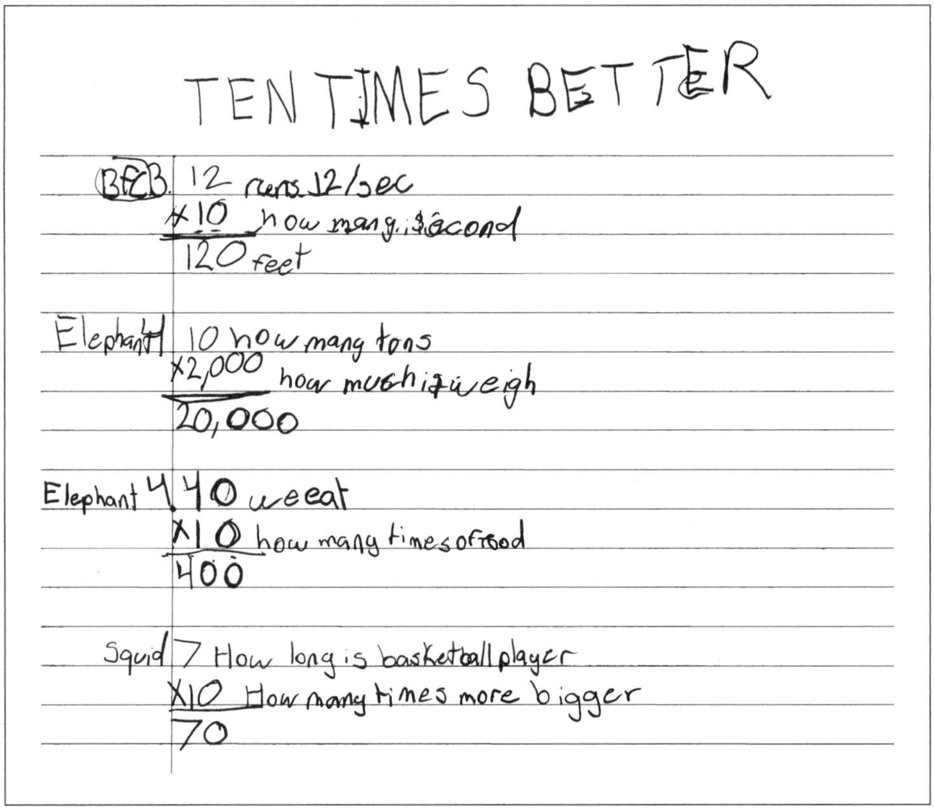

Figure 18–10: Lorenzo was confident using multiplication to solve each problem.

TEN TIMES BETTER

BFB 12 runs 12/sec
×10 how many isecond
120 feet

Elephant 10 how many tons
×2,000 how much it weigh
20,000

Elephant 4 40 we eat
×10 how many times of food
400

Squid 7 How long is basketball player
×10 How many times more bigger
70

Tiger Math

Taught by Stephanie Sheffield

Tiger Math: Learning to Graph from a Baby Tiger, written by Ann Whitehead Nagda and Cindy Bickel (2000), has two purposes. The right-hand pages tell the story of T. J., a Siberian tiger born at the Denver Zoo whose mother dies when it is just ten weeks old. Graphs on the left-hand pages provide general information about tigers and depict how T. J. grows and how the staff at the zoo monitors his growth. This lesson, taught in a third-grade class, gives students a concrete experience with creating a circle graph from information presented in a picture graph.

MATERIALS

removable white correction tape or sticky notes

small round counters, about 1-inch in diameter, 15 per student

plastic two-liter bottle, weighted by being half filled with water, sand, rice, or dried beans

yarn or string, 4 pieces each about 4 feet long, all tied to the neck of the two-liter bottle

12-by-18-inch white construction paper, 1 sheet, cut into fourths, each 6-by-9 inches

Day 1

Before presenting *Tiger Math*, I turned to page eight, which shows a picture graph about tigers in the wild, and covered parts of the graph with removable correction tape. I covered the title; the key, which indicates that one tiger in the graph represents five hundred tigers; and the words and numbers along the bottom and left side of the graph.

What remained visible were the two axes of the graph and the four columns of pictures of tigers. Covering parts of the graph would allow me to introduce the children to the graph in a way that would help them make sense of its various parts.

I gathered the third graders in the meeting area and held up the book to show them the back cover, which is orange with black tiger stripes and leaves little doubt about the book's subject. "It's a tiger book!" I heard someone say. I turned the book around to show the children the photograph of T. J., the Siberian tiger cub, on the front cover. The children responded with oohs and ahhs. There were more excited remarks as I showed the children the photographs on the front and back end papers and on the title page.

The introduction explains that the book uses graphs to help tell the story of T. J., and it suggests reading all the right-hand pages first to learn his story, then looking at the graphs on the left-hand pages to learn more. I followed this suggestion. Reading and discussing every page in one sitting would require a greater attention span than third graders have.

When I finished reading the story aloud, I returned to the beginning of the book and reread the page that introduces T. J. and his mother, Buhkra. We learned that T. J. weighed only three pounds when he was born and looked tiny next to his father, Matthew, who weighed three hundred fifty pounds.

"That's quite a difference in weight," I said. "How much would T. J. have to gain to weigh as much as his father?" I waited a moment and then asked, "How could you figure that out?" After waiting a bit more, I called on Rex.

"You do three hundred fifty minus three," Rex said. "And that's three hundred forty-seven. I know that because fifty minus three is forty-seven, so it's three hundred forty-seven." I wrote $350 - 3 = 347$ on the board.

"Is there another way to do it?" I asked.

"Well," Venisha said, "not unless you do it backwards."

"What do you mean by backwards?" I asked.

"Like three minus three hundred fifty?" Anton asked.

"No," Vanessa clarified. "I mean like three plus something equals three hundred fifty. T. J. weighs three pounds now, and he gains some weight, and someday he weighs three hundred fifty pounds." As I wrote $3 + ? = 350$ on the board, Vanessa added, "It's three hundred forty-seven again." I changed what I had written to $3 + 347 = 350$.

"So you can think about it as a subtraction problem or as an addition problem," I said. "Does anyone have another idea?" Although students had given the two responses I expected, I've learned to continue asking for other ideas. I'm often surprised by children's thinking, and I try to remember that just because an idea hasn't occurred to me doesn't mean it isn't a good idea. Even incorrect responses give me insight into students' thinking. Sure enough, Shellie raised her hand with a new idea.

"You could do three hundred fifty divided by three," she said. I wrote $350 \div 3 = ?$ on the board under the other equations.

Martin spoke as I was writing. "Hey, it's a fact family!" he observed.

"Can you explain what you mean, Martin?" I asked.

"Well, if you just put three times three hundred fifty up there, you'll have a fact family. All of the problems have the same numbers, so it's a fact family," he explained.

As I recorded $3 \times 350 = ?$ on the board, I thought about how to respond to Martin's confusion about fact families, which are number sentences that relate either to addition and subtraction, or to multiplication and division, but not to all four operations.

Jeanne had an idea to share: "I don't think that multiplying one works," she said. "The answer would be much higher than the subtraction problem."

"What's wrong with that?" I asked.

Jeanne responded, "If he gains that much, he'll be bigger than his father."

"If you did three hundred fifty plus three," Aren observed, "you would have T. J.'s father's weight and then three pounds more. That wouldn't work." I wrote $350 + 3 = 353$ on the board.

"The division one doesn't work, either," Kyra said. "Three hundred divided by three is only one hundred, so that answer would be bigger but not much. It's too small."

The children seemed satisfied that the first two suggestions were right, and they were ready to move on. I decided to let Martin's comment slide and address fact families at another time.

I had been holding the book so that the children could see only the right-hand page, which has a photograph of T. J. and Buhkra, his mother, and not the graph on the facing page. I then showed them page eight, on which I had used correction tape to cover everything except for the four columns of pictures of tigers. The graph has eight tigers in the first column, three in the second, and one each in the third and fourth columns.

"What do you think this is?" I asked.

The students answered, almost in unison, "It's a graph!"

"What's a graph?" I asked.

Taletha answered, "It's something that tells you how many of something there is."

Aren added, "It's a math picture that can tell about somebody's life."

"It can show how much someone did something," Ryan added. "Like how much they went to the movies."

No one else had an idea to share, so I asked, "What do you think this graph tells us?"

"It might tell the age T. J. was, or how many pounds he weighed," Sam said.

"But it doesn't have any numbers," Carissa observed.

"Or a title," Hayley chimed in.

Joanna wasn't sure how to say what she was thinking. "It's kind of like . . . it doesn't tell what it's about," she said.

Jon added, "It doesn't say how much each thing represents."

"The key!" Taletha exclaimed. "You need a key!" She clapped her hand over her mouth.

"That's right, Taletha," I said. "The key is the part of a graph that tells what each symbol represents. Would it help if I gave you the key?"

The students clamored, "Yes!" I carefully peeled the tape away to reveal the key: a picture of one tiger followed by = *500 tigers*. I repeated my earlier question, "What do you think this graph is about?" Students offered different ideas.

"It might be about where the tigers live."

"It could be about how many tigers are born each year."

"Or how many tigers are in the zoo."

"Or how many different kinds of tigers there are."

"Maybe it's about how many cubs are born each month."

"Or about how many stripes each tiger has."

"I think it's about how much tigers eat, or maybe about how many tigers died in a year."

After the students had offered these ideas, I uncovered the left side of the graph, where the axis is labeled "Number of Tigers" and marked in increments of five hundred up to four thousand. At first the students were excited about getting this new information, but it dawned on them that this wasn't such a big revelation after all. Janie voiced her frustration.

"That doesn't tell us anything," she said. "We already know that each tiger picture was five hundred tigers, so we just had to count them to get those numbers." Janie pointed to the numbers at the side of the graph.

Kyra, Jon, and Victor were up on their knees gesturing toward the book excitedly. "Show us the bottom of the graph!" Jon said.

I smiled at their enthusiasm and slowly peeled the last pieces of correction tape off the page, revealing the title—*Tigers in the Wild*—and the information along the bottom of the graph. All at once the graph made sense to the students. They read aloud the names of the four kinds of tigers at the bottom of the columns—Bengal tigers, Indo-Chinese tigers, Sumatran tigers, and Siberian tigers—and commented on which ones they were familiar with. Since none of the children had heard of Sumatran tigers, I pulled down the wall map of the world and pointed out Sumatra. The students noticed that the different kinds of tigers all came from the same general part of the world.

"What do you know from the information on this graph?" I asked. As the students commented on the graph I recorded their statements on the board:

There are lots more Bengal tigers than the other kinds of tigers.
There are about the same number of Sumatran tigers as Siberian tigers.
They probably estimated the numbers of tigers because they probably don't really live in groups of 500.
There are more Bengal tigers than all the other kinds put together.
There are 4,000 Bengal tigers in the wild.
There are 2,500 more Bengal tigers than Indo-Chinese tigers.

The paragraph at the bottom of the page explains how to read the graph, but our discussion made the explanation unnecessary. I was sure that my students understood the graph's message.

Third graders can sit only so long, and I knew we were nearing the end of their sit time. I asked the students to stand, move the desks to the sides of the room, and leave an open space in the middle of the room. Then I said, "I'm going to ask some of you to represent the tiger groups on the graph, and some of you will be tiger wranglers." I held up the book so that the students could see the graph on page eight. "Each person whose name I call will represent five hundred tigers, just the way one tiger picture on the graph represents five hundred tigers." I called the names of eight students and identified them as representing Bengal Tigers. Then I called five other children to represent the Indo-Chinese, Sumatran, and Siberian tigers, because there were a total of five hundred tigers of these three types. I asked the rest of the students to be tiger wranglers and help the tiger children line up to make a picture graph like the one in the book. I watched as the students moved into position, the wranglers helping them line up in straight lines.

When the tiger children were all in place and the others had moved to the side, I again asked for their attention. "Now I'll show you how to rearrange yourselves so that we can make a circle graph," I said. I directed the tiger students in the graph to make one long straight line, Bengal tigers first, then Indo-Chinese tigers, then Sumatran, then Siberian.

I chose two of the tiger wranglers and said, "Help move the ends of this line around into a circle, so that the first Bengal tiger child is standing next to the Siberian tiger child."

When the tiger children were in a circle, I told them, "Sit down right where you are and move together into a tight circle, with the knees of your crossed legs almost touching the person next to you."

Then I asked Aren, one of the wranglers, to put the weighted two-liter pop bottle with the yarn attached in the center of the circle. I said, "A moment ago, our tiger children were in four columns, but now they're in a circle and we're going to construct a new kind of graph, a circle graph, with the same data. This graph will display the same information, but in a different way. I have four pieces of yarn tied to this pop bottle and I'm going to use the yarn to divide the circle into groups of tigers. Aren, take one piece of yarn to the spot between the last Bengal tiger and the first Indo-Chinese tiger." Aren stretched the yarn out and put it down on the floor between two children.

"OK," I said, "now I want you to find where the Bengal tigers begin. This will be where the Bengal tigers and the Siberian tigers meet. Put another piece of yarn there." Aren did so, creating a wedge-shaped area marked on the floor by the two pieces of yarn.

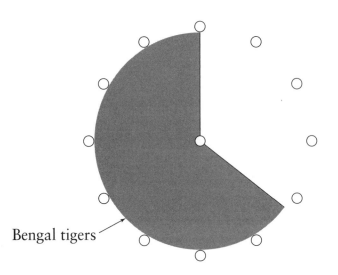
Bengal tigers

Standing outside the circle, I indicated the students sitting in the wedge-shaped area. "What kind of tigers do all these children represent?" I asked.

"They are the Bengals," Arden said.

I handed Janie, one of the wranglers, a piece of white construction paper and a marker. I said, "Janie, please write *Bengal tigers* on this paper to make a label for this area of the graph," I said. Janie wrote *Bengal tigers* on the paper and placed it outside the circle near the wedge.

I had other tiger wranglers place the yarn between the last Indo-Chinese tiger and the Sumatran tiger, and then between the Sumatran and Siberian tigers. I asked other children to make labels for the three tiger groups and place them near the appropriate wedges. By doing this, we completed a circle graph.

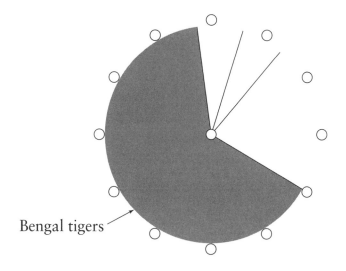

Bengal tigers

The students seemed pleased with their accomplishment. To end the class, I said, "Tomorrow you'll each have the chance to make a circle graph by yourself."

Day 2

I started class the next day by reminding the students how we had constructed the circle graph the day before: "We started with columns, then joined them into one line. What did we do next?" A few students didn't remember, but most hands were in the air. I called on Taletha.

"We put all the tigers in a circle and made lines between the groups with yarn," she said. "And then we put papers to show which tigers they were."

"They were labels," Jasmine said.

"That's right," I said. "Today you're each going to create a circle graph on paper that tells about tigers in the wild. I'll put a bowl of counters on each table for you to use to represent the tigers. There are different colors of counters, and you need to pick one color to represent each type of tiger. You'll have to cooperate with the others at your table so you all have the number of each color counter you need. Does anybody have an idea about how many counters you'll need?"

Ryan replied, "If it's like yesterday, we'll need one color for the Siberian tigers, one for the...." His voice faded. Then he asked, "What's that other kind of tiger that starts with an S?"

"Sumatran," I answered.

Ryan continued, "A different color for the Sumatran tigers and a different color for the other ones, too. We need four colors because there are four kinds of tigers."

I nodded and said, "Remember that each counter represents five hundred tigers, just like yesterday when each person represented five hundred tigers. First you should make four columns of counters on your desk, one column for each type of tiger, representing each kind of tiger with a different color of counter. Then take the counters and arrange them into a circle the way we did yesterday with people."

On the overhead I arranged four piles of colored counters into columns to represent the information shown on the graph in the book.

Next I moved the counters on the overhead projector into a circle. I demonstrated how to draw around the outside edges of the circular counters to make a circle, then to draw lines from the center of the circle to the places where the different colors met.

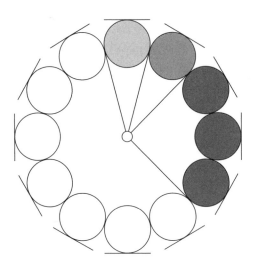

I then removed the counters, wrote a title, and labeled each section in the circle.

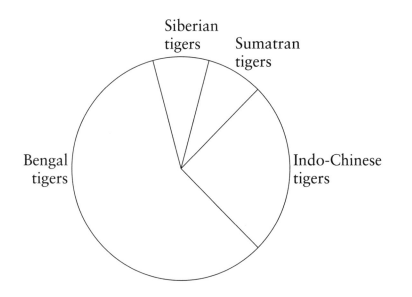

"For your graph," I told the children, "remember that each counter counts for five hundred tigers." I wrote on the board:

Bengal tigers: 4,000
Indo-Chinese tigers: 1,500
Sumatran tigers: 500
Siberian tigers: 500

The students began creating their graphs, most counting carefully by five hundred to be sure that they had the correct total in each column. Drawing the circle around the counters was tricky for some students, but they helped each other hold the counters in place. The students completed their graphs by labeling the sections of the circle and coloring the sections to make them distinctive. (See Figures 19–1, 19–2, 19–3.)

After all of the students had completed their graphs, I called them together to share their work. They passed their papers around and admired each other's graphs. Then I turned to page ten in the book and showed the class the circle graph titled "Tigers in the Wild." The children were surprised to see that a fifth kind of tiger, South China tigers, was shown on the graph, occupying a tiny sliver of the circle.

"Hey, what does that mean?" Carissa exclaimed.

"Yeah, why weren't those tigers on the other graph?" Jacob asked. There was a lot of excited talking as the children all tried to get closer to the book to examine the graph.

If Jacob hadn't asked this question, I would have raised it. I said, "Jacob poses an interesting question. Why do you think there weren't any South China tigers on the picture graph? Talk to the person next to you about your ideas." After a few minutes of conversation, I asked if anyone had an idea to share.

Figure 19–1: Jeanne labeled her sections with the actual numbers of tigers left in the wild.

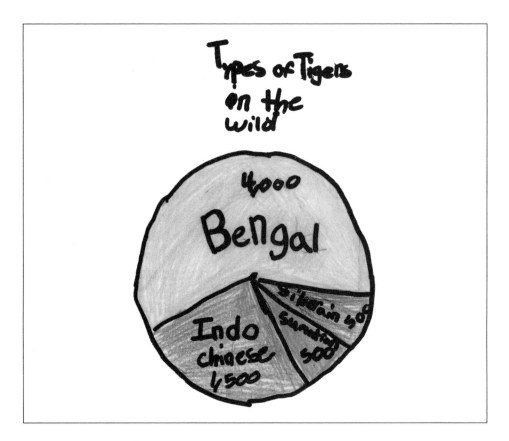

Figure 19–2: Taletha made a detailed key for her circle graph.

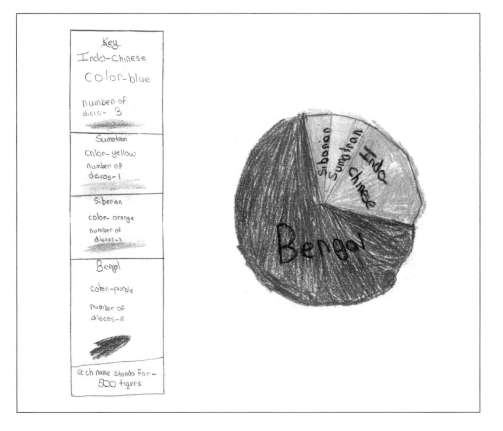

Math and Nonfiction, Grades 3–5

Figure 19–3: Haley had difficulty creating her circle and keeping her lines straight, but the result was similar to the graph in the book.

"We think maybe there aren't enough of that kind of tiger to put on the other graph," Kyra said.

Jeanne continued, "If there were two hundred fifty of them, they could have just drawn half a tiger."

Shellie added, "Maybe there weren't even two hundred fifty of them."

I read the last sentence in the text at the bottom of the page: "There are so few South China tigers left (about forty) that they couldn't be shown on the picture graph on page eight—they would have been just a small piece of a tiger picture."

"That's not even half a tiger's worth," Ryan said.

I had the students compare their own papers with the circle graph in the book, and they realized that their graphs were quite similar.

This graphing lesson referred to only the first few pages of the book. I continued reading and the children enjoyed revisiting the book. This time, I focused more on the graphs, which represent information about tigers in general and specifically about T. J. For each graph, we read the information the authors provide and discussed it.

Wilma Unlimited

Taught by Kathleen Gallagher

In *Wilma Unlimited* (1996), Kathleen Krull tells the inspiring story of Wilma Rudolph, who weighed just four pounds when she was born. When she contracted polio at the age of five, everyone thought that she would never walk again. But Wilma not only overcame her condition, she became the first woman to win a gold medal in the Olympics—in running. In this lesson, fourth-grade students collect data on birth weights and organize the data so it can be compared and discussed.

MATERIALS

2-by-2-inch squares of paper in multiple colors, 36 per pair of students

Birth Weight Record Sheet (see Blackline Masters)

#10 envelopes, 1 per pair of students

graph paper

Two days before teaching this lesson, I gave the fourth graders the homework assignment of finding out their birth weights and recording them on a special sheet I gave them. (See Figure 20–1.)

Giving the children two days to collect the data gave those who forgot another chance to bring the information to class before the lesson. I began the lesson by giving the students an overview of how they were going to work. "Today we're going to work with some data," I said. "Does anyone have an idea about what data we might be working with today?" Since we had gone to the trouble of gathering data that all of them could relate to, I wanted to make sure I connected their experience to the correct math terminology. Several children raised their hands and I called on Paul.

Fourth Grade Students,

We are going to do a math lesson on Friday that requires you to know your birth weight. Please fill in the following information and return this paper tomorrow.

Name _Danny M._

Birth weight

_6_ lbs. _13_ oz.

"Information?" he offered, remembering that the word *data* had something to do with information.

"Data is information," I encouraged, "but today we're going to work with some very specific data."

"Ooh, ooh, I know," said Jason excitedly, barely able to stay in his seat. "Is it our birth weights?"

"What do you think?" I asked Priscilla, who was quietly raising her hand.

"I think our birth weights," she said.

"Yes," I confirmed. "Today we are going to work with the data about your birth weights. In a minute, I'm going to have you come to the meeting area and listen to the beginning of a story I have to share with you. But first, clear off your desk top and place your homework sheet with your birth weight right in the center. Then come to the rug and bring a pencil with you. You probably won't return to your own desk until the end of the period, so I want you to make sure before you come to the meeting area that your desk is clear except for your data, and that you have a pencil. Does everyone understand what to do?"

The students nodded and followed my instructions. When everyone was seated in the meeting area, I showed the children the book and read them the title: *Wilma Unlimited: How Wilma Rudolph Became the World's Fastest Woman.* The children were immediately drawn to the illustrations.

"He's a runner!" exclaimed Frederick.

"I think it's not a boy if it's called *Wilma Unlimited,*" corrected Karen.

"I love this book because I think that both the writing and the pictures are really interesting and extremely well done," I told the class. "I'm just going to read a little bit of the book today, and we'll finish it tomorrow." I read the first paragraph: "No one expected such a tiny girl to have a first birthday. In Clarksville, Tennessee, in 1940, life for a baby who weighed just over four pounds was sure to be limited." I paused, looking at the class and asked, "What are you thinking?"

"She was probably sick when she was born," suggested Julias.

"Maybe she had breathing problems and they thought she was going to die," added Marcus.

"How many years ago was that?" Javier wanted to know.

"It was 1940. So how many years ago *was* that?" I asked the class.

Many children raised their hands immediately. I said, "Raise your hand when you know the answer. I'm going to wait until everyone has an idea about the answer." I think it's important for the students to learn that when I ask a question, I expect everyone to think about the answer. Before I call on students to share their ideas, I wait until every child has had an opportunity to think about it. Since some children were taking longer than others, I said, "If you already have an answer, think about what your brain did to figure it out and be prepared to share that, too."

After about a minute I pointed to Lucia. "What do you think?"

"Sixty-four," she replied. I pointed to several different children, and each of them agreed that sixty-four was the correct answer.

"Who can explain how they figured it out?" I asked. I called on Priscilla, but before she spoke, I said to the class, "Listen carefully to how Priscilla solved the problem and then be prepared to explain what she did to someone sitting next to you."

Priscilla said, "First I thought only about if it was two thousand, and I knew it would be sixty because forty plus sixty is one hundred. Then I added four more to make sixty-four."

"Raise your hand if you understand what Priscilla did," I said.

Many children raised their hands. I asked them all to turn and talk with a partner and see if they could explain what Priscilla did. After a minute, I called on Paul to explain Priscilla's method.

Paul said, "First she had to figure out how many were between nineteen forty and two thousand, and she knew it was sixty because forty plus sixty is one hundred. Then she had to add four more to get to two thousand four." I recorded on the board what Paul said.

$$1940 + 60 = 2000$$
$$2000 + 4 = 2004$$
$$60 + 4 = 64 \text{ years}$$

We then talked a bit about how life was different sixty-four years ago. We connected our discussion to a recent discussion we had had about Martin Luther King Jr., and we figured out that this book took place prior to the civil rights movement.

Because we were going to work with birth weights, I focused the discussion on Wilma's birth weight: "I'm going to read this paragraph again and I want you to listen carefully to find out how much Wilma Rudolph weighed when she was born."

After reading, I wondered aloud, "How much is 'just over four pounds'?"

"I think she weighed four pounds, one ounce, because it said 'just over.' That means just a teeny tiny bit more," said Daisy.

"It could have been two or three ounces over," added Julias, "because that's still just a little more than four pounds."

"How high do you think her birth weight could go before it wouldn't be 'just over'?" I asked.

"I think it would just be one or two," said Javier.

"I think if it was half, it would be too much," added Carmen.

"Half of what?" I asked.

"I think half a pound wouldn't be just over, because then they would say four and a half," she explained.

"How many pounds and ounces would that be?" I asked. "Let's say someone in our class weighed four and a half pounds when they were born and they had to fill out the homework sheet like the one you all filled out. What would they write in the spaces?" On the board, I wrote: __ lbs. __ oz.

"Four and a half is four point five," Julia said, "so I think you should write four pounds five ounces." Most of the children agreed with Julia. I thought for a moment about how to deal with this misconception. Then I drew a number line on the board. I wrote 4 lbs. beneath the mark I had made at the left side of the number line and 5 lbs. beneath the mark at the right end.

I said, "You're right that four and a half is the same as four point five." I made a mark halfway between the 4- and 5-pound marks and wrote 4.5 lbs. underneath. I continued, "But four point five pounds doesn't equal four pounds, five ounces." On the top of the first mark, I wrote 0 oz., corresponding with the 4 lbs. I pointed to the mark that I had labeled 5 lbs. and asked, "How many ounces are in a whole pound?"

Although the class had had a lesson or two from the textbook about weight, I don't think much of the information had really sunk in. Their answers ranged from 8 to 20 ounces. I told the class there were 16 ounces in a whole pound and wrote 16 oz. above the 5 lbs. on the number line.

I asked, "So how many ounces are there in half a pound?"

The class agreed that there must be 8 ounces in half a pound. I drew an arc from the 4 lbs. mark to the 5 lbs. mark and wrote 8 oz. at the top of the arc.

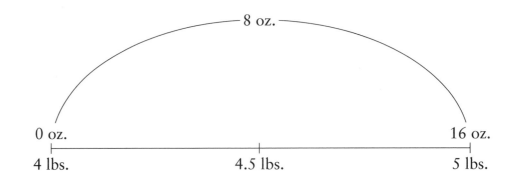

"Four pounds five ounces is less than four and a half," said Robert.

"Half is eight. So four pounds, eight ounces would be four and a half pounds," Ruben added.

Armando was confused. "How could four pounds, eight ounces be four point five?" he wondered aloud.

I acknowledged that it was confusing, because when we use decimals, we divide the whole into equal tens, hundreds, or some other power of ten. But pounds are divided into sixteen ounces. "You always have to think about what the numbers mean," I told the students. "In this context, four point five means four pounds eight ounces because the whole is sixteen, not ten."

"Now," I said, "let's say we use Javier and Daisy's idea and agree that Wilma Rudolph weighed four pounds, one ounce when she was born. I wonder how the rest of your birth weights compare to Wilma Rudolph's birth weight." I explained the procedure for creating a class set of data. I showed the children the envelopes I had prepared, each with thirty-six small squares of paper. "Your job is to work with a partner and collect data from every other student in the class." Let's say Frederick and I are partners. He's going to take half of the squares and go to each of the desks at tables one and two and copy down the birth weights of each of those children, one weight on a slip of paper. I'm going to do the same at tables three and four." (This class has four table groups.)

I modeled how I would record the pounds and ounces for one student, then use another slip of paper for the next person's data. "I used several different colors for the slips of papers," I told the children. "So that your data won't get mixed up with the data of someone else who might be working close to you, don't work near someone who has the same color you have."

I continued with the directions. "After you and your partner have recorded each student's birth weight on a piece of paper, find a place to work where you can organize the data in some way so that we can talk about it. When you have the data organized, I'd like each of you to choose a piece of paper to record what you did." I showed the

Math and Nonfiction, Grades 3–5

students the three kinds of paper that were available to them—plain white copy paper, loose-leaf lined paper, and graph paper.

"This is the important part of the lesson. When we clean up, all of the squares are going to be put away. I want to be able to understand from your papers how you had the data arranged. Then I'm going to have you do some writing about what you did."

I reminded the students to be quiet as they moved around the room so others could think. I excused Daisy and Julia first. Their envelope contained yellow slips of paper, so I reminded them not to sit next to other students working with yellow to prevent their data from getting mixed up. I passed out the remaining envelopes to pairs of students and watched as they began to work.

The classroom buzzed with whispering as the children figured out how to share the responsibility of writing down the data. As they finished writing the birth weights, I encouraged them to find a place to work at organizing their data. All of the children began ordering their data either greatest-to-least or vice versa. Some did this by first grouping the birth weights by pounds, then putting the slips of paper in order to create lines resembling a bar graph. Others added one piece of data at a time, creating a long line of paper slips.

I walked over to Marcus and Ashton and said, "Explain to me what you've done so far."

"We're organizing them by number order," replied Marcus. They had a long line of pieces of paper and were running out of room for data on their table.

"Is there a way you could group them so you don't have such a long line?" I asked.

"Hmm," they said. They studied their data for a few seconds, then Ashton said, "We could put the ones that are the same together, like this." Since there were three pieces of data that each said 6 pounds, 5 ounces (which they had recorded as *6/5*), he moved the second and third squares of paper above the first one to create a column.

"Oh, that helps," I said. "Are there a lot of duplicates?"

"Yeah," Marcus said. "There's four of these and four of these." He pointed to the slips with *6/8* and *6/9* on them.

I didn't make it back to Marcus and Ashton until the end of the period, but was amazed at how they had recorded their work. Although they didn't finish, their paper clearly represents the work they did. (See Figure 20–2.)

Frederick and Alex's thinking was similar to Ashton and Marcus's, but they represented it differently. At first, Frederick hadn't put numbers going up the left side of his graph. When I asked him, he said, "This is one, this is two, this is three," as he pointed to the lines. When I suggested that he write the numbers in he said, "Hey, it's like a graph!" I thought it was interesting that he had organized his data into

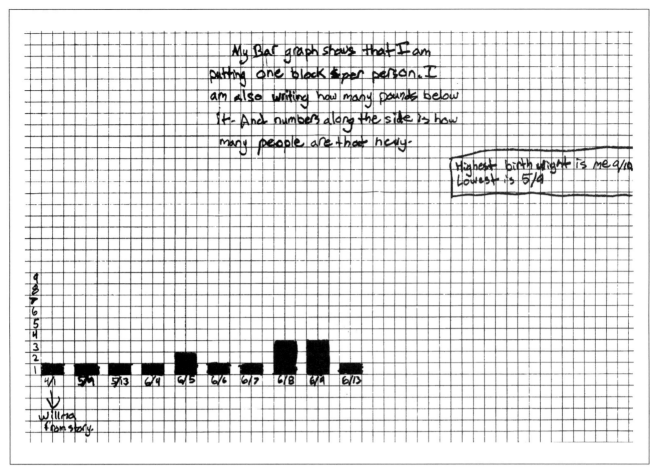

My Bar graph shows that I am
putting one block per person. I
am also writing how many pounds below
it. And numbers along the side is how
many people are that heavy.

Highest birth weight is me 9/10
Lowest is 5/4

4/1 5/9 5/13 6/4 6/5 6/6 6/7 6/8 6/9 6/13

Wilma
from story.

Figure 20–2: Ashton and Marcus's paper wasn't complete, but it represented their work well.

a graph but didn't think about it as such until he began labeling it. I pointed to the numbers on the bottom of his graph and said, "You might want to tell what these numbers are, too, and then try to give your paper a title," which he did. (See Figure 20–3.)

Diego used the same strategy, but built his graph going down. (See Figure 20–4.) When I walked over to him, he had the picture drawn, but no numbers attached to it. I pointed to the first box and asked, "What does this square represent?"

"That's Wilma's weight," he replied.

"How much was that?" I asked.

"Four pounds, one ounce."

"Can you show that on your paper?" I asked.

Diego wrote *4* and *1*, then continued to add the rest of the numbers.

"What are these?" I asked, pointing to the numbers in the top row.

"Pounds," he replied.

"Write that on your paper so the reader knows what it is," I told him. He did so, and added the word *ounces* without being prompted.

Karen and her partner decided to order the numbers from least to greatest and recorded that on their papers. (See Figure 20–5.)

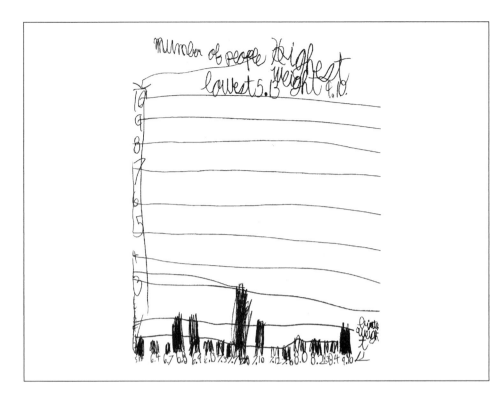

Figure 20–3: Frederick used the idea of a basic graph to show the data he and Alex had gathered.

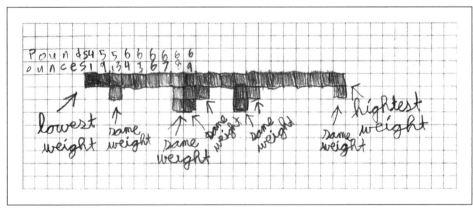

Figure 20–4: Diego needed help adding numbers to his graph to give it meaning.

Javier and Duane recorded their whole process. First they grouped the numbers by pounds, then they organized the groups by ounces. Their final order looked similar to Karen's. (See Figure 20–6.)

Although Priscilla forgot to include Wilma's weight, her graph is quite sophisticated. She labeled the top of each column to indicate pounds and ounces and organized the numbers from least to greatest. This graphic representation resembles a stem and leaf plot, which the children will be expected to understand in sixth grade. Priscilla's note about the average being "in the 6 pound area" could facilitate a useful discussion about the definition and purpose of different types of averages. (See Figure 20–7.)

Both Lucia and Julias made graphs similar to Priscilla's, but they look slightly different. I thought that it would be interesting to have

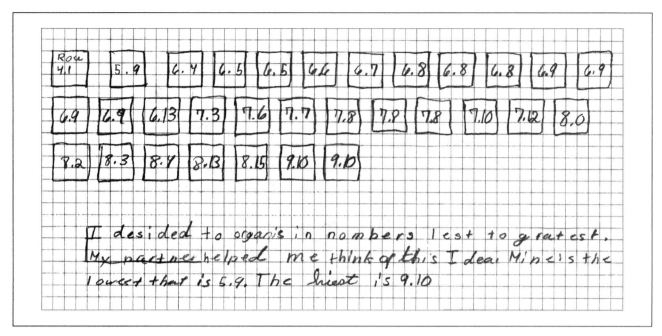

Figure 20–5: Karen and her partner organized the numbers from least to greatest.

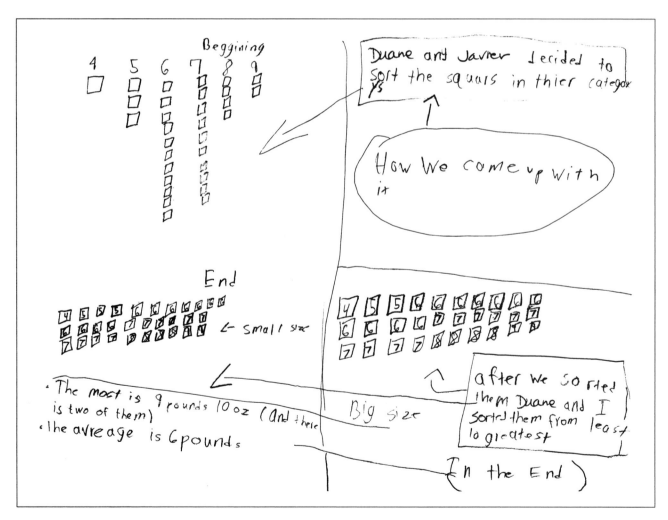

Figure 20–6: Javier and Duane recorded the process they went through to come up with their final order.

Math and Nonfiction, Grades 3–5

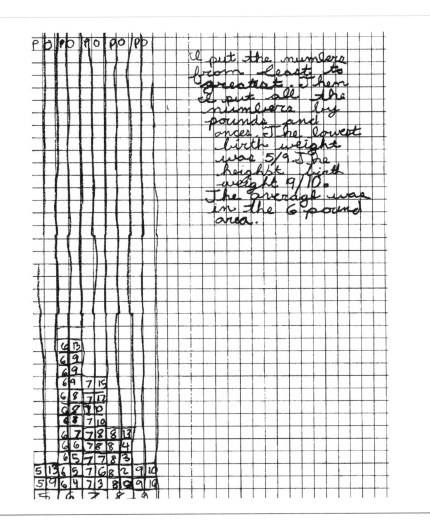

Figure 20–7: Priscilla
ordered the numbers
from least to greatest, then
by pounds and ounces.

the students discuss the different ways that they had represented the same data. Julias's horizontal representation (Figure 20–8) matches Priscilla's (Figure 20–7) and Lucia's (Figure 20–9) vertical representations, but the data is rotated. These representations are the opposite of Alex's graph, which displays the data vertically but moving down from the baseline rather than up.

Many children decided to clump the data together differently, trying to create groups that were more equal. Judge wrote: *There were a lot of kids that had 6 or 7 so I thought we could make a graph and put 5 and under together and 8 and over together.* I think it's important that children maintain ownership of their work. Although many of their notations are not consistent with customary methods, for example, writing 6 lbs., 13 oz. as 6/13, their work provides a meaningful context for discussing the reasoning behind and importance of customary notations.

The next day, I read the rest of the book. The children enjoyed the story. They concluded that you can't predict what will happen to a person based on how much they weigh when they're born.

Figure 20–8: Julias represented his data horizontally.

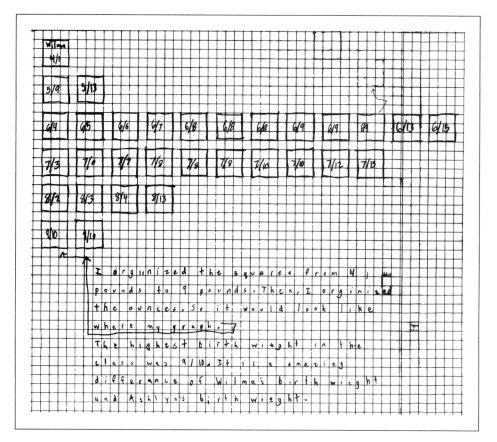

Figure 20–9: Lucia put the
pounds in separate columns
then stacked them from
least to greatest by ounces.

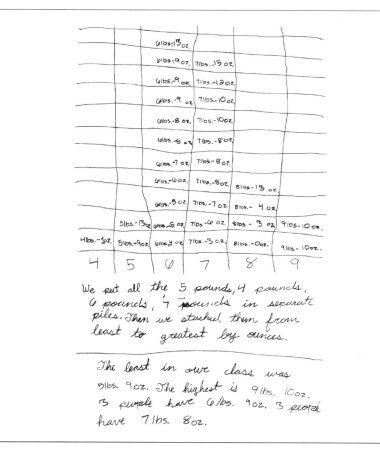

Math and Nonfiction, Grades 3–5

Blackline Masters

One-Inch Grid Paper
My Baby Milestones
Hottest, Coldest, Highest, Deepest Worksheet
Grid and Circle Worksheet
Half-Inch Grid Paper
1–100 Chart
Birth Weight Record Sheet

One-Inch Grid Paper

My Baby Milestones

Dear Parents,

Today we read a book which used information about a baby chimp to help us learn math. We are going to gather information about our childhoods to compare them to Jiggs the Chimp. Please help your child fill in his or her ages for each of the milestones below. If you can't remember exact ages, please give us your best guess. We will use this information for a graphing activity.

Thank you.

1. How old was I when I first sucked my thumb or pacifier? _____

2. How old was I when I got my first tooth? _____

3. How old was I when I ate solid food for the first time? _____

4. How old was I when I could sit up by myself? _____

5. How old was I when I began crawling? _____

6. How old was I when I took my first steps? _____

7. How old was I when I could walk alone? _____

Hottest, Coldest, Highest, Deepest Worksheet

1. Use cubes to build a representation of the two places you are comparing.

2. Draw a picture of your model. Try to make your drawing to scale.

3. Label your drawing with numbers to show how it relates to the actual measurements.

4. Explain in words how you know your drawing makes sense.

Grid and Circle Worksheet

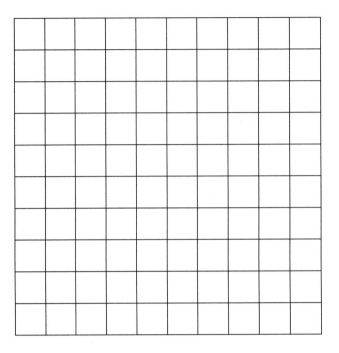

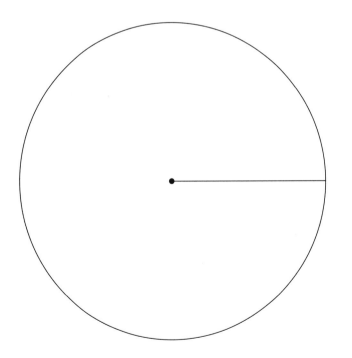

From *Math and Nonfiction, Grades 3–5* by Stephanie Sheffield and Kathleen Gallagher. © 2004 Math Solutions Publications.

Half-Inch Grid Paper

1–100 Chart

1	2	3	4	5	6	7	8	9	10
11	12	13	14	15	16	17	18	19	20
21	22	23	24	25	26	27	28	29	30
31	32	33	34	35	36	37	38	39	40
41	42	43	44	45	46	47	48	49	50
51	52	53	54	55	56	57	58	59	60
61	62	63	64	65	66	67	68	69	70
71	72	73	74	75	76	77	78	79	80
81	82	83	84	85	86	87	88	89	90
91	92	93	94	95	96	97	98	99	100

Birth Weight Record Sheet

We are going to do a math lesson that requires you to know your birth weight. Please fill in the following information and return this paper tomorrow.

Name _____

Birth weight

_____ lbs. _____ oz.

References

Burns, Diane L. 1996. *Berries, Nuts, and Seeds*. Illus. John F. McGee. Chanhassen, MN: NorthWord.

Davies, Nicola. 2001. *One Tiny Turtle*. Illus. Jane Chapman. Cambridge, MA: Candlewick.

Emberley, Ed. 1984. *Ed Emberley's Picture Pie: A Circle Drawing Book*. Boston: Little, Brown.

Farmer, Jacqueline. 1999. *Bananas*. Illus. Page Eastburn O'Rourke. Watertown, MA: Charlesbridge.

Geisert, Arthur. 1996. *Roman Numerals I to MM: Numerabilia Romana Uno ad Duo Mila*. Boston: Houghton Mifflin.

Giesecke, Ernestine. 2003. *From Seashells to Smart Cards: Money and Currency (Everyday Economics)*. Illus. Daniel Condon. Chicago: Heinemann Library.

Jenkins, Steve. 1995. *Biggest, Strongest, Fastest*. Boston: Houghton Mifflin.

———. 1998. *Hottest, Coldest, Highest, Deepest*. Boston: Houghton Mifflin.

Krull, Kathleen. 1996. *Wilma Unlimited: How Wilma Rudolph Became the World's Fastest Woman*. Illus. David Diaz. San Diego: Voyager.

Long, Lynette. 1998. *Dealing with Addition*. Watertown, MA: Charlesbridge.

Maestro, Betsy, and Giulio Maestro. 1990. *A More Perfect Union: The Story of Our Constitution*. New York: HarperTrophy.

Michelson, Richard. 2000. *Ten Times Better*. Illus. Leonard Baskin. New York: Marshall Cavendish.

Morgan, Rowland, comp. 1997. *In the Next Three Seconds . . . Predictions for the Millennium*. Illus. Rod and Kira Josey. New York: Puffin.

Nagda, Ann W., and Cindy Bickel. 2000. *Tiger Math: Learning to Graph from a Baby Tiger*. New York: Henry Holt.

———. 2002. *Chimp Math: Learning About Time from a Baby Chimpanzee*. New York: Henry Holt.

Nolan, Helen. 1997. *How Much, How Many, How Far, How Heavy, How Long, How Tall Is 1000?* Illus. Tracy Walker. Tonawanda, NY: Kids Can Press.

Schwartz, David M. 1998. *G Is for Googol: A Math Alphabet Book*. Illus. Marissa Moss. Berkeley, CA: Tricycle.

———. 1999. *If You Hopped Like a Frog*. Illus. James Warhola. New York: Scholastic.

Simon, Seymour. 1999. *Icebergs and Glaciers*. New York: HarperTrophy.

Smith, David J. 2002. *If the World Were a Village: A Book About the World's People*. Illus. Shelagh Armstrong. Tonawanda, NY: Kids Can Press.

Index

acute angles, 51, 68, 71–73, 75–76
addends, 42
addition in number combinations lesson with playing cards, 39–46
Africa, populations, 116, 117
ages, in lesson on averaging, 140–47
American Revolution, 138–47
A More Perfect Union, lesson, 138–47
Angel Falls (Venezuela), 83, 85, 86, 87
angles, 68. *See also individual angles*
  classification of, 51–52, 66–77
  defined, 74
  estimating, lesson, 66–77
  in real world, lesson about finding, 68–77
animal to human comparisons, lesson, 118–31
Antarctica, 83
ants, 131, 171–73
apples, lesson comparing nutritional data of bananas with, 4–9
art, lesson on geometric figures in, 50–57
Asia, populations, 114–17

averages, 140
  ages, lesson averaging, 138–47
  in lesson using bananas, 2

Baikal, Lake (Russia), 80–82, 85, 86, 87
bananas, lesson, 1–9
Bananas, lesson, 1–9
bar graphs lesson using weight, 29–38, 206
Barr, Tamara, 128
berries, graphing lesson with, 10–18, 205
Berries, Nuts, and Seeds, lesson, 10–18, 205
Bickel, Cindy, 29, 181
biggest, comparison lesson using concept of, 19–28
Biggest, Strongest, Fastest, lesson, 19–28
birth weights, collecting and organizing data on, lesson, 192–202, 209, 211
Blackline Masters, 203–11
Burns, Diane L., 10

calendars, 31–38
camels, 173–74
Canada, 116, 117
  populations, 115
cards, playing, number combinations lesson with, 39–46

centipedes, 174–77

chameleons, 130

charts, 31–38

chimpanzees, 29–38, 206

Chimp Math, lesson,
  29–38, 206

circle graphs
  creating, from picture graphs,
    lesson, 181–91, 208
  with human population lesson,
    107–17

circles, picture-making lesson
  with fractional, 47–57

classifying, berries, nuts and
  seeds, lesson, 10–18, 205

comparison
  in *Biggest, Strongest, Fastest*
    lesson, 19–28
  in *Hottest, Coldest, Highest,*
    Deepest lesson, 78–87, 207
  money lesson, comparing
    salaries to hourly wages,
    58–65
  nutritional data on bananas
    and apples, 4–9

Constitutional Convention,
  lesson, 138–47

Constitution (United States), 138

countable numbers, 95

cranberries, 11

cranes, 126, 128–30

data
  averaging ages, lesson,
    138–47
  birth weights, collecting and
    organizing data on, lesson,
    209, 211
  graphing, lessons, 29–38, 206
  picture graph lesson, 10–18, 205

Davies, Nicola, 148

Dayton, Jonathon, 140

Dead Sea (Israel, Jordan), 83

Dealing with Addition, lesson,
  39–46

Death Valley (California), 78, 83

degrees, 68

depth, in *Hottest, Coldest,*
  Highest, Deepest lesson,
  78–87, 207

dinosaurs, 119

Discovery Channel, 101

distributive property, 82

division, multiple ways of writing
  problems, 120–22

Ed Emberley's Picture Pie, lesson,
  47–57
  fifth-grade lesson, 50–57
  third-grade lesson, 47–50

elephants, weight lessons with,
  20–28, 177–80

Emberley, Ed, 47

Empire State Building (New York
  City), 80–83, 86–87

estimation, with turtle egg-laying
  lesson, 148–59

Europe, populations, 116, 117

Everest, Mount (Nepal, Tibet),
  78, 84, 85, 86, 87

Farmer, Jacqueline, 1

fastest, comparison lesson using
  concept of, 19–28

Fibonacci, Leonardo, 67

fractions
  circles, lesson with fractional,
    47–57
  in lesson for determining
    underwater portion
    of icebergs, 100–106
  writing division problems
    as, 121–23

Franklin, Benjamin, 140

frogs' leaps, measurement
  of, 118–20

From Seashells to Smart Cards,
  lesson, 58–65

fruit, lesson comparing
  nutritional data of, 4–9

Gallagher, Kathleen
  Biggest, Strongest, Fastest,
    teaching, 19–28

G Is for Googol, teaching, 66–77
Hottest, Coldest, Highest, Deepest, teaching, 78–87, 207
If the World Were a Village, teaching, 107–17
A More Perfect Union, teaching, 138–47
One Tiny Turtle, teaching, 148–59
Wilma Unlimited, teaching, 192–202, 209, 211
Geisert, Arthur, 160
genre, 100
geometry
  angles (*see* angles)
  circles, lesson with fractional, 47–57
Giesecke, Ernestine, 58
G Is for Googol, lesson, 66–77
glaciers and icebergs, lessons, 100–106
goods, 58–59
graphing
  bar graphs lesson, 29–38, 206
  circle graphs lessons, 107–17, 181–91, 208
  half-inch grid paper (Blackline Master), 209
  human population data, lesson, 107–17
  in lesson on birth weights, 197–202
  one-inch grid paper (Blackline Master), 205
  picture graphs lessons, 10–18, 181–91, 205, 208
grids
  grid and circle worksheet (Blackline Master), 208
  half-inch grid paper (Blackline Master), 209
  one-inch grid paper (Blackline Master), 205

height
  animal to human comparisons, lesson, 118–22

in *Hottest, Coldest, Highest, Deepest* lesson, 78–87, 207
in *How Much, How Many, How Far, How Heavy, How Long, How Tall Is 1000?* lesson, 88–99
Hottest, Coldest, Highest, Deepest, lesson, 78–87, 207
How Much, How Many, How Far, How Heavy, How Long, How Tall Is 1000?, lesson, 88–99
human populations, lesson on, 107–17
human to animal comparisons, lesson, 118–31
hundreds, lesson for exploring, 88–94
hundreds chart
  Blackline Master, 210
  with human population lesson, 108–9
  with turtle egg-laying lesson, 148–59

Icebergs and Glaciers, lessons, 100–106
If the World Were a Village, lesson, 107–17
If You Hopped Like a Frog, lesson, 118–31
infinity, 95
In the Next Three Seconds . . . Predictions for the Millennium, lesson, 132–37

Jenkins, Steve, 19, 27–28, 78, 79

Karnick, Mary, 11–18
Krull, Kathleen, 192

Latin language, 161
linear measurement
  animal to human comparisons, lesson, 118–31

linear measurement (*contd.*)
  in *How Much, How Many, How Far, How Heavy, How Long, How Tall Is 1000?* lesson, 88–99
lines, 68, 74
line segments, 68, 74
Long, Lynette, 39

Maestro, Betsy, 138
Maestro, Giulio, 138
Marianas Trench (Pacific Ocean), 83, 84, 85, 86–87
means, 141
measurement
  animal to human comparisons, lesson, 118–31
  height (*see* height)
  in *Hottest, Coldest, Highest, Deepest* lesson, 78–87, 207
  in *How Much, How Many, How Far, How Heavy, How Long, How Tall Is 1000?* lesson, 88–99
  linear measurement (*see* linear measurement)
medians, 140
Michelson, Richard, 169–80
milestones, 31–32
minimum wage, 59
modeling underwater portions of icebergs, lesson, 103–6
modes, 140, 141
money
  comparing salaries to hourly wages, lesson, 58–65
  in *How Much, How Many, How Far, How Heavy, How Long, How Tall Is 1000?* lesson, 88–99
Morgan, Rowland, 132
multiplication
  distributive property, 82
  lesson using bananas with, 3–9
  multiples of ten, lesson involving, 169–80
  partial products, 82

Nagda, Ann Whitehead, 29, 181
Nile River (Africa), 79, 84, 85
Nolan, Helen, 88
North Pole, 78
numbers, human population lessons using large, 107–17
numerals
  Arabic and Roman numerals compared, lesson, 165–68
  Roman numerals, lesson, 160–68
nutrition information, lesson comparing, 4–9
nuts, graphing lesson with, 10–18, 205

obtuse angles, 51, 67–74, 76
Oceania, 108
  populations, 115
one hundred, lesson for exploring, 88–94
one thousand, lesson for exploring, 88–99
One Tiny Turtle, lesson, 148–59
1–100 chart
  Blackline Master, 210
  with human population lesson, 108–9, 113, 116–17
  with turtle egg-laying lesson, 148–59

partial products method, 82
percent circles, with human population lesson, 110–17
picture graphs
  creating circle graphs from, lesson, 181–91, 208
  lesson, 10–18, 205
pie charts
  in fractions lesson, 101–3
  in human population lesson, 109–10, 113–17
playing cards, number combinations lesson with, 39–46
populations, lesson on human, 107–17

prediction in lesson using time, 132–37

proportional reasoning, in *Highest, Coldest, Highest, Deepest* lesson, 78–87, 207

range, 4
right angles, 68–70, 72–75
right triangles, 68
Roman and Arabic numerals compared, lesson, 165–68
Roman Numerals I to MM, lesson, 160–68
Rudolph, Wilma, 192

salaries, lesson comparing hourly wages to, 58–65
Schwartz, David M., 66, 118, 119
seeds, graphing lesson with, 10–18, 205
services, 59
Sheffield, Stephanie
  Bananas, teaching, 1–9
  Berries, Nuts, and Seeds, teaching, 10–18, 205
  Chimp Math, teaching, 29–38, 206
  Dealing with Addition, teaching, 39–46
  Ed Emberley's Picture Pie, teaching, 47–57
  How Much, How Many, How Far, How Heavy, How Long, How Tall Is 1000?, teaching, 88–99
  Icebergs and Glaciers, teaching, 100–106
  If You Hopped Like a Frog, teaching, 118–31
  In the Next Three Seconds . . . Predictions for the Millennium, teaching, 132–37
  Roman Numerals I to MM, teaching, 160–68
  From Seashells to Smart Cards, teaching, 58–65

Ten Times Better, teaching, 169–80
Tiger Math, teaching, 181–91, 208
shrews, 131
Simon, Seymour, 100
skip counting, 154–56
  with multiples of ten, lesson, 169–80
Smith, David J., 107
sorting, in berries, nuts and seeds, lesson, 10–18, 205
South America, 116
  populations, 117
spiders, 128, 129
squids, giant, 180
strongest, comparison lesson using concept of, 19–28
symmetry, 49–50, 51

temperature in hottest, coldest, highest, deepest, lesson, 78–87, 207
ten
  lesson on number combinations up to, 39–46
  multiples of, lesson involving, 169–80
Ten Times Better, lesson, 169–80
thousands, lesson for exploring, 88–99
Tiger Math, lesson, 181–91, 208
tigers, lesson, 181–91, 208
time, predicting, 132–37
time lines, 31–38
Titanic, 101
turtles, loggerhead, lesson, 148–59

United States, populations, 115, 117

Venn diagrams, with Roman numerals lesson, 166–68

wages, lesson comparing salaries to hourly, 58–65

Washington, George, 139
weight
   birth weights, collecting and
     organizing data on, lesson,
     192–202, 209, 211
   with elephants lessons, 20–28,
     177–80
   graphing, in chimpanzee lesson,
     30–31

   in *How Much, How Many,*
     How Far, How Heavy, How
     Long, How Tall Is 1000?
     lesson, 88–99
whales, blue, 21–22, 27
Wilma Unlimited, lesson,
   192–202, 209, 211